More praise for *Winners, Losers & Microsoft*...

"Liebowitz and Margolis's **WINNERS, LOSERS & MICROSOFT** *is instructive for all participants—the judge, defendants, plaintiffs and experts in the DOJ vs. Microsoft tragicomedy. For the rest of us, including Microsoft customers and competitors, it is not too late to learn, as well as be entertained by, the Liebowitz-Margolis explanation and histories of several presumptive 'monopolies' of 'networks' and 'entrenched universal users.'"*
— **ARMEN A. ALCHIAN**, Professor of Economics, UCLA

"If only the Justice Department read **WINNERS, LOSERS & MICROSOFT**, *the American economy would be spared much pain and legal expense. Stan Liebowitz and Stephen Margolis really know their stuff, and they can write too."*
— **PAUL A. GIGOT**, columnist, *The Wall Street Journal*

"Innovative and utterly convincing, their dismantling of commonly accepted myths about the QWERTY typewriter keyboard and the VHS-versus-Beta video struggle makes fascinating and illuminating reading." — **AMERICAN WAY**

*"***WINNERS, LOSERS & MICROSOFT** *features what appears to be the first systematic look at the real-world history of the software industry—and the results are sure to give Department of Justice trial attorneys the heebie-jeebies. An invaluable addition to the bookshelf of anyone interested in the Microsoft trial and future high-tech antitrust cases, the book is the best compilation that anyone's offered."* — **WIRED**

*"***WINNERS, LOSERS & MICROSOFT** *collects in a single volume the impressive scholarly work of Stan Liebowitz and Stephen Margolis on network effects and path dependence. This book is extremely important and useful."*
— **BRUCE H. KOBAYASHI**, Professor of Law, George Mason University

"In **WINNERS, LOSERS & MICROSOFT**, *Liebowitz and Margolis take aim at the common understanding of network effects—in particular, the belief that vast user bases and compatibility can allow inferior technologies to drive superior ones out of the marketplace. Their arguments, such as their history of software applications, will be of interest to executives in virtually any field."* — **UPSIDE**

"Liebowitz and Margolis's **WINNERS, LOSERS & MICROSOFT** *is an all-out attack on the intellectual and empirical basis for 'path dependence,' with particular application to Microsoft's role in the software market. The book serves a useful purpose in throwing cold water on the idea that markets routinely pick inferior technologies and in providing the first thorough summary of what really happens in software markets."* — **REASON**

"WINNERS, LOSERS & MICROSOFT gives 'path dependence' a cold shower and sheds much-needed empirical light. The book is also a pleasure to read because it serve up course after course of exquisite historical and institutional detail." — **GEORGE BITTLINGMAYER**, Prof. of Econ, Univ. of Kansas

"In WINNERS, LOSERS & MICROSOFT, economists Liebowitz and Margolis present powerful evidence that Microsoft lowered prices." — **NEWSWEEK**

"In WINNERS, LOSERS & MICROSOFT, Liebowitz and Margolis argue that path dependence is something of a myth, or at least far less important than Microsoft-bashers make out. . . . Ironic, isn't it, how often anti-monopoly actions to correct alleged market failures end up hurting the little guy?"
— *FINANCIAL TIMES*

"Economists Liebowitz and Margolis find no convincing examples that network effects are at all important in establishing and maintaining monopoly of inferior products. This excellent volume is recommended for academic and professional collections." — **CHOICE**

"Respected economists Stan Liebowitz and Stephen Margolis use plenty of statistics to examine the key tenets surrounding the Microsoft antitrust trial. Their research makes a compelling case and argues that their voluminous research proves that consumers don't get 'locked in' to inferior standards, à la the popular economic theory of 'network effects.'" — **INDUSTRY STANDARD**

"Powerful stuff, WINNERS, LOSERS & MICROSOFT will have an important impact on the debate about antitrust in high technology. It exhibits a very high calibre of scholarship and bases its conclusions on a wealth of new empirical evidence."
— **WILLIAM SHUGHART II**, Professor of Economics, U. of Mississippi

"WINNERS, LOSERS & MICROSOFT is a timely book on competition and antitrust issues in high-technology industries. It is highly recommended for managers interested in a better understanding of the impact of network effects, technology lock-in, and path dependence."
— *JOURNAL OF PRODUCT INNOVATION AND MANAGEMENT*

"In their book, WINNERS, LOSERS & MICROSOFT, economists Liebowitz and Margolis argue that not only did Microsoft's products earn superior reviews, their entry into the market sent prices plunging. This is what the Justice Department is protecting the world from? Better products and lower prices?"
— *WASHINGTON TIMES*

Winners, Losers & Microsoft

Competition and Antitrust
in High Technology

Winners, Losers & Microsoft

Competition and Antitrust in High Technology

Revised Edition

Stan J. Liebowitz
Stephen E. Margolis

Foreword by Jack Hirshleifer

The INDEPENDENT INSTITUTE

Oakland, California

CABRINI COLLEGE LIBRARY
610 KING OF PRUSSIA ROAD
RADNOR, PA 19087

HD
9696.63
.U64
M5364
2001

#46823338

Copyright ©1999, 2001 by The Independent Institute

The Independent Institute
100 Swan Way, Oakland, CA 94621-1428
Telephone: 510-632-1366 • Fax 510-568-6040
E-mail: info@independent.org
Website: http//www.independent.org

All rights reserved. No part of this book may be reproduced or transmitted in
any form by electronic or mechanical means now known or to be invented,
including photocopying, recording, or information storage and retrieval
systems, without permission in writing from the publisher, except by a
reviewer who may quote brief passages in a review.

Library of Congress Catalog Number: 99-73414
ISBN: 0-945999-84-4

Published by The Independent Institute, a nonprofit, nonpartisan, scholarly
research and educational organization that sponsors comprehensive studies
on the political economy of critical social and economic issues. Nothing
herein should be construed as necessarily reflecting the views of the Institute
or as an attempt to aid or hinder the passage of any bill before Congress.

The INDEPENDENT INSTITUTE

THE INDEPENDENT INSTITUTE is a non-profit, scholarly research and educational organization that sponsors comprehensive studies of the political economy of critical social and economic problems.

The politicization of decision-making in society has too often confined public debate to the narrow reconsideration of existing policies. Given the prevailing influence of partisan interests, little social innovation has occurred. In order to understand both the nature of and possible solutions to major public issues, the Independent Institute's program adheres to the highest standards of independent inquiry and is pursued regardless of prevailing political or social biases and conventions. The resulting studies are widely distributed as books and other publications, and are publicly debated through numerous conference and media programs.

Through this uncommon independence, depth, and clarity, the Independent Institute pushes at the frontiers of our knowledge, redefines the debate over public issues, and fosters new and effective directions for government reform.

FOUNDER & PRESIDENT
David J. Theroux

RESEARCH DIRECTOR
Alexander T. Tabarrok

SENIOR FELLOWS
Bruce L. Benson
Robert Higgs
Richard K. Vedder

ACADEMIC ADVISORS
Stephen E. Ambrose
University of New Orleans
Martin Anderson
Hoover Institution
Herman Belz
University of Maryland
Thomas E. Borcherding
Claremont Graduate School
Boudewijn Bouckaert
University of Ghent,
Belgium
James M. Buchanan
George Mason University
Allan C. Carlson
Rockford Institute
Robert W. Crandall
Brookings Institution
Arthur A. Ekirch, Jr.
State University of New
York, Albany
Richard A. Epstein
University of Chicago
B. Delworth Gardner
Brigham Young University

George Gilder
Discovery Institute
Nathan Glazer
Harvard University
Ronald Hamowy
University of Alberta
Steve H. Hanke
Johns Hopkins University
Ronald Max Hartwell
Oxford University
H. Robert Heller
Int'l. Payments Institute
Lawrence A. Kudlow
ING Barings
Deirdre N. McCloskey
University of Iowa
J. Huston McCulloch
Ohio State University
Forrest McDonald
University of Alabama
Merton H. Miller
University of Chicago
Thomas Gale Moore
Hoover Institution
Charles Murray
American Enterprise
Institute
William A. Niskanen
Cato Institute
Michael J. Novak, Jr.
American Enterprise
Institute
Charles E. Phelps
University of Rochester

Paul Craig Roberts
Institute for Political Economy
Nathan Rosenberg
Stanford University
Simon Rottenberg
University of Massachusetts
Pascal Salin
University of Paris, France
Arthur Seldon
Institute of Economic Affairs
England
William F. Shughart II
University of Mississippi
Joel H. Spring
State University of New York
Old Westbury
Richard L. Stroup
Montana State University
Thomas S. Szasz
State University of New York
Syracuse
Robert D. Tollison
George Mason University
Arnold S. Trebach
American University
Gordon Tullock
University of Arizona
Richard E. Wagner
George Mason University
Sir Alan A. Walters
AIG Trading Corporation
Carolyn L. Weaver
American Enterprise Institute
Walter E. Williams
George Mason University

THE INDEPENDENT INSTITUTE
100 Swan Way, Oakland, CA 94621-1428, U.S.A.
Telephone: 510-632-1366 • Fax: 510-568-6040
E-mail: info@independent.org • Website: http://www.independent.org

INDEPENDENT STUDIES IN POLITICAL ECONOMY

For further information and a catalog of publications, please contact:
THE INDEPENDENT INSTITUTE
100 Swan Way, Oakland, CA 94621-1428, U.S.A.
Telephone: 510-632-1366 • Facsimile: 510-568-6040
E-mail: info@independent.org • Website: http://www.independent.org

Table of Contents

Foreword

History matters. This is an unexceptionable assertion, surely, but one that has also become a slogan in the current economic literature, intended to epitomize a newly discovered flaw in the market system. The flaw is this: the merest of historical accidents, perhaps an early engineering choice by a technology pioneer responding to some random influence or ephemeral advantage, locks in future generations to an inefficient technology owing to *path dependence*. Examples of such supposed market failures include the notorious QWERTY keyboard that has bedeviled typists for nearly a century, failure of the Beta videotape format to replace the inferior VHS design, and the strangely persistent quirky English inches, ounces, and quarts in the face of the more rational metric system of measures.

Analytically, path dependence is blamed on network effects. An initial mistaken (or only temporarily correct) choice retains a kind of natural monopoly over a superior one. Electric autos might be better than gasoline-driven ones. But given that there are almost no recharging stations, a private individual does not find it sensible to buy an electric car. Nor can any firm profitably install recharging stations when there are so few electric cars around to use them. Everyone is supposedly aware of the inefficiency, yet no single rational decision-maker—having to conform to the actions of everyone else—is in a position to correct it.

Stan Liebowitz and Stephen Margolis show that inefficient outcomes due to network effects are indeed theoretically possible in a market economy, though only under rather stringent conditions. These outcomes are a matter for empirical study. How frequently do such inefficient lock-ins actually happen? Liebowitz and Margolis's fascinating historical review of the leading reported instances demonstrates that several of them, notably the QWERTY problem, are essentially mythical while other widely accepted stories represent misinterpretations of the evidence.

To begin with, path dependence is inefficient only when an inferior product survives at the expense of a superior one *and* if the costs of changing over do not exceed the value of the postulated quality improvement. Omitting this rather obvious qualification represents what Harold Demsetz has called the Nirvana fallacy: comparing a real-world actuality with a hypothetical ideal not within the range of feasible opportunities.

Network effects constitute a possible source of natural monopoly and lock-in that operates on the demand side. (In contrast with the traditional explanation of natural monopoly as due to decreasing average cost, increasing returns on the supply side.) These demand-side increasing returns stem from the advantages of synchronization. The value of a good to a consumer may depend not only on the characteristics of the commodity itself but also on how many other users have adopted the same product. This is evidently true of literal networks such as the telephone system (there is no point having a phone if there is no one else to call). And to a degree the same logic applies to any product for which person-to-person compatibility and standardization are advantageous. Notably, in computer hardware and software there are efficiency gains to be made if people can exchange files with one another or move from machine to machine without worrying about incompatible standards and formats.

Liebowitz and Margolis explore the range and limits of these network effects. Suppose product A is superior to B, in the sense that all consumers prefer the former at each and every possible given ratio of market shares. Thus, A would be preferred over B if they each had 10 percent of the market, or if each had 20 percent, and so on. Yet such a superior product may indeed fail to displace an inferior one if the incumbent starts with a sufficient initial preponderance. (With 90 percent of the market to begin with, B might be preferred by most consumers over a superior newcomer A with only 10 percent.) That is the essence of the market failure due to network effects, and it can happen.

But Liebowitz and Margolis do not stop at this point. They go on to ask what rational consumers and rational suppliers, faced with such a situation, would be expected to do—and whether we actually observe such responses. Manufacturers of innovative superior products are not powerless; there are ways to enlarge market share. For a firm aiming to acquire the critical mass needed to tip consumers' decisions in its direction, evident possibilities include offering a low introductory price or money-back guarantee. And because by hypothesis the new product really is superior, the new entrant might profitably subsidize the cost of the user's changeover, and even commit to pay the cost of changing back should that be desired. All of these devices are observed in real-world markets. Furthermore, just as suppliers can often find ways to escape the stasis trap, so can buyers. Users can and do remain alert to technological progress; in the computer field, Liebowitz and Margolis show, published product reviews in magazines aimed at consumers have had very significant effect on market share. Given the likelihood of the superior product eventually winning the battle, foresighted purchasers may well (among other things) demand the same return and exchange privileges from incumbents as from newcomers B thereby attenuating the market advantage of simply having been first in the field.

In what for many readers will be the most exciting portion of the book, the authors go on to examine histories of alleged market failures, starting with QWERTY. Were producers and consumers actually locked into inferior market solutions? And if not, what devices were employed to escape the supposed trap? I will say no more on this topic here, so as not to take the edge off the authors' accounts of the creativity and ingenuity displayed by both suppliers and consumers in the competitive battle for critical mass.

Finally, there are important implications for economic theory and public policy. High-tech markets, the authors show, do challenge some of the old textbook verities, though in ways somewhat different from those emphasized in most recent discussions. In a high-tech world, all market participants must anticipate continuing product changes. Incumbent suppliers have to decide how often to put improvements on the market, how big a change to make each time (among other things, how to balance between optimality and compatibility), and what to do about prices. And rational consumers must correspondingly anticipate such supplier decisions, taking into account the likely entry of market contenders with entirely new offerings.

Turning from decision-making to overall market effects, one implication is that economists need to reconsider notions of competition. The authors show that, in tech markets, predominant market share may be the consequence and hallmark of effective competition. This often takes the paradoxical form of serial monopoly, as instanced by WordStar giving way to WordPerfect, which in turn lost out to Microsoft Word.

As for economic policy, a firm's having dominant market share need not lead to exploitation of consumers by high prices or low-quality products. In support of their argument, what better evidence can there be than the history of rapidly improving products and falling prices in high-tech industries, even where single firms have had dominant shares in particular markets? This point has obvious implications for antitrust issues, as elaborated by the authors, with particular attention to the Microsoft story.

So increasing returns/synchronization effects and consequent tendencies toward market concentration are indeed important in tech markets. But equally important and more in need of analytic appreciation are the steps that consumers and firms can take to deal with these effects. Dominant market share attracts competitors anxious to offer new and improved products to watchful and alert users. The situation may be one of natural monopoly, but no firm can retain such a monopoly position unless it matches or surpasses what hungry outsiders are ready and anxious to provide. In an increasingly high-tech world, competition does not take the textbook form of many suppliers offering a single fixed product to passive consumers. Instead it becomes a struggle to win, by entrepreneurial innovation and sensitivity to consumer needs, the big prize of dominant market share. It is this form of competition that has been mainly responsible for the success of the modern American economy in recent decades.

Jack Hirshleifer
Professor of Economics
University of California
Los Angeles

Preface to the Revised Edition

When we were finalizing the proof for the first edition, the Microsoft trial had just begun, but it was already well on its way from a narrow examination of certain business practices to a broad examination of the Microsoft's role as the provider of the standard platform for desktop computing. Not long after publication, the court issued its findings of fact. As we prepare revisions for this second edition, not quite a year later, the appeals process has not yet begun.

The trial brought a surprising amount of attention to the first edition, attention that is in part responsible for the paperback edition. We anticipated that chapters 8, 9, and 10 (which deal directly with some of the reasons for Microsoft's market position) and the appendix (which examines antitrust issues) would be of interest to people who followed the trial. We did not suspect, however, that the subject of network effects would play a role in the court's decision. Although the ideas of lock-in, path dependence, and network effects—ideas that we examine critically throughout the book—underpinned the government's claim on economic justification for its activism in high-technology markets, we thought that the judgment would most likely hang on more-established antitrust doctrines.

But in fact, the trial and the especially the court's decision did rest heavily on lock-in explanations of various sorts. The court's findings are peppered with phrases such as "the collective action problem," "the chicken and egg problem," and the "applications barrier to entry." Such phrases indicate that the appellate process may have to decide, among other things, whether it is appropriate to build antitrust doctrines on such unseasoned foundations.

Although the courtroom activity has moved apace, market activity has moved even faster. Technological development has moved away from the desktop and toward communications channels and other data-handling devices. Generation changes—what we refer to as "paradigm changes" in chapter 7—seem to be upon us in several areas, most notably in the rise of the Internet as the possible central focus of computer activity, and the movement away from PCs to personal-information managers, cellular phones, and game machines. Additionally, AOL, after its purchase of Netscape, has merged with Time-Warner, removing any David-versus-Goliath component from the browser wars.

This edition adds another appendix that considers some economic issues the trial raised and a discussion of the court's remedy. Otherwise, it is largely unchanged form the first edition, except for the correction of some typographical and other minor errors.

Acknowledgments

This book would not have been written without the encouragement, even prodding, of David Theroux. As this project developed, David had a continuing influence on its shape and scope. We thank David and the Independent Institute for his enduring confidence in this project and for his support of our research efforts.

We owe a deep debt to Jack Hirshleifer who has provided his encouragement, wisdom and advice over the years. He has been a mentor, a role model, and tireless advocate of our work. We wish to publicly thank him for all the times he has circulated our papers or otherwise injected our arguments into various debates on the workings of social systems. We are thrilled that he agreed to write the forward.

Various journal editors, referees, and others have helped us in our writings on these subjects over the years. We extend our gratitude to Bill Landes, Oliver Williamson, Richard Zerbe, Peter Newman, Timothy Taylor, Virginia Postrel, Nick Gillespie, Bill Niskanen, and anonymous referees who have helped us improve our thoughts and ideas. Nancy Margolis deserves special thanks for applying her expertise as an editor and writer to salvage our prose. Bruce Kobayashi, George Bittlingmayer, William Shughart and Alex Tabarrok read the manuscript thoroughly and provided many detailed comments. We have relied heavily on their work and we thank them for their efforts.

The software chapters benefited from insights and encouragement from two software veterans, Bob Frankston, co-inventor of the spreadsheet, and Gene Callahan, who was in charge of various aspects of "Managing Your Money" before moving on to his own company.

We thank our colleagues for their encouragement over the years as we wrote the papers that form the core set of ideas exposited here. We particularly would like to thank: Craig Newmark, John Lott, Ed Erickson, Lee Craig, Chuck Knoeber, David Flath, John Seater and Joel Mokyr. We also acknowledge contributions from George Stigler in the early states of this research. We thank our respective universities for their support, and to the UTD Management School which provided some financial support.

Chapters 8 and 9 could not have been written without a great deal of research support. We first thank our two main research assistants, both students at the time at UTD, Greg Bell (now at IBM) and Chris McAnally, for doing a fabulous job. Xiaojin Chu, provided clean-up support. We also need to thank Deborah Robinson, the chief librarian at Microsoft, who provided access to much of the data.

Over the years we have benefited from comments by participants at seminars presented at: Clemson University, the Fuqua School of Business, George Mason University, Harvard University, the Kennan Flagler School of Business, New York University, North Carolina State University, Southern Economic Association, Southern Methodist University, UCLA, University of California at Santa Barbara, Simon Fraser University, University of Georgia, University of Michigan Business School, and Wake Forest University.

Errors of course are our own. We have, unfortunately, been unable to pursue all of the good suggestions we have received and have meddled with the text right to the end.

Finally we thank our wives, Nancy and Vera, and families for enduring occasional absences and frequent crabbiness in the final stages of this project.

PART ONE

The Paradigm

In laissez-faire economies, resources are allocated by the independent decision-making of firms and individuals—what we often call the free market. Beginning with Adam Smith, one of the central questions of economics has been whether all this independence of consumers and producers leads to anything that we could judge to be good, or more precisely, whether it leads to the greatest achievable wealth and efficiency. For Smith, and for much of economics since, the conclusion has been that for the most part it does.

That is not to say, however, that economists never find imperfections in free markets. On the contrary, much energy has been spent answering the policy question: How can we improve upon independent decision making? This quest for improvement, however, has proven to be difficult. Economists have sometimes spent time and energy analyzing some purported market imperfection, only to have it shown decades later that the imperfection doesn't occur, or that there is no realistic means of overcoming it.

In Part One we present an overview of the most recent claim of a market imperfection. The claim is that free markets are not capable of making good choices among competing products, technologies, and standards where the values of these things depend upon interactions among users. Instead, markets are alleged to "lock in" to inferior choices.

The paradigm-setting case for this claim of market failure is the typewriter keyboard. This section presents our treatment of the history of the typewriter keyboard, which was first published in 1990. As we show, the keyboard story concisely illustrates not a market failure but rather a market success.

1

Networked World

"Build a better mousetrap and the world will beat a path to your door." This adage, most often attributed to Ralph Waldo Emerson, is implicit in enough economic thinking that it might well take its place alongside "Incentives matter" and "Marginal returns eventually decline" as a fundamental building block. In the past decade, however, some journalists, bureaucrats, and even some economists have begun to doubt Emerson's adage. The markets for new technologies, they say, seem to behave differently from the markets for traditional goods and services. Laissez-faire policies may have produced good results in other times, but they cannot be relied on in the Age of Technology. Emerson, they say, may have been right about mousetraps, but his adage doesn't hold up so well if the only mouse in sight is a computer mouse.

Doubts, of course, are niggling things, but once they gain a footing, it's only human nature to look for evidence that doubts may be facts. And the evidence seems to be everywhere. Consider the typewriter keyboard. Everybody knows that the QWERTY keyboard arrangement is completely arbitrary. We'd all be better off if we had a different one, but changing now would just be too much trouble. We stick to the old, inefficient arrangement only out of unhappy habit. The market failed us on that one, didn't it?

And what about VCR format? Surely you've heard that the Beta format was much, much better than the VHS format that dominates the market today. Another market failure?

Or let's look at the war between Apple and DOS operating systems. Talk to any Mac owner. He'll be quick to tell you that Macintosh was a whole lot better than DOS. We'd all be using the Mac today except for one thing: The market failed. Didn't it?

If such stories were true, the evidence would be incontrovertible: In markets for technology, the best does not always prevail. And in this unpredictable New World, quality would lose out to the oddest things: a trivial head start, an odd circumstance, a sleight of hand. When there are benefits to compatibility, or conformity, or certain other kinds of interaction that can be categorized as *network effects*, a single product would tend to dominate in the market. Moreover, this product would enjoy its privileged position whether or not it was the best available.

Thus, the new technology gives economics, the dismal science, a chance to forge an unhappy marriage with the bad-news media. Journalists have been quick to file the bad-news story of how the world is not only unfair, but also illogical. Private litigants in the antitrust arena file suits alleging unfair competition. Incumbents, they say, are using unfair advantages to foist inferior products on an unsuspecting public. The U.S. Justice Department has been quick to second the notion, using it to support their cases against Microsoft and other successful U.S. firms.

The good news for consumers, though the bad news for the failure-mongers and the U.S. Justice Department (and possibly for consumers if the Department of Justice should prevail), is that the economic theory of a high-tech market locked in to failure has its foundation only in shallow perceptions—not in facts. A hard look at the claims of real-world market failures shows that they are not failures at all. The winners in the high-tech world have won not by chance, but rather by the choices of consumers in an open market. A responsible examination of the historical record provides evidence that entrepreneurship and consumer sovereignty work as well in high-tech markets as they do in more traditional ones—which is to say, very well indeed.

Does Wheat Separate from Chaff?

The prospect that the mediocre prevail is certainly intuitively intriguing. Anyone who has spent any time watching the celebrity talk shows, where celebrities talk about being celebrities, has already confronted a version of the world where cream doesn't seem to rise to the top. Do television commentators really represent our best intellects? How many of these people are famous for being famous? How many of them just look and sound good, inasmuch as they merely need to read statements over a teleprompter?

One might also ask how many political leaders represent the pinnacle of the talent pool. It is easy to suspect that success might be arbitrary. Alternatively, if success is not perfectly arbitrary, perhaps it is imperfectly arbitrary: the consequence of a head start, being in the right place at one particularly right time, or having the right connections.

On the other hand, television viewers might not necessarily want to watch someone who reminds them of a teacher in school, no matter how erudite that teacher might have been. Instead, they might want to be entertained. They might prefer a politician they like over one who might better understand the issues. They might prefer Metallica to Mozart, or Sidney Sheldon to Shakespeare. If we want to, we can conclude that they have bad taste, but we can't conclude that they are not getting the products that provide *them* the most quality for their money. So we need to be careful when defining quality.

Quality might well be in the eye of the beholder, but for certain utilitarian products, consumers can be expected to prefer the ones that perform tasks the most economically. Who wants a car that breaks down, or doesn't accelerate, or fails to stop when the brakes are pushed? Who prefers a television with a fuzzy picture, or an awkward-to-use tuner, or garbled sound? We ought to expect some agreement about quality among these utilitarian products. But even here we need to distinguish between efficient solutions and elegant solutions. In 1984, a Macintosh operating system might have ranked highest in terms of elegance, but DOS might have gotten the job done most cost effectively.

Still, it is natural to suspect that things—products, technologies, standards, networks—might be successful independent of their quality. It might be even more predictable that intellectuals, who prefer Mozart and Shakespeare, or at least Norman Mailer and Woody Allen, might disdain markets as reliable arbiters of product quality.

One part of the answer seems clear. Success sometimes does breed more success. It's human nature to get on a bandwagon—as any parent who has tried to track down a Cabbage Patch doll, a Beanie Baby, or a Furby can tell you. And bandwagons can be more than mob mentality. Some things are more useful when lots of people have them. The owner of the first telephone or fax machine found his purchase a lot more useful when a lot more people jumped on that particular consumer bandwagon.

A different and more interesting question, however, is whether it is possible for a product like a telephone or fax machine to continue to be successful only because it has been successful. If this can happen, it could be that in some important aspects of our economic lives, we have the things we have for no particularly good reason, and, what is more important, we might be doing without better things, also for no particularly good reason.

Let's look at the VCR example again. People benefit from using video-tape recorders that are compatible with other people's videotape recorders. That way they can rent tapes more readily at the video store and send tapes of the grandkids to mom. If some early good luck in the marketplace for VHS leads people to buy mostly VHS machines, VHS might come to pre-vail completely over Beta, the alternative, in the home-use market. Fur-ther, Beta might never recover because no one would want to go it alone: No one buys Beta because no one buys Beta. Some people allege that not only can this happen but also that it did happen, in spite of the fact that Beta (it is alleged) offered advantages over VHS.

Although this story is at odds with the actual history of VCRs in a num-ber of important ways (which we will examine in detail in chapter 6), it does illustrate the kinds of allegations that are often made about market performance regarding new technologies. First, if there are benefits to do-ing or using what other people are doing or using, it is more likely that we will all do and use the same things. This condition might lead to a kind of monopoly. Second, it is possible that for some kinds of goods, it is only by chance that the resulting market outcomes are good ones.

If in fact these allegations about market performance could be borne out, we would indeed have a problem. But these scenarios are not true stories; they are mere *allegations* of problems that *could* occur. The thrust of our research for the last decade, and that of a several other scholars, shows that in the real world, the marketplace is remarkably free of such disasters. Nevertheless, the fearmongers' allegation of possible problems has begun to exert a powerful influence on public policy—particularly antitrust policy.

Where's the Beef?

Almost everyone will acknowledge that the market is a pretty efficient arbi-ter of winners and losers for most goods. If two brands of fast-food ham-burgers are offered in the market, we expect people who like McDonald's better to buy McDonald's, and people who like Burger King better to buy Burger King. No one is much concerned about how many other people are buying the same brand of hamburger that they are buying, so each person buys what he wants. If one product is, in everyone's estimation, better than the other and also no more costly to produce, then the better one will survive in the market and the other one will not. If it is possible for new companies to enter the industry, they probably will choose to produce products that have characteristics more like the one that is succeeding.

But many other outcomes are possible. If some people like McDonald's and some like Burger King, then both brands may endure in the market. If Wendy's comes along, and everyone likes Wendy's better, Wendy's will displace them both. If some people like Wendy's better and others are happy with what they've had, then all three may survive. None of this is terribly complicated: May the best product win. It might be that VCRs can be successful merely because they are successful, but hamburgers are different. They have to taste good.

The VCR and hamburger stories appear to be different in three important ways. First, the tendency toward monopoly is alleged only in the VCR story, not in the hamburger story. Second, the possibility of the best product failing is alleged only in the VCR story, not in the hamburger story. Third, the impossibility of a new champion replacing the old one is alleged only in the VCR story, not in the hamburger story.

Size Matters: The Economics of Increasing Returns

If, for some activity, bigger is better, we say that the activity exhibits *increasing returns to scale*. Economists have long observed that increasing returns can pose special problems in a market economy. In the best-understood cases of increasing returns, the average or unit cost of producing a good—the average cost of a good—decreases as the level of output increases. Such effects can be witnessed within firms—for example, there are often economies to mass production. They can also be observed at the industry level—a whole industry may experience lower costs per unit of output as industry scale increases.

Most production exhibits this increasing-returns property to some degree. As we go from extremely small quantities of output to somewhat larger outputs, the cost per unit of output decreases. A great deal of direct evidence supports this claim. It explains why a homemaker might make two pie crusts at once: one to fill right away; one to put in the freezer. It explains why two might live almost as cheaply as one. It explains why we don't see a television manufacturer or a tire plant in every town. Instead, larger plants serve broad geographical markets. Regions specialize.

For most activities, however, we expect that these increasing returns will run out, or will be exhausted as output gets very large: Bigger is better—but only up to a point. This is why we do not satisfy the nation's demand for steel from a single plant or satisfy the world's demand for wheat from a single farm. Some constraint—land, labor, transportation cost, management ability—ultimately imposes limits on the size of a single enterprise.

On the other hand, it is possible for a special case to arise where a single company enjoys decreasing production costs all the way up to outputs large enough to satisfy an entire market. This circumstance is what economists call a *natural monopoly*. A natural monopoly arises as the inevitable outcome of a competitive process. Bigger is better, or bigger is at least cheaper, so a large firm can drive out any smaller competitors. Many of the so-called public utilities were once thought to exhibit this property, and some are still monopolies. Generation and distribution of electricity, for example, was once understood to enjoy increasing returns all the way up to the point of serving entire regions of the country. This was, at least according to textbook explanations, the reason that these public utilities were established as price-regulated monopolies.

Even for public utilities, we now think that the benefits of increasing returns are more limited than we once believed. The result has been a public-policy decision to restructure and deregulate many of the utility industries, separating the increasing-returns parts of those industries from the rest. But even as deregulation in these industries proceeds, a number of analysts have begun to argue that we ought to get involved in regulating modern high-technology industries, basing their argument on the claim that high-tech industries are particularly prone to increasing returns.

The software industry, they argue, is subject to increasing returns that are almost inexhaustible: Once the code for a software product is written, a software firm has very low costs of producing additional copies of that product. But while the relationship between the fixed costs of designing a software product and the direct costs of making additional copies may explain increasing returns over some range, the idea that software production is subject to inexhaustible economies of scale merits careful scrutiny. After all, the cost of serving an additional customer is not confined to the cost of reproducing the software. It also includes the costs of service and technical support, the costs of marketing, and the design costs of serving a larger, and therefore more diverse, user population. In this way, the software industry is a lot like many older, traditional industries that have large fixed and low variable costs, including book, newspaper, and magazine publishing; radio and television broadcasting; and university lecturing.

Two's Company, Three's a Network

Many of our newest industries involve information technologies. In one way or another, they allow us to access, process, and distribute large amounts of information at high speeds and low costs. Many of these industries exhibit one variety or another of increasing returns.

One important form of these increasing returns results from what is called a *network effect*.[1] If consumers of a particular good care about the number of other consumers that consume the same good, that good is subject to network effects. The telephone, though hardly a new technology, is an obvious example. Your telephone is more valuable to you if many other people have telephones. Telephones are, in fact, extremely important because almost everyone has one, and everyone expects everyone else to have one. The VCR problem that we discussed also relies on a network effect. Similarly, fax machines are much more valuable as more people get them—another network effect.

A particular kind of network effect occurs as technology develops. As more firms or households use a technology, there is a greater pool of knowledge for users to draw upon. As we gain experience and confidence in a technology, the expected payoff to someone who adopts it may become greater. Once a few people have tried a technology, others know what can be expected. Working knowledge of a technology, availability of appropriate equipment and supplies, and more widespread availability of expertise all make a well-worked technology more useful to businesses and consumers.

A special kind of network effect is the establishment of *standards*. Standard systems of building products allow projects to go together more quickly and more cheaply, make building materials more immediately and more assuredly available, and make design easier. Standard dimensions for nuts and bolts make it easier to find hardware and easier to fill a toolbox. In very much the same way, software standards make it much easier to build computers, design peripherals, and write applications.

Network effects, including technology development and standards, are examples of increasing returns that extend beyond individual firms to entire industries. Each of the firms in an industry may enjoy advances in technology, or they all may benefit from the establishment of networks where products are compatible, or they all may benefit from the emergence and consolidation of a standard.

Certainly network effects, scale economies, standards, and technology development are important ideas that correspond to important features of our economy. One cannot observe the emergence of the Internet without being impressed with the power of networks. One cannot survey developments in microelectronics or biotechnology without understanding that the rate and direction of technological development has a profound influence on our standard of living. Furthermore, it is in this world with network effects and increasing returns that the VCR type of problem that we described above is a theoretical possibility. It is precisely this possibility that has become an important influence on policy, particularly in the area of antitrust.

Conventional versus Serial Monopoly

Because bigger is better in increasing-returns industries, such industries tend to evolve into monopolies. Monopoly, however, does not lead inevitably to a bad economic outcome for society. The harm of a monopoly is not that it exists, but rather that it exploits its advantage by restricting the quantities of goods or services that it produces in order to elevate price. It is this decrease in quantity and increase in price that constitutes the economic inefficiency of monopoly power. If there is an objective in antitrust that can be argued from well-established economic principles, avoiding this particular inefficiency is it. But rising prices, of course, are not characteristics of high-tech industries. On the contrary, prices for high-tech products and services have drifted (and sometimes plummeted) down over time. Why is this?

Sometimes an industry develops in such a way that monopoly is not only a likely outcome but also a desirable one. In such industries, what we are likely to witness is not conventional monopoly, but rather serial monopoly: one monopoly or near monopoly after another. WordStar gave way to WordPerfect, which gave way to Word. Beta gave way to VHS, which will, in time, give way to some digital format. In such a world, anything that a firm does to compete can be, at some point, viewed as an attempt to monopolize. And anything that a firm does to improve its products, extend its standards, or reach additional markets will look like an attempt to monopolize. It will look like an attempt to monopolize because it *is* an attempt to monopolize.[2] But where standards or networks or other sources of increasing returns are sufficiently important, such actions might be socially desirable. In fact, these actions are the very things that allow more valuable societal arrangements—standards, networks, and new technologies—to replace less valuable ones.

In the special environment of serial monopoly, monopolistic-looking firms that offer an inferior deal to consumers are readily replaced. In such circumstances, an attempt to exploit a monopoly by restricting output and raising prices is suicidal. Furthermore, in the environment of serial monopoly, firms, even monopolistic ones, will end up decreasing their profits if they handicap their products in some way. For example, if they unwisely bundle goods into their product that cost more than they are worth, given the available alternatives, they will lose out. In short, in the environment of serial monopoly (unlike conventional monopoly) the punishment for inferior products, elevated prices, or inefficient bundling is obsolescence and replacement.

The Typewriter Keyboard

In academic, legal, and popular circles, the possibility of products locking in to inefficient standards generally comes around to the paradigmatic story of the history of the typewriter keyboard. This story serves as the teaching example, the empirical foundation for any number of theorems that have been served up in economics journals, and the label for an entire way of thinking.

As a popular book on the economics of policy issues concludes, "In the world of QWERTY, one cannot trust markets to get it right."[3] This statement captures two important features of economic orthodoxy. First, the paradigm-setting case is the story of the typewriter keyboard. Second, academic thinking about these models and the policy discussions surrounding them are inextricably tied up with a kind of market failure. Although markets may work with conventional goods, where individual interactions are unimportant, markets cannot be trusted to make good choices in QWERTY worlds, where one person's consumption or production choice has implications for what others can consume or how others can produce.

The standard typewriter keyboard arrangement owes its existence to the Remington typewriter, which was introduced in 1873. Christopher Latham Sholes had patented a typewriter in 1867, developed the machine for a while, and ultimately sold it to the Remington company, a manufacturer of firearms. The story is told that the arrangement of the typewriter keys had been chosen by Sholes in order to mitigate a problem with jamming of the typing hammers. Remington had a good deal of trouble marketing the typewriter, but it did begin to catch on toward the end of the nineteenth century. There were a number of typewriters that competed with Remington, some of them produced by Sholes's original collaborators. In 1888 a contest in Cincinnati pitted a very fast hunt-and-peck typist who used the rival Caligraph typewriter against one of the world's first touch-typists, who used the Sholes-Remington design. According to the tale, an overwhelming victory for the Sholes-Remington typewriter helped establish touch-typing on the Remington machine as the proper way to type. The QWERTY arrangement, so called because of the order of the letters in the left top row, became the standard, and the world has not looked back.

QWERTY remains the standard, it is claimed, in spite of the fact that a vastly superior alternative is available. In 1936 August Dvorak, a professor of education at the University of Washington, patented an alternative keyboard arrangement. Dvorak's arrangement was alleged to follow ergonomic principles to achieve a keyboard layout that allowed faster typing and was easier to learn. Nevertheless, the Dvorak keyboard has never caught on. The failure of the Dvorak keyboard, it is alleged, is an example of lock-in. No one learns to type on the Dvorak machine because Dvorak machines are hard to find, and Dvorak machines are hard to find because so few typists learn to type on the Dvorak keyboard. Thus, the superior latecomer has never been able to displace the inferior incumbent; we are locked in to a bad standard.

If true, the keyboard story would be the perfect illustration of lock-in. First, the failure to change to a better outcome rests on an interdependence across users. It might be costly to know only an odd typewriter configuration. Second, there are few performance characteristics that matter, and better would be fairly unambiguous, so better would be well defined.

But the keyboard story, as outlined above and retold in any number of places, is simply not true. The Dvorak keyboard is not, as urban legend has it, vastly superior to the standard QWERTY configuration.

When we first began our research on the economics of standards in the late 1980s we, like others, took the typewriter story we have just outlined as one of the illustrative lessons on the topic. Our interests at the time were how institutions such as standards were shaped by the benefits and costs— demand and supply—that they generated. As we began to look into this case to get a more precise measure of the benefits that Dvorak offered, we began to discover a body of evidence that indicates that Dvorak, in fact, offered no real advantage. As we dug further, we discovered that the evidence in favor of a Dvorak advantage seems to be very unscientific in character and came mostly from Dvorak himself. Eventually, we encountered claims that Dvorak himself had been involved in one study that had been given prominence by other writers, a study attributed to the U.S. Navy. After some struggle, we found a copy of the study—not an official U.S. Navy publication—and found that it was shot through with error and bias. Our conclusion, based on a survey of various ergonomic studies, computer simulations, and training experiments, is that the Dvorak keyboard offers no significant advantage over the standard Sholes or QWERTY keyboard.

Our research into the QWERTY keyboard was published as "The Fable of the Keys," the lead article in the *Journal of Law and Economics,* in April 1990. For a time after the paper was published, it was ignored by many economists who had a stake in the theory of lock-in. Even though the article had appeared in one of the most influential economics journals, and was appearing on graduate reading lists in graduate economics courses throughout the country, it was seldom cited in the theoretical literature. Instead, the flawed version of QWERTY continued to be cited as evidence of the empirical importance of lock-in. It was only with our publication in 1994 of an article in the *Journal of Economic Perspectives,* a journal that goes to all members of the American Economics Association, that it became more common to acknowledge that the received history of the typewriter keyboard might be flawed. We made further progress with publications in *Regulation* and *Upside* magazines, both in 1995, which introduced our findings to policy and business audiences.

Yet the myth lives on. In the January 1996 issue of *Harvard Law Review,* Mark Roe makes much of QWERTY as an example of market failure. In February 1996 Steve Wozniak explained Apple's problems by analogy to the Dvorak keyboard: "Like the Dvorak keyboard, Apple's superior operating system lost the market share war." In spring of 1997, Jared Diamond published a lengthy discussion in *Discover* magazine in which he fretted over the demise of the "infinitely better" Dvorak keyboard. Other recent references to the paradigmatic story appear in the *New York Times, Washington Post, Boston Globe, PBS News Hour with Jim Lehrer,* and even *Encyclopedia Britannica.*

Indeed, what may be the most telling feature of the QWERTY keyboard story is its staying power. Lock-in theory suggests that in an increasing-returns world, the market selects good alternatives only by good luck. If there are lots of so-called QWERTY worlds, there should be no problem finding plenty of examples of inferior technologies or products that have prevailed against superior alternatives. If the QWERTY story does not illustrate the point, it ought to be possible for lock-in theorists to replace it with another, just as compelling, story. Such a story has not been forthcoming. But this does not keep the lock-in theories from pouring forth. Nor does it keep the lock-in theorists from broadly applying these theories to sweeping policy prescriptions.

Application to Antitrust

Theories of lock-in, network effects, and increasing returns have come to greater public prominence as a result of their very conspicuous, and sometimes inconsistent application to antitrust. As we write, the Microsoft antitrust case is in district court. There is no telling how the court case will come out, but it is now thought that it is very likely that the case will affect very profoundly how antitrust law is applied to information technologies and other industries that involve some degree of increasing returns.

The government's case against Microsoft depends heavily on network effects. Franklin Fisher, the economic expert witness for the government, begins the substantive portion of his report as follows: "The dominance of Microsoft's windows 9x operating system in the market for operating systems for Intel compatible desktop personal computers is protected, among other things, by what are sometimes referred to as network effects." Nothing about the argument we present here would dispute the claim that there are network effects, although the ability of these effects to "protect" a firm's market position is very much in dispute. The very heart of our argument is that network effects do not "protect" market participants from competition. The essence of the lock-in claim is that inferior products are "protected" from superior newcomers. As we will see, however, there is neither convincing theory nor even minimal empirical support for the lock-in proposition.

Weak as the lock-in argument is as an economic foundation for an anti-trust case, it is a foundation that antitrust enforcers cannot really do with-out. The usual monopoly concern—low output and high price—is simply not much in evidence in the computer software market, as we show in chapters 8 and 9. It is particularly not in evidence in markets where Mi-crosoft has become dominant. Instead, prices continue to fall and products keep getting better, all while the number of users keeps getting larger. This would seem to be the opposite of the monopoly inefficiency problem. In-stead, it is evidence of sharp rivalry assuring that consumers get a better and better deal.

If that problem is not fundamental enough, network effects or increas-ing returns-to-scale industries pose a still more basic conflict for antitrust practice. If industries really do have network effects, we would expect them to gravitate toward monopoly. If we all really do want to use the same word processor, or the same VCR, then we probably will. And should. So, in fighting monopolies that would arise in some network industries, antitrust enforcers are not only fighting against the workings of the marketplace, they are fighting against efficient outcomes as well.

These monopolies, we would argue, are efficient outcomes in network industries, where the network effect, or scale economy, is strong. It is not our argument that such monopolies would never arise, but rather that these monopolies would not be locked in. Such industries are serial mo-nopolies; one monopoly after another. One firm occupies a monopoly position for a while, only to be replaced when something else comes along. The stakes are always very high in such industries. The new en-trant seeks not to coexist with the incumbent, but rather to replace it. These high stakes, and the rivalry that they create, is apparently sufficient discipline to hold monopoly prices in check and to keep the rate of inno-vation very rapid.

This condition—that network effects, if strong enough, will give us a succession of monopolies—alters the antitrust world considerably. As we write, the government's expert witness in the Microsoft case is testifying that Microsoft has monopoly power. As evidence of monopoly power, he cites a Microsoft internal e-mail in which a Microsoft employee expresses concern that the price of the Windows NT operating system may induce the entry of a rival that would replace NT. The e-mail is, however, not evidence of monopoly power "protected," to use Franklin Fisher's term, by network effects. Instead, it is the inevitable manifestation of competition in an industry with important network effects, a world of serial monopoly. In this world, the firm competes not to take its share of today's market; it competes to take the market for its share of days. Legislatures and courts may choose to make some ways of competing legal and some not, but the old structuralist approaches to antitrust will only be misleading. In a world of strong network effects, all competition is monopolization, though perhaps short-lived monopolization.

The Plan of This Book

Because of the importance of the keyboard story for this debate, we have included "The Fable of the Keys" in its entirety as chapter 2, which along with this opening chapter constitutes Part One of the book. "The Fable of the Keys" presents in detail the history of the QWERTY keyboard, and the relationship of that history to economic thought.

Part Two, "The Theory" develops the theoretical background for the arguments that we present in "The Fable." In chapters 3 and 4 we discuss the assumptions, logic, and limitations of the theory of network effects, path dependence, and lock-in. In chapter 5 we examine how these theories come together in a simple model that we construct for two hypothetical competing standards. These three chapters explain why it is reasonable to expect that the keyboard arrangement, and any other network product that survives in competitive markets, would be at least passably efficient. They also explain why lock-in theorists have had a difficult time providing examples of inefficient lock-in.

Part Three, "The Real World," begins with chapter 6, which examines the histories of several alleged lock-ins to inferior arrangements, including Beta versus VHS, and Macintosh versus Windows. These cases build a record in which claim after claim of harmful lock-in turn out to be faulty. Although we cannot prove the negative proposition that there are no cases of harmful lock-in, the fact that the best cases for lock-in are not lock-in at all suggests that the theoretical possibility of lock-in may not have a great deal of relevance in the real world.

The final three chapters in Part Three focus on the software market. They provide a strong factual basis on which to judge the Microsoft case. Chapter 7 describes a method for examining software markets. Chapter 8 applies the method to spreadsheets and word processing. Chapter 9 extends the method to personal finance, desktop publishing, online services, and browsers. We find that a firm can succeed in the software market only when its product is better than the competition's. Furthermore, this rule applies even to Microsoft. When a Microsoft product is judged the best available, it displaces incumbent standards and dominates its product segment. When another firm's product is judged the best available, the Microsoft product fails.

The appendix describes the general antitrust principles raised by the new technologies and examines some of the specific claims that are being raised in the Microsoft case.

NOTES TO CHAPTER 1

1. Originally, these were called *network externalities* by a number of writers. That term reflected the presumption that these effects constituted a kind of market failure. Much of our writing argues that these effects most often are not market failures. Our 1994 paper suggested that *network effects* is a more appropriate term for the general concept, relegating *network externalities* to a subset of cases where markets were demonstrated to work incorrectly.

2. We should point out that almost all competitive actions could be construed as attempts to monopolize an industry. The difference is that market shares grow sufficiently large in network industries that the possibility of monopolizing an industry appears much more real.

3. Paul Krugman, page 235, contained within a chapter aptly titled "The Economics of QWERTY," in *Peddling Prosperity* (1994). We quote Krugman's statement as typical of the treatments. We note, however, that Krugman does suggest caution in drawing policy conclusions from the typewriter story, and has since indicated that he thinks the force and frequency of the QWERTY problem may be limited. See Gomes in the *Wall Street Journal* (1998), and Krugman in *Slate* (1998).

2

The Fable of the Keys

The term *standard* can refer to any social convention (standard of conduct, legal standards), but it most often refers to conventions that require exact uniformity (standards of measurement, computer operating systems). Current efforts to control the development of high-resolution television, multitasking computer-operating systems, and videotaping formats have heightened interest in standards.

The economics literature on standards has focused recently on the possibility of market failure with respect to the choice of a standard. In its strongest form, the argument is essentially this: An established standard can persist over a challenger, even where all users prefer a world dominated by the challenger, if users are unable to coordinate their choices. For example, each of us might prefer to have Beta-format videocassette recorders as long as prerecorded Beta tapes continue to be produced, but individually we do not buy Beta machines because we don't think enough others will buy Beta machines to sustain the prerecorded tape supply. I don't buy a Beta format machine because I think that you won't; you don't buy one because you think that I won't. In the end, we both turn out to be correct, but we are both worse off than we might have been. This, of course, is a Catch-22 that we might suppose to be common in the economy. There will be no cars until there are gas stations there will be no gas stations until there are cars. Without some way out of this conundrum, joyriding can never become a favorite activity of teenagers.[1]

The logic of these economic traps and conundrums is impeccable as far as it goes, but we would do well to consider that these traps are often avoided in the market. Obviously, gas stations and automobiles do exist, so

---

This is a very lightly edited version of our article "The Fable of the Keys," which appeared in the October 1990 issue of the *Journal of Law and Economics*. We have retained the complete article even though there is some minor duplication of material with other sections of the book, because "Fable" is, in a way, a microcosm of the rest of the book, and we wanted the reader to get the gist of the story up front.

participants in the market must use some technique to unravel such conundrums. If this Catch-22 is to warrant our attention as an empirical issue, at a minimum we would hope to see at least one real-world example of it. In the economics literature on standards,[2] the popular real-world example of this market failure is the standard QWERTY typewriter keyboard[3] and its competition with the rival Dvorak keyboard.[4] This example is noted frequently in newspaper and magazine reports, seems to be generally accepted as true, and was brought to economists' attention by the papers of Paul David.[5] According to the popular story, the keyboard invented by August Dvorak, a professor of education at the University of Washington, is vastly superior to the QWERTY keyboard developed by Christopher Sholes that is now in common use. We are to believe that, although the Dvorak keyboard is vastly superior to QWERTY, almost no one trains on Dvorak because there are too few Dvorak machines, and there are almost no Dvorak machines because there are too few Dvorak typists.

This chapter examines the history, economics, and ergonomics of the typewriter keyboard. We show that David's version of the history of the market's rejection of the Dvorak keyboard does not report the true history, and we present evidence that the continued use of QWERTY is efficient given the current understanding of keyboard design. We conclude that the example of the Dvorak keyboard is what beehives and lighthouses were for earlier market-failure fables. It is an example of market failure that will not withstand rigorous examination of the historical record.[6]

Some Economics of Standards

Some standards change over time without being impaired as social conventions. Languages, for example, evolve over time, adding words and practices that are useful and winnowing features that have lost their purpose. Other standards are inherently inflexible. Given current technologies, it will not do, for example, for broadcast frequencies to drift in the way that orchestral tuning has. A taste for a slightly larger centimeter really cannot be accommodated by a sequence of independent decisions the way that increased use of contractions in academic writing can. Obviously, if standards can evolve at low cost, they would be expected to evolve into the forms that are most efficient (in the eyes of those adopting the standards).

Conversely, an inappropriate standard is most likely to have some permanence where evolution is costly.

In their influential article on standards, Joseph Farrell and Garth Saloner presented a formal exploration of the difficulties associated with changing from one standard to another.[7] They constructed hypothetical circumstances that might lead to market failure with respect to standards. To refer to the condition in which a superior standard is not adopted, they coined the phrase *"excess inertia"*. Excess inertia is a type of externality: Each nonadopter of the new standard imposes costs on every other potential user of the new standard, and there is no third party (entrepreneur) in the model who can rearrange incentives to achieve efficient adoption. In the case of excess inertia, the new standard can be clearly superior to the old standard, and the sum of the private costs of switching to the new standard can be less than the sum of the private benefits, and yet the switch does not occur. This is to be distinguished from the far more common case where a new standard is invented that is superior to the old, but for which the costs of switching are too high to make the switch practicable. Users of the old standard may regret their choice of that standard, but their continued use of the old standard is not inefficient if the costs of switching are greater than the benefits.

Farrell and Saloner's construct is useful because it shows the theoretical possibility of a market failure and also demonstrates the role of information. There is no possibility of excess inertia in their model if all participants can communicate perfectly.[8] In this regard, standards are not unlike other externalities in that costs of transacting are essential. Thus, standards can be understood within the framework that Ronald Coase offered decades ago in his paper on externalities.[9]

By their nature, this model and others like it must ignore many factors in the markets they explore. Adherence to an inferior standard in the presence of a superior one represents a loss of some sort. Such a loss implies a profit opportunity for someone who can figure out a means of appropriating some of the value made available from changing to the superior standard. Furthermore, institutional factors such as head starts from being first on the market, patent and copyright law, brand names, tie-in sales, discounts, and so on, can also lead to appropriation possibilities (read "profit opportunities") for entrepreneurs, and with these opportunities we expect to see activity set in motion to internalize the externalities. The greater the gap in performance between two standards, the greater are these profit opportunities, and the more likely that a move to the efficient standard will take place. As a result, a clear example of excess inertia is apt to be very hard to find. Observable instances in which a dramatically inferior standard prevails are likely to be short-lived, imposed by authority, or fictional.

The creator of a standard is a natural candidate to internalize the externality.[10] If a standard can be "owned," the advantage of the standard can be appropriated, at least in part, by the owner. Dvorak, for example, patented his keyboard. An owner with the prospect of appropriating substantial benefits from a new standard would have an incentive to share some of the costs of switching to a new standard. This incentive gives rise to a variety of internalizing tactics. Manufacturers of new products sometimes offer substantial discounts to early adopters, offer guarantees of satisfaction, or make products available on a rental basis. Sometimes manufacturers offer rebates to buyers who turn in equipment based on old standards, thus discriminating in price between those who have already made investments in a standard and those who have not. Internalizing tactics can be very simple: Some public utilities once supplied light bulbs, and some UHF television stations still offer free UHF indoor antennas. In many industries firms provide subsidized or free training to assure an adequate supply of operators. Typewriter manufacturers were an important source of trained typists for at least the first fifty years of that technology.[11]

Another internalizing tactic is convertibility. Suppliers of new-generation computers occasionally offer a service to convert files to new formats. Cable-television companies have offered hardware and services to adapt old televisions to new antenna systems for an interim period. Of interest in the present context, for a time before and after the Second World War, typewriter manufacturers offered to convert QWERTY typewriters to Dvorak for a very small fee.[12]

All of these tactics tend to unravel the apparent trap of an inefficient standard, but there are additional conditions that can contribute to the ascendancy of the efficient standard. An important one is the growth of the activity that uses the standard. If a market is growing rapidly, the number of users who have made commitments to any standard is small relative to the number of future users. Sales of audiocassette players were barely affected by their incompatibility with the reel-to-reel or eight-track players that preceded them. Sales of sixteen-bit computers were scarcely hampered by their incompatibility with the disks or operating systems of eight-bit computers.

Another factor that must be addressed is the initial competition among rival standards. If standards are chosen largely through the influence of those who are able to internalize the value of standards, we would expect, in Darwinian fashion, the prevailing standard to be the fittest economic competitor. Previous keyboard histories have acknowledged the presence of rivals but they seem to view competition as a process leading to results indistinguishable from pure chance.

Consideration of the many complicating factors present in the market suggests that market failure in standards is not as compelling as many of the abstract models seem to suggest. Theoretical abstraction presents candidates for what might be important, but only empirical verification can determine if these abstract models have anything to do with reality.

The Case for the Superiority of the Dvorak Keyboard

Paul David, a leading economic historian, with his 1985 paper introduced economists to the conventional story of the development and persistence of the current keyboard standard, known as the Universal, or QWERTY, keyboard. The key features of that story are as follows. The operative patent for the typewriter was awarded in 1868 to Christopher Latham Sholes, who continued to develop the machine for several years. Among the problems that Sholes and his associates addressed was the jamming of the type bars when certain combinations of keys were struck in very close succession. As a partial solution to this problem, Sholes arranged his keyboard so that the keys most likely to be struck in close succession approached the type point from opposite sides of the machine. Because QWERTY was designed to accomplish this now obsolete mechanical requirement, maximizing speed was not an explicit objective. Some authors even claim that the keyboard is actually configured to minimize speed since decreasing speed would have been one way to avoid the jamming of the typewriter. At the time, however, a two-finger hunt-and-peck method was probably all that was contemplated, so the keyboard speed envisioned was quite different from touch-typing speeds.

The rights to the Sholes patent were sold to E. Remington & Sons in early 1873. The Remingtons added further mechanical improvements and began commercial production in late 1873.

A watershed event in the received version of the QWERTY story is a typing contest held in Cincinnati on July 25, 1888. Frank McGurrin, a court stenographer from Salt Lake City, who was apparently one of the first typists to memorize the keyboard and use touch-typing, won a decisive victory over Louis Taub. Taub used the hunt-and-peck method on a Caligraph, a machine that used seventy-two keys to provide upper- and lower-case letters. According to popular history, the event established once and for all that the Remington typewriter, with its QWERTY keyboard, was technically superior. More important, the contest created an interest in touch-typing, an interest directed at the QWERTY arrangement. Reportedly, no one else at that time had skills that could even approach McGurrin's, so there was no possibility of countering the claim that the Remington keyboard arrangement was efficient. McGurrin participated in typing contests and demonstrations throughout the country and became something of a celebrity. His choice of the Remington keyboard, which may well have been arbitrary, contributed to the establishment of the standard. So it was, according to the popular telling, that a keyboard designed to solve a short-lived mechanical problem became the standard used daily by millions of typists.[13]

In 1936 August Dvorak patented the Dvorak Simplified Keyboard (DSK), claiming that it dramatically reduced the finger movement necessary for typing by balancing the load between hands and loading the stronger fingers more heavily. Its inventors claimed advantages of greater speed, reduced fatigue, and easier learning. These claims have been accepted by most commentators including David, who refers, without citation, to experiments done by the U.S. Navy that showed that the increased efficiency obtained with the DSK would amortize the cost of retraining a group of typists within ten days of their subsequent full-time employment.[14] In spite of its claimed advantages the Dvorak keyboard has never found much acceptance.

This story is the basis of the claim that the current use of the QWERTY keyboard is a market failure. The claim continues that a beginning typist will not choose to train in Dvorak because Dvorak machines are likely to be difficult to find, and offices will not equip with Dvorak machines because there is no available pool of typists.

This is an ideal example. The number of dimensions of performance are few and in these dimensions the Dvorak keyboard appears overwhelmingly superior. These very attributes imply, however, that the forces to adopt this superior standard should also be very strong. It is the failure of these forces to prevail that warrants our critical examination.

The Myth of Dvorak

Farrell and Saloner mention the typewriter keyboard as a clear example of market failure. So too does the textbook by Tirole.[15] Both works cite David's article as the authority on this subject. Yet there are many aspects of the QWERTY-versus-Dvorak fable that do not survive scrutiny. First, the support for the claim that Dvorak is a better keyboard is both scant and suspect. Second, studies in the ergonomics literature find no significant advantage for Dvorak that can be deemed scientifically reliable. Third, the competition among producers of typewriters, out of which the standard emerged, was far more vigorous than is commonly reported. Fourth, there were far more typing contests than just the single Cincinnati contest. These contests provided ample opportunity to demonstrate the superiority of alternative keyboard arrangements. That QWERTY survived significant challenges early in the history of typewriting demonstrates that it is at least among the reasonably fit, even if not the fittest that can be imagined.

Gaps in the Evidence for Dvorak

Like most of the historians of the typewriter, David seems to assume that Dvorak is decisively superior to QWERTY. He never questions this assertion, and he consistently refers to the QWERTY standard as inferior. His most tantalizing evidence is his undocumented account of the U.S. Navy experiments. After recounting the claims of the Navy study, he adds "if as Apple advertising copy says, DSK 'lets you type 20 to 40% faster,' why did this superior design meet essentially the same resistance as the previous seven improvements on the QWERTY typewriter keyboard?"[16]

Why indeed? The survival of QWERTY is surprising to economists only in the presence of a demonstrably superior rival. David uses QWERTY's survival to demonstrate the nature of path dependency, the importance of history for economists, and the inevitable oversimplification of reality imposed by theory. Numerous theorists have used his historical evidence to claim empirical relevance for their versions of market failure. But on what foundation does all this depend? All we get from David is an undocumented assertion and some advertising copy.

Although the view that Dvorak is superior is widely held, this view can be traced to a few key sources. A book published by Dvorak and several co-authors in 1936 included some of Dvorak's own scientific inquiry.[17] Dvorak and his co-authors compared the typing speed achieved in four different and completely separate experiments conducted by various researchers for various purposes.[18]

One of these experiments examined the typing speed on the Dvorak keyboard and three examined typing speed on the QWERTY keyboard. The authors claimed that these studies established that students learn Dvorak faster than they learn QWERTY. A serious criticism of their methodology is that the various studies they compared used students of different ages and abilities (for example, students learning Dvorak in grades 7 and 8 at the University of Chicago Lab School were compared with students in conventional high schools), in different school systems taking different tests, and in classes that met for different periods of time. Still more serious is that they did not stipulate whether their choice of studies was a random sample or the full population of available studies. So their study really establishes only that it is possible to find studies in which students learning to type on QWERTY keyboards appear to have progressed less rapidly in terms of calendar time than Dvorak's students did on his keyboard. Even in this Dvorak study, however, the evidence is mixed as to whether students, as they progress, retain an advantage when using the Dvorak keyboard, since the differences seem to diminish as typing speed increases.

In general it is desirable to have independent evaluation, and here the objectivity of Dvorak and his co-authors seems particularly open to question. Their book seems to be more in the vein of an inspirational tract than a scientific work. Consider the following passages taken from their chapter about relative keyboard performances):

> The bare recital to you of a few simple facts should suffice to indict the available spatial pattern that is so complacently entitled the universal [QWERTY] keyboard. Since when was the universe lopsided? The facts will not be stressed, since you may finally surmount most of the ensuing handicaps of this [QWERTY] keyboard. Just enough facts will be paraded to lend you double assurance that for many of the errors that you will inevitably make and for much of the discouraging delay you will experience in

longed-for speed gains, you are not to blame. If you grow indignant over the beginner's role of innocent victim, remember that a little emotion heightens determination.[19]

Analysis of the present keyboard is so destructive that an improved arrangement is a modern imperative. Isn't it obvious that faster, more accurate, less fatiguing typing can be attained in much less learning time provided a simplified keyboard is taught. [20]

The Navy study, which seems to have been the basis for some of the more extravagant claims of Dvorak advocates, is also flawed. Arthur Foulke, Sholes's biographer, and a believer in the superiority of the Dvorak keyboard, points out several discrepancies in the reports coming out of the Navy studies. He cites an Associated Press report of October 7, 1943, to the effect that a new typewriter keyboard allowed typists to "zip along at 180 words per minute" but then adds, "However, the Navy Department, in a letter to the author October 14, 1943, by Lieutenant Commander W. Marvin McCarthy, said that it had no record of and did not conduct such a speed test, and denied having made an official announcement to that effect."[21] Foulke also reports a *Business Week* story of October 16, 1943, that reports a speed of 108, not 180, words per minute.

We were able to obtain, with difficulty, a copy of the 1944 Navy report.[22] The report does not state who conducted the study. It consists of two parts, the first based on an experiment conducted in July 1944 and the second based on an experiment conducted in October of that year. The report's foreword states that two prior experiments had been conducted but that "the first two groups were not truly fair tests." We are not told the results of the early tests.

The first of the reported experiments consisted of the retraining of fourteen Navy typists on newly overhauled Dvorak keyboards for two hours a day. We are not told how the subjects were chosen, but it does not appear to be based on a random process. At least twelve of these individuals had previously been QWERTY typists with an average speed of thirty-two words per minute although the Navy defined competence as fifty words per minute. The typists had IQs that averaged 98 and dexterity skills with an average percentile of 65. The study reports that it took fifty-two hours for typists to catch up to their old speed. After completing an average of eighty-three hours on the new keyboard, typing speed had increased to an average of fifty-six net words per minute compared to their original thirty-two words per minute, a 75 percent increase.

The second experiment consisted of the retraining of eighteen typists on the QWERTY keyboard. It is not clear how these typists were picked or even if members of this group were aware that they were part of an experiment. We are not told whether this training was performed in the same manner as the first experiment (the Navy retrained people from time to time and this may just have been one of these groups). The participants' IQs and dexterity skills are not reported. It is difficult to have any sense whether this group is a reasonable control for the first group. The initial typing scores for this group averaged twenty-nine words per minute but these scores were not measured identically to those from the first experiment. The report states that because three typists initially had net scores of zero words per minute, the beginning and ending speeds were calculated as the average of the first four typing tests and the average of the last four typing tests. In contrast, the initial experiment using Dvorak simply used the first and last test scores. This truncation of the reported values reduced the measured increase in typing speed on the QWERTY keyboard by a substantial margin and raises further suspicion upon the motives and abilities of the researchers.[23]

The measured increase in net typing speed for QWERTY retraining was from twenty-nine to thirty-seven words per minute (28 percent) after an average of 158 hours of training, considerably less than the increase that occurred with the Dvorak keyboard.

The Navy study concludes that training in Dvorak is much more effective than retraining in QWERTY. But the experimental design leaves too many questions for this to be an acceptable finding. Do these results hold for typists with normal typing skills or only for those far below average? Were the results for the first group just a regression to the mean for a group of underperforming typists? How much did the Navy studies underestimate the value of increased QWERTY retraining due to the inconsistent measurement? Were the two groups given similar training? Were the QWERTY typewriters overhauled, as were the Dvorak typewriters? There are many possible biases in this study. All, suspiciously, seem to be in favor of the Dvorak design.

The authors of the Navy study do seem to have their minds made up concerning the superiority of Dvorak. In discussing the background of the Dvorak keyboard and prior to introducing the results of the study, the report claims on page 2: "Indisputably, it is obvious that the Simplified Keyboard is easier to master than the Standard Keyboard." Later, on page 24, the report's authors refer to QWERTY as an "ox" and Dvorak as a "jeep" and add, "no amount of goading the oxen can materially change the end result."

There are other problems of credibility with these Navy studies, having to do with potential conflicts of interest. Foulke (p. 103) identifies Dvorak as Lieutenant Commander August Dvorak, the Navy's top expert in the analysis of time and motion studies during World War II. Earle Strong, a professor at Pennsylvania State University and a one-time chairman of the Office Machine Section of the American Standards Association, reports that the 1944 Navy experiment and some Treasury Department experiments performed in 1946 were conducted by none other than Dr. Dvorak.[24] We also know that Dvorak had a financial stake in this keyboard. He owned the patent on the keyboard and had received at least $130,000 from the Carnegie Commission for Education for the studies performed while he was at the University of Washington.[25]

But there is more to this story than the weakness of the evidence reported by the Navy, or Dvorak, or his followers. A 1956 General Services Administration study by Earle Strong, which was influential in its time, provides the most compelling evidence against the Dvorak keyboard. This study is ignored in David's history for economists and is similarly ignored in other histories directed at general audiences. Strong conducted what appears to be a carefully controlled experiment designed to examine the costs and benefits of switching to Dvorak. He concluded that retraining typists on Dvorak had no advantages over retraining on QWERTY.

In the first phase of Strong's experiment, ten government typists were retrained on the Dvorak keyboard. It took well over twenty-five days of four-hours-a-day training sessions for these typists to catch up to their old QWERTY speed. When the typists had finally caught up to their old speed, Strong began the second phase of the experiment. The newly trained Dvorak typists continued training and a group of ten QWERTY typists began a parallel program to improve their skills. In this second phase, the Dvorak typists progressed less quickly with further Dvorak training than did QWERTY typists training on QWERTY keyboards. Thus, Strong concluded that Dvorak training would never be able to amortize its costs. He recommended that the government provide further training in the QWERTY keyboard, for QWERTY typists. The information provided by this study was largely responsible for putting Dvorak to rest as a serious alternative to QWERTY for many firms and government agencies.[26]

Strong's study does leave some questions unanswered. Because it uses experienced typists, it cannot tell us whether beginning Dvorak typists could be trained more quickly than beginning QWERTY typists. Further, although one implication of Strong's study is that the ultimate speed achieved would be greater for QWERTY typists than for Dvorak typists (because the QWERTY group was increasing the gap over the Dvorak group in the second phase of the experiment), we cannot be sure that an experiment with beginning typists would provide the same results.[27]

Nevertheless, Strong's study must be taken seriously. It attempts to control the quality of the two groups of typists and the instruction they receive. It directly addresses the claims that came out of the Navy studies, which consider the costs and benefits of retraining. It directly parallels the decision that a real firm or a real government agency might face: Is it worthwhile to retrain its present typists? The alleged market failure of the QWERTY keyboard as represented by Farrell and Saloner's excess-inertia notion is that all firms would change to a new standard if only they could each be assured that the others would change. If we accept Strong's findings, it is not a failure to communicate that keeps firms from retraining its typists or keeps typists from incurring their own retraining costs. If Strong's study is correct, it is efficient for current typists not to switch to Dvorak.

Current proponents of Dvorak have a different view when they assess why the keyboard has not been more successful. Hisao Yamada, an advocate of Dvorak who is attempting to influence Japanese keyboard development, gives a wide-ranging interpretation to the Dvorak keyboard's failure. He blames the Depression, bad business decisions by Dvorak, World War II, and the Strong report. He goes on to say:

> There were always those who questioned the claims made by DSK followers. Their reasons are also manifold. Some suspected the superiority of the instructions by DSK advocates to be responsible (because they were all holders of advanced degrees); such a credential of instructors is also apt to cause the Hawthorne effect. Others maintain that all training experiments, except the GSA one as noted, were conducted by the DSK followers, and that the statistical control of experiments was not

well exercised. This may be a valid point. It does not take too long to realize, however, that it is a major financial undertaking to organize such an experiment to the satisfaction of statisticians. . . . The fact that those critics were also reluctant to come forth in support of such experiments . . . may indicate that the true reason of their criticism lies elsewhere.[28]

Nevertheless, Yamada as much as admits that experimental findings reported by Dvorak and his supporters cannot be assigned much credibility and that the most compelling claims cited by Yamada for DSK's superiority come from Dvorak's own work. Much of the other evidence Yamada uses to support his views of DSK's superiority actually can be used to make a case against Dvorak. Yamada refers to a 1952 Australian post office study that showed no advantages for DSK, when it was first conducted. It was only after adjustments were made in the test procedure (to remove "psychological impediments to superior performance") that DSK did better.[29] He cites a 1973 study based on six typists at Western Electric, where after 104 hours of training on DSK, typists were 2.6 percent faster than they had been on QWERTY.[30] Similarly, Yamada reports that in a 1978 study at Oregon State University after 100 hours of training typists were up to 97.6 percent of their old QWERTY speed. Both of these retraining times are similar to those reported by Strong and not to those in the Navy study. Yamada, however, thinks the studies themselves support Dvorak.[31] But unlike the Strong study, neither of these studies included parallel retraining on QWERTY keyboards. As the Strong study points out, even experienced QWERTY typists increase their speed on QWERTY if they are given additional training. Even if that problem is ignored, the possible advantages of Dvorak are all much weaker than those reported from the Navy study.

Evidence from the Ergonomics Literature

The most recent studies of the relative merits of keyboards are found in the ergonomics literature. These studies provide evidence that the advantage of the Dvorak layout is either small or nonexistent. For example, A. Miller and J. C. Thomas conclude that "the fact remains, however, that no alternative has shown a realistically significant advantage over the QWERTY for general purpose typing."[32] In two studies based on analysis of hand-and-finger motions, R. F. Nickells, Jr. finds that Dvorak is 6.2 percent faster than QWERTY,[33] and R. Kinkhead finds only a 2.3 percent advantage for

Dvorak.[34] Simulation studies by Donald Norman and David Rumelhart find similar results:

> In our studies . . . we examined novices typing on several different arrangements of alphabetically organized keyboards, the Sholes (QWERTY) keyboard, and a randomly organized keyboard (to control against prior knowledge of Sholes). There were essentially no differences among the alphabetic and random keyboards. Novices type slightly faster on the Sholes keyboard, probably reflecting prior experience with it. We studied expert typists by using our simulation model. Here, we looked at the Sholes and Dvorak layouts, as well as several alphabetically arranged keyboards. The simulation showed that the alphabetically organized keyboards were between 2% and 9% slower than the Sholes keyboard, and the Dvorak keyboard was only about 5% faster than the Sholes. These figures correspond well to other experimental studies that compared the Dvorak and Sholes keyboards and to the computations of Card, Moran, and Newell . . . for comparing these keyboards. . . . For the expert typist, the layout of keys makes surprisingly little difference. There seems no reason to choose Sholes, Dvorak, or alphabetically organized keyboards over one another on the basis of typing speed. It is possible to make a bad keyboard layout, however, and two of the arrangements that we studied can be ruled out.[35]

These ergonomic studies are particularly interesting because the claimed advantage of the Dvorak keyboard has been based historically on the claimed ergonomic advantages in reduced finger movement. Norman and Rummelhart's discussion offers clues to why Dvorak does not provide as much of an advantage as its proponents have claimed. They argue,

> For optimal typing speed, keyboards should be designed so that:
>
> A. The loads on the right and left hands are equalized.
>
> B. The load on the home (middle) row is maximized.
>
> C. The frequency of alternating hand sequences is maximized and the frequency of same-finger typing is minimized.

The Dvorak keyboard does a good job on these variables, especially A and B: 67% of the typing is done on the home row and the left-right hand balance is 47–53%. Although the Sholes (QWERTY) keyboard fails at conditions A and B (most typing is done on the top row and the balance between the two hands is 57% and 43%), the policy to put successively typed keys as far apart as possible favors factor C, thus leading to relatively rapid typing.

The explanation for Norman and Rummelhart's factor C is that during a keystroke, the idle hand prepares for its next keystroke. Thus, Sholes's decision to solve a mechanical problem through careful keyboard arrangement may have inadvertently satisfied a fairly important requirement for efficient typing.

The consistent finding in the ergonomic studies is that the results imply no clear advantage for Dvorak. These studies are not explicitly statistical, yet their negative claim seems analogous to the scientific caution that one exercises when measured differences are small relative to unexplained variance. We read these authors as saying that, in light of the imprecision of method, scientific caution precludes rejection of the hypothesis that Dvorak and QWERTY are equivalent. At the very least, the studies indicate that the speed advantage of Dvorak is not anything like the 20–40 percent that is claimed in the Apple advertising copy cited by David. Moreover, the studies suggest that there may be no advantage of the Dvorak keyboard for ordinary typing by skilled typists. It appears that the principles by which Dvorak "rationalized" the keyboard may not have fully captured the actions of experienced typists largely because typing appears to be a fairly complex activity.

A final word on all of this comes from Frank McGurrin, the world's first known touch-typist:

> Let an operator take a new sentence and see how fast he can write it. Then, after practicing the sentence, time himself again, and he will find he can write it much faster: and further practice on the particular sentence will increase the speed on it to nearly or quite double that on the new matter. Now let the operator take another new sentence, and he will find his speed has dropped back to about what it was before he commenced practicing the first sentence. Why is this? The fingers are capable of

the same rapidity. It is because the mind is not so familiar with the keys.[36]

Of course, performance in any physical activity can presumably be improved with practice. But the limitations of typing speed, in McGurrin's experiment, appear to have something to do with a mental or, at least, neurological skill and fairly little to do with the limitations on the speeds at which the fingers can complete their required motions.

Typewriter Competition

The Sholes typewriter was not invented from whole cloth. Yamada reports that there were fifty-one inventors of prior typewriters, including some earlier commercially produced typewriters. He states: "Examination of these materials reveals that almost all ideas incorporated into Sholes' machines, if not all, were at one time or another already used by his predecessors."[37]

Remington's early commercial rivals were numerous, offered substantial variations on the typewriter, and in some cases enjoyed moderate success. There were plenty of competitors after the Sholes machine came to market. The largest and most important of these rivals were the Hall, Caligraph, and Crandall machines. The Yost, another double-keyboard machine, manufactured by an early collaborator of Sholes, used a different inking system and was known particularly for its attractive type. According to production data assembled by Yamada, the machines were close rivals, and they each sold in large numbers.[38] Franz Xavier Wagner, who also worked on the 1873 Remington typewriter, developed a machine that made the type fully visible as it was being typed. This machine was offered to, but rejected by, the Union Typewriter Company, the company formed by the 1893 merger of Remington with six other typewriter manufacturers.[39] In 1895, Wagner joined John T. Underwood to produce his machine. Their company, which later became Underwood, enjoyed rapid growth, producing 200 typewriters per week by 1898.[40] Wagner's offer to Union also resulted in the spinoff from Union of L. C. Smith, who introduced a visible-type machine in 1904.[41] This firm was the forerunner of the Smith-Corona company.

Two manufacturers offered their own versions of an ideal keyboard: Hammond in 1893 and Blickensderfer in 1889.[42] Each of these machines survived for a time, and each had certain mechanical advantages. Blickens-derfer later produced what may have been the first portable and the first electric typewriters. Hammond later produced the Varityper, a standard office type-composing machine that was the antecedent of today's desktop publishing. The alternative keyboard machines produced by these manu-facturers came early enough that typewriters and, more important, touch-typing were still not very popular. The Blickensderfer appeared within a year of the famous Cincinnati contest that first publicized touch-typing.

In the 1880s and 1890s typewriters were generally sold to offices not already staffed with typists or into markets in which typists were not readily available. Because the sale of a new machine usually meant training a new typist, a manufacturer that chose to compete using an alternative keyboard had an opportunity. As late as 1923, typewriter manufacturers operated placement services for typists and were an important source of operators. In the earliest days, typewriter salesmen provided much of the limited training available to typists.[43] Because almost every sale required the train-ing of a typist, a typewriter manufacturer that offered a different keyboard was not particularly disadvantaged. Manufacturers internalized training costs in such an environment, so a keyboard that allowed more rapid train-ing might have been particularly attractive.

Offering alternative keyboards was not a terribly expensive tactic. The Blickensderfer used a type-bar configuration similar in principle to the IBM Selectric type ball, and so could easily offer many different configura-tions. The others could create alternative keyboard arrangements by sim-ply soldering the type to different bars and attaching the keys to different levers. So apparently the problem of implementing the conversion was not what kept the manufacturers from changing keyboards.

The rival keyboards did ultimately fail, of course.[44] But the QWERTY keyboard cannot have been so well established at the time the rival key-boards were first offered that they were rejected because they were non-standard. Manufacturers of typewriters sought and promoted any technical feature that might give them an advantage in the market. Certainly, shorter training and greater speed would have been an attractive selling point for a typewriter with an alternative keyboard. Neither can it be said that the rival keyboards were doomed by inferior mechanical characteristics, because these companies went on to produce successful and innovative, though QWERTY-based, typing machines. Thus we cannot attribute our inheritance of the QWERTY keyboard to a lack of alternative keyboards or the chance association of this keyboard arrangement with the only mechanically adequate typewriter.

Typing Competitions

Typing competitions provided another test of the QWERTY keyboard. These competitions are somewhat underplayed in the conventional history. David's history mentions only the Cincinnati contest. Wilfred Beeching's history, which has been very influential, also mentions only the Cincinnati contest and attaches great importance to it: "Suddenly, to their horror, it dawned upon both the Remington Company and the Caligraph Company officials, torn between pride and despair, that whoever won was likely to put the other out of business!" Beeching refers to the contest as having established the four-bank keyboard of the Remington machine "once and for all."[45]

In fact, typing contests and demonstrations of speed were fairly common during this period. They involved many different machines, with various manufacturers claiming to hold the speed record.

Under the headline "Wonderful Typing," the *New York Times* reported on a typing demonstration given the previous day in Brooklyn by a Mr. Thomas Osborne of Rochester, New York.[46] The *Times* reported that Mr. Osborne "holds the championship for fast typing, having accomplished 126 words a minute at Toronto August 13 last." This was a mere three weeks after the Cincinnati contest. In the Brooklyn demonstration he typed 142 words per minute in a five-minute test, 179 words per minute in a single minute. and 198 words per minute for 30 seconds. He was accompanied by a Mr. George McBride, who typed 129 words per minute blindfolded. Both men used the non-QWERTY Caligraph machine. The *Times* offered that "the Caligraph people have chosen a very pleasant and effective way of proving not only the superior speed of their machine, but the falsity of reports widely published that writing blindfolded was not feasible on that instrument."

There were other contests and a good number of victories for McGurrin and Remington. On August 2, 1888, a mere week after the Cincinnati contest, the *Times* reported a New York contest won by McGurrin with a speed of 95.8 words per minute in a five-minute dictation. In light of the received history, according to which McGurrin is the only person to have memorized the keyboard, it is interesting to note the strong performance of his rivals. Miss May Orr typed 95.2 words per minute, and M. C. Grant typed 93.8 words per minute. Again, on January 9, 1889, the *Times* reported a McGurrin victory under the headline "Remington Still Leads the List."

We should probably avoid the temptation to compare the Caligraph speed with the Remington speeds, given the likely absence of any serious attempts at standardizing the tests. Nevertheless, it appears that the issue of speed was not so readily conceded as is reported in Beeching's history. Typists other than McGurrin could touch-type, and machines other than Remington were competitive. History has largely ignored events that did not build toward the eventual domination by QWERTY. This focus may be reasonable for the history of the Remington Company or the QWERTY keyboard. But if we are interested in whether the QWERTY keyboard's existence can be attributed to more than happenstance or an inventor's whim, these events do matter.

Conclusions

The trap constituted by an obsolete standard may be quite fragile. Because real-world situations present opportunities for agents to profit from changing to a superior standard, we cannot simply rely on an abstract model to conclude that an inferior standard has persisted. Such a claim demands empirical examination.

As an empirical example of market failure, the typewriter keyboard has much appeal. The objective of the keyboard is fairly straightforward: to get words onto the recording medium. There are no conflicting objectives to complicate the interpretation of performance. But the evidence in the standard history of QWERTY versus Dvorak is flawed and incomplete. First, the claims for the superiority of the Dvorak keyboard are suspect. The most dramatic claims are traceable to Dvorak himself, and the best-documented experiments, as well as recent ergonomic studies, suggest little or no advantage for the Dvorak keyboard.[47]

Second, by ignoring the vitality and variety of the rivals to the Remington machine with its QWERTY keyboard, the received history implies that Sholes's and McGurrin's choices, made largely as matters of immediate expediency, established the standard without ever being tested. A more careful reading of historical accounts and checks of original sources reveal a different picture: There were touch-typists other than McGurrin; there were competing claims of speed records; and Remington was not so well established that a keyboard offering significant advantages could not have gained a foothold. If the fable is to carry lessons about the workings of markets, we need to know more than just who won. The victory of the tortoise is a different story without the hare.

There is more to this disagreement than a difference in the evidence that was revealed by our search of the historical record. Our reading of this history reflects a more fundamental difference in views of how markets, and social systems more generally, function. David's overriding point is that economic theory must be informed by events in the world. On that we could not agree more strongly. But ironically, or perhaps inevitably, David's interpretation of the historical record is dominated by his own implicit model of markets, a model that seems to underlie much economic thinking. In that model an exogenous set of goods is offered for sale at a price, take it or leave it. There is little or no role for entrepreneurs. There generally are no guarantees, no rental markets, no mergers, no loss-leader pricing, no advertising, no marketing research. When such complicating institutions are acknowledged, they are incorporated into the model piecemeal. And they are most often introduced to show their potential to create inefficiencies, not to show how an excess of benefit over cost may constitute an opportunity for private gain.

In the world created by such a sterile model of competition, it is not surprising that accidents have considerable permanence. In such a world, embarking on some wrong path provides little chance to jump to an alternative path. The individual benefits of correcting a mistake are too small to make correction worthwhile, and there are no agents who might profit by devising some means of capturing a part of the aggregate benefits of correction.

It is also not surprising that in such a world there are a lot of accidents. Consumers are given very little discretion to avoid starts down wrong paths. A model may assume that consumers have foresight or even that they are perfectly rational, but usually in a very limited sense. For example, in the model of Farrell and Saloner, consumers can predict very well the equilibrium among the two candidate standards. But they are attributed no ability to anticipate the existence of some future, better standard. We are not led to ask how the incumbent standard achieved its status; like Topsy, "It jes' growed."

But at some moment, users must commit resources to a standard or wait. At this moment, they have clear incentives to examine the characteristics of competing standards. They must suffer the consequences of a decision to wait, to discard obsolete equipment or skills, or to continue to function with an inferior standard. Thus, they have a clear incentive to consider what lies down alternative paths. Though their ability to anticipate future events may not be perfect, there is no reason to assume that their judgments are any more faulty than those of any other observers and there are reasons to believe their judgments are likely to be better.

Finally, it is consistent that, in a world in which mistakes are frequent and permanent, "scientific approaches" cannot help but make big improvements to market outcomes. In such a world, there is ample room for enlightened reasoning, personified by university professors, to improve on the consequences of myriad independent decisions. What credence can possibly be given to a keyboard that has nothing to accredit it but the trials of a group of mechanics and its adoption by millions of typists? If we use only sterilized models of markets, or ignore the vitality of the rivalry that confronts institutions, we should not be surprised that the historical interpretations that result are not graced with truth.

NOTES TO CHAPTER 2

1. This trap is treated more seriously in the literature on standards than in other economics literature. This reflects a supposition that foresight, integration, or appropriation are more difficult in the case of standards.

2. See, for example, Farrell and Saloner (1985), Katz and Shapiro (1985), or Tirole (1988).

3. QWERTY stands for the arrangement of letters in the upper left-hand portion of the keyboard below the numbers. This keyboard is also known as the Sholes, and Universal.

4. This is also sometimes known as the DSK keyboard for Dvorak Simplified Keyboard. The keys are arranged in a different order.

5. See Paul David (1985) and (1986).

6. See Ronald Coase (1974) and Steven N. Cheung (1973). These two papers examine how the market provided the services of lighthouses and beehives respectively. These examinations were important because these two examples had been put forward as instances where markets could not work, just as the QWERTY example has been put forward. Our debt is obvious.

7. Farrell and Saloner (1985).

8. Inertia is not necessarily inefficient. Some delay in settling on a standard will mean that relatively more is known about the associated technology and the standards themselves by the time most users commit to a technology. See the well-known discussion of Harold Demsetz (1969) on the nature of efficiency. If God can costlessly cause the adoption of the correct standard, any inertia is excessive (inefficient) in comparison. But it seems ill advised to hold this up as a serious benchmark. Excessive inertia should be defined relative to some achievable result. Furthermore, some reservation in committing to standards will allow their creators to optimize standards rather than rushing them to the market to be first. If the first available standard were always adopted, then standards, like patents, might generate losses from the rush to be first. Creators might rush their standards to market, even where waiting would produce a better and more profitable product.

9. Coase (1960). This paper is one of the most influential economics articles of the century. Coase pointed out that what may appear to be externalities often will be taken care of in the market.

10. We may ask ourselves why new standards are created if not with the idea of some pecuniary reward. One would hardly expect nonobvious and costly standards to proliferate like manna from heaven.

11. Herkimer County Historical Society (1923) notes that in the early 1920s a single typewriter company was producing 100,000 typists a year.

12. Foulke (1961) notes on p. 106, "Present day keyboard machines may be converted to the simplified Dvorak keyboard in local typewriter shops. It is now available on any typewriter. And it costs as little as $5 to convert a Standard to a simplified keyboard."

13. This history follows David (1985), but see Beeching (1974) as an example of an account with the features and emphasis described here.

14. David (1985), p. 332. If true, this would be quite remarkable. A converted Sholes typist will be typing so much faster that whatever the training cost, it is repaid every ten days. Counting only working days, this would imply that the investment in retraining repays itself approximately twenty-three times in a year. Does this seem even remotely possible? Do firms typically ignore investments with returns in the range of 2200 percent?

15. Tirole states (p. 405), "Many observers believe that the Dvorak keyboard is superior to this QWERTY standard even when retraining costs are taken into account. However it would be foolish for a firm to build this alternative keyboard and for secretaries to switch to it individually." Under some circumstances it might have been foolish for secretaries and firms to act in this manner but this type of behavior hardly seems foolish in many real-world situations. For example, large organizations (federal, state, and local governments, Fortune 500 companies, and the like) often have tens of thousands of employees. And these organizations could have undertaken the training if the costs really were compensated in a short time.

16. David (1986), p. 34.

17. Dvorak et al. (1936).

18. Dvorak et al. (1936), p. 226.

19. Dvorak et al. (1936), p. 210.

20. Dvorak et al. (1936), p. 221.

21. Foulke, p. 103.

22. We tried to have the Navy supply us with a copy when our own research librarians could not find it. The Navy research librarian had no more success even though she checked the Navy records, the Martin Luther King Library, the Library of Congress, the National Archives, the National Technical Communication Service, and other agencies. We were finally able to locate a copy held by an organization, Dvorak International. We would like to thank its director, Virginia Russell, for her assistance. She believes that they obtained their copy from the Underwood Company. We would be more sanguine about the question of the document's history had it been available in a public archive. The copy we received was "A Practical Experiment in Simplified Keyboard Retraining—A Report on the Retraining of Fourteen Standard Keyboard Typists on the Simplified Keyboard and a Compari-

son of Typist Improvement from Training on the Standard Keyboard and Retraining on the Simplified Keyboard," Navy Department, Division of Shore Establishments and Civilian Personnel, Department of Services, Training Section, Washington, D.C. (July and October 1944).

23. It is not an innocuous change. We are told (p. 20) that three QWERTY typists initially scored zero on the typing test but that their scores rose to twenty-nine, thirteen, and sixteen within four days. We are also told that several other typists had similar improvements in the first four days. These improvements are dismissed as mere testing effects that the researchers wished to eliminate. But the researchers made no effort to eliminate the analogous testing effect for the Dvorak typists. Truncating the measurements to the average of the first four days reduces the reported speed increases for the three typists with zero initial speed by at least thirteen, twelve, and fourteen words per minute. Assuming the existence of two other typists with similar size testing effects, removing this testing effect would reduce the reported speed improvements by 3.6 words per minute, lowering the gain from 46 percent to 28 percent. We are not supplied sufficient data to measure the effect of the truncation at the end of the measuring period. But the problem is worse than just this. Not only were the improvements measured differently, but truncation at this stage is also entirely unjustified inasmuch as there is no testing effect to be removed at this stage of the experiment after many tests have been taken. Although the apparent effect of these measurement differences is significant, the indisputable problem is that they were not applied equally to the QWERTY and Dvorak typists.

24. Earle P. Strong (1956). Yamada (1980), trying to refute criticisms of Dvorak's keyboard, claims that Dvorak did not conduct these studies, but only provided the typewriters. Yamada admits that Dvorak was in the Navy and in Washington when the studies were conducted but denies any linkage. We do not know whom to believe, but we are skeptical that Dvorak would not have had a large influence on these tests, based on the strong circumstantial evidence and given Foulke's identification of Dvorak as the Navy's top expert on such matters. Interestingly, Yamada accuses Strong of being biased against the Dvorak keyboard (p. 188). He also impugns Strong's character. He accuses Strong of refusing to provide other (unnamed) researchers with his data. He also implies that Strong stole money from Dvorak because in 1941, when Strong was a supporter of Dvorak's keyboard, he supposedly accepted payment from Dvorak to conduct a study of the DSK keyboard without ever reporting his results to him.

25. Yamada (1980).

26. At the time of Strong's experiment, Dvorak had attracted a good deal of attention. At least one trade group had taken the position that pending confirmation from the Strong study it would adopt Dvorak as its new standard. See "US Plans to Test New Typewriter," *New York Times*, November 1, 1955; "Revolution in the Office," *New York Times*, November 30, 1955; "Key Changes Debated," *New York Times*, June 18, 1956; "US Balks at Teaching Old Typists New Keys," *New York Times*, July 2, 1956; and Peter White, "Pyfgcrt vs. Qwertyuiop," *New York Times*, January 22, 1956.

27. In fact, both the Navy and General Service Administration studies found that the best typists take the longest time to catch up to their old speed and showed the smallest percentage improvement with retraining.

28. Yamada (1980), p. 189.

29. Yamada (1980), p. 185.

30. Yamada (1980), p. 188.

31. Yamada interprets the Oregon study to support the Dvorak keyboard. To do so he fits an exponential function to the Oregon data and notes that the limit of the function as hours of training goes to infinity is 17 percent greater than the typist's initial QWERTY speed. This function is extremely flat, however, and even modest gains appear well outside the range of the data. A 10 percent gain, for example, would be projected to occur only after 165 hours of training.

32. Miller and Thomas (1977).

33. Cited in Yamada (1983), p. 336.

34. Cited in Yamada (1983), p. 365.

35. Norman and Rumelhart (1983).

36. Mares (1909).

37. Yamada (1983), p 177.

38. Yamada (1983), p. 181.

39. Beeching (1974), p. 165.

40. Beeching (1974), p. 214.

41. Beeching (1974), p. 165.

42. David (1986), p. 38. Also see Beeching (1974), pp. 40, 199. Yamada (1983), p. 184, discussing the Hammond keyboard arrangement, states, "This 'ideal' arrangement was far better than QWERTY but it did not take root because by then Remington Schools were already turning out a large number of QWERTY typists every year." In 1893, Blickensderfer offered a portable typewriter with the Hammond keyboard.

43. Herkimer County Historical Society (1923), p. 78.

44. We should also take note of the fact that the QWERTY keyboard, although invented in the United States, has become the dominant keyboard throughout the world. Other countries, when introduced to typewriters, need not have adopted this keyboard if superior alternatives existed since there would not yet have been any typists trained on QWERTY. Yet all other keyboard designs fell before the QWERTY juggernaut. In France and some other countries, the keyboard is slightly different from the QWERTY keyboard used in the United States. The major difference is that the top left-hand keys are Azerty (that is also what these keyboard designs are called) and several letters are transposed, but most of the keys are identical.

45. Beeching (1974), p. 41.

46. *New York Times*, February 28, 1889.

47. There are several versions of the claim that a switch to Dvorak would not be worthwhile. The strongest, which we do not make, is that QWERTY is proven to be the best imaginable keyboard. Neither can we claim that Dvorak is proven to be inferior to QWERTY. Our claim is that there is no scientifically acceptable evidence that Dvorak offers any real advantage over QWERTY. Because of this claim, our assessment of a market failure in this case is rather simple. It might have been more complicated. For example, if Dvorak were found to be superior, it might still be the case that the total social benefits are less than the cost of switching. In that case, we could look for market failure only in the process that started us on the QWERTY keyboard (if the alternative were available at the beginning). Or we might have concluded that Dvorak is better and that all parties could be made better off if we could costlessly command both a switch and any necessary redistribution. Such a finding would constitute a market failure in the sense of mainstream welfare economics. Of course, this circumstance still might not constitute a market failure in the sense of Demsetz, which requires consideration of the costs of feasible institutions that could effect the change.

The Theory

Economists create models of markets to help us understand the way the world works.

Ideally, these models capture the essential ingredients of a market while ignoring less important things. The hoped-for result is a simplification that allows us to think more clearly and make predictions about the real world. Such simplification is constructive only if it captures the things that matter for the phenomena that we are trying to explain. We can't know whether a model has achieved this goal without testing it against reality.

In Part Two we examine several models of path dependence, networks, and standards. We examine critically several models that imply lock-in to inferior products. We explain how these models yield lock-in as an implication. We then show that the implication of lock-in is readily reversed once we acknowledge certain features of real-world markets that these models assume away. The lesson from this is that economists' claims to have "proven" something must be taken with a grain of salt. Those particular assumptions—those simplifications that we talked about—may or may not capture what is important.

Parts of the next three chapters may be a bit difficult for those unfamiliar with economics. We hope we have made chapters 3 and 4 intuitive enough to be accessible with a bit of effort. Chapter 5 is the most demanding in the book. Although the exposition there relies mainly on diagrams, it may prove tough going to some readers. We hope that many of our readers will find insights offered in chapter 5 are worth the effort, but others should feel no shame just reading the introductory sections of the chapter and then skipping to chapter 6.

3

Theories of Path Dependence

     Some economic decisions are self-reinforcing: You buy a VHS videotape recorder because many other people have VHS videotape recorders.[1] Then someone else buys a VHS videotape recorder because members of a group of people, larger now by one, have VHS videotape recorders. If the influence of self-reinforcement is powerful enough, it is theoretically possible that important outcomes might be controlled by mere quirks of history.

But this controlling influence need not be pure happenstance. A settler might choose to build a provisions store at a particular crossing, or by a particular water source, for reasons that are fairly compelling—but only in regard to his own circumstances. A short time later, a stable, a saloon, and a dance hall might be established to take advantage of the availability of the provisioner's customers. Those things might well attract other facilities, and soon the settlement might qualify as a village, a town, or even a city. The choice of the specific location was rational enough, but the reasons for that original choice may be largely irrelevant for the activities that subsequently locate there.

This is an example of path dependence. Outcomes depend critically on history. Efficiency—the economic "goodness" of the location—takes a back seat to a specific sequence of decisions. Each private decision is a good one, conditional on the prior commitments of resources, but the achieved larger outcome need not be the best version of that larger outcome from the set of possible outcomes available at the outset.

The Character of an Economic Model

Economists often like to make their work appear to offer the same certainty as mathematics, presenting much of their work as "proofs." But there is a difference between economics and mathematics. In mathematics, it is always explicit that the proofs apply inside a hypothetical world that is clearly specified in a set of postulates. Mathematicians make no claim that these hypothetical worlds capture some real or experiential world, and in fact often take pains to avoid giving that impression. They are not unhappy if people find that their work is helpful in some endeavors (and this possibility of applicability probably is, in the long run, why they get paid), but realism is not central for much of mathematics. This is where economics is different—or ought to be.

Unlike a mathematical model, an economic model is constructed to explain some behavior that can be observed in the real world. The success of an economic model is determined by examining whether it connects in some important way to that behavior. Economists continue to argue about how to examine that connection, but most economists acknowledge that connecting to reality is a central goal of their science.

This is where economists run into trouble with proofs. Proofs, in economics or anywhere else, are proofs only within the context of certain maintained hypotheses. In formal models, this means that proofs are proofs only in that, given the particular set of assertions about the world that underlie the formal model, the model works in a particular way. Proofs in economic models are not proofs about the world. To learn something about the world, we have to look at the world—at least every now and then.

However much a model may prove, it can never prove that the assumptions it starts off with are the right ones. The assertions that define the model may make a strong appeal to our common sense, or they may not. In any case, models are extraordinary simplifications of the underlying economic world. By what they leave in, they assert what is important. And by what they leave out, either explicitly or implicitly, they also assert what is unimportant. Assertions of both sorts may be wrong. This is why it is important to understand the character of the claim whenever the claim is made that economics has "proven" something or other.

In what follows we argue that the economic models of path dependence fail to capture what is important about the working of real-world markets. This is why, for all their formal correctness, for all their internal consistency, these models fail to capture what is borne out in the real world. Taken on their own merits, these models tell us that there should be "many more QWERTY worlds," to use Paul David's phrase. But as we showed in the previous chapter, not even QWERTY offers us a QWERTY world, and as we show later, other QWERTY worlds are awfully hard to find.

Defining Path Dependence

The term *path dependence* is common in the literature of both economics and law. In general, an assertion of path dependence amounts to some version of "History matters": Where we are today is a result of what has happened in the past. For example, the statement "We saved and invested last year and therefore we have assets today" might be expressed in contemporary economics jargon as "The capital stock is path dependent."

As an idea, path dependence spilled over to economics from intellectual movements that arose elsewhere. In physics and mathematics, related ideas arose in chaos theory. One potential of the nonlinear models of chaos theory is sensitive dependence on initial conditions—determination, and perhaps lock-in, by small, apparently insignificant events. This is the proverbial butterfly wing-flapping in the Sahara that causes a hurricane in the Atlantic. In biology, the related idea is called *contingency*—the irreversible character of natural selection. Scientific popularizations such as Gleick (1987) and Gould (1991) have moved such ideas into the public view.

But path dependence in the physical sciences is not completely analogous to path dependence in the economy. If turtles become extinct, they will not reappear suddenly when circumstances change to make it advantageous to have a shell. But if people stop using large gas-guzzling engines because gasoline has become expensive, they can always revert to their old ways if they come to regret the switch when gasoline prices fall.

In mathematics, *path independence* is a condition for the existence of exact solutions for differential equations. In probability theory, a stochastic process is path independent if the probability distribution for period $t + 1$ is conditioned only on values of the system in period t. In both cases, path independence means that it doesn't matter how you got to a particular point, only that you got there. What is interesting is that in both of these mathematical uses of path independence, history does matter in the ordinary sense. History matters in that it is what gets us to the present state. In a game of coin tossing, for example, the history of coin tosses does determine the winnings of each player. But the particular sequence of winnings does not influence the probabilities on the next toss.

In contrast, if a process is path dependent, the sequence does influence the next step. So in mathematics, path dependence is a stronger claim than simply that history matters. The particulars of the past, and not just the current values of the explicit (state) variables, exercise an influence on what happens next.

Unfortunately, as the idea of path dependence has been borrowed into the social sciences, it has taken on several different and often conflicting meanings. Sometimes it means only that history matters in the very narrowest sense, and other times it means something more.

Economics has always recognized that history matters. The wealth of nations has much to do with the accumulation of capital of every sort: our saving, investing, studying, and inventing. But the current path-dependence literature raises the concern that the quirks and accidents of history may affect economic circumstances in important, and perhaps perverse, ways. The present that we inherit or the future that we build may come about not as a result of endowments and preferences—which set in play the inevitable forces brought about by the maximizing behavior of consumers and producers assumed by most economists—but rather from little things that we might easily change if we only realized how they affected us.

One settler locates at a particular spot for no very important reason, and that leads to the development of a city. Similarly, a chance experiment with one technology might lead to additional experimentation with that technology, which will increase its advantages over untried alternatives. In both cases, we build on what we have, making the best of it. In such contexts, individuals may have limited incentives to examine whether what we have is what we ought to have and limited opportunity to effect a change. Are we optimizing in some global sense, or are we just finding some minor, local, and insignificant optimum? This is the concern raised by path dependence as it has been applied to economic allocations.

The path-dependence literature of economics has been sloppy about specifying the claims that underlie the term "path dependence." Some writers use "path dependence" to denote a failure of the market system to select good outcomes. Others use "path dependence" simply to denote the fact that some things last a long time. But these very different claims have very different implications and must not be confounded. It is possible to specify a taxonomy to organize the discussion of these issues.[2]

First-Degree Path Dependence

A minimal form of path dependence is present whenever there is an element of persistence or durability in a decision. A house, for example, is a very durable good. You don't alter your consumption of housing services every day in response to a change in your income or in prices. Your exact consumption of housing is largely determined by a rental or purchase decision made some time in the past. As a result, an outside observer could not expect to determine the values of your housing consumption today just from the knowledge of the current values that enter your optimization problem. That is to say, we could not predict the size or quality of your house just from knowing your current income, wealth, and the set of prices that you currently face. So here we have something that could be called path dependence: What you have today depends upon conditions that prevailed and decisions you made at some time in the past.

The observation that the size of your house is narrowly wrong, given today's income and prices, would not, however, prompt anyone to claim that you are irrational, nor would it prompt us to discard consumer rationality as a basis for analysis. In any practical approach to modeling a consumer's choice problem, we would recognize the presence of some fixed or quasi-fixed factors and the presence of transaction costs, and examine the consumer's action as a rational pursuit of his interests. Here we have persistence and perhaps nothing else.

You may well have properly predicted all future prices, incomes, family-size developments, and so on. Your house might have been a bit too big at first, then just right, then too small, and then a bit too big later on. But you may have predicted all this fairly well. If so, there is no error or inefficiency. This is what we term *first-degree path dependence*—you made decisions based on correct predictions about the future but because of those decisions your position at any moment may not seem optimal. Path dependence here does no harm; it is simply a consequence of durability.

Second-Degree Path Dependence

Because information is never perfect, there are other possibilities. When individuals fail to predict the future perfectly, it is likely that decisions made before all the information is available (*ex ante* decisions), but that are efficient given the information that is available at the time of the decision, may not turn out to be efficient in retrospect. You may build a house without knowing that five years hence a sewage treatment plant will be built nearby, lowering property values and the neighborhood amenities available. Here the inferiority of a chosen path is unknown at the time a choice is made, but you later recognize that some alternative path would have yielded greater wealth. In such a situation, there is a dependence on past conditions that leads to outcomes that are regrettable and costly to change. You would not have built the house had you known in advance what was going to happen. This dependence is not, however, inefficient in any meaningful sense, given the assumed limitations on knowledge. This is what we call *second-degree path dependence.*

Third-Degree Path Dependence

The strongest kind of path-dependence claim alleges the existence of inefficiencies that are remediable. You know a sewage plant is going to be built, but build a house nearby anyway since all of your friends are buying houses there and you value being part of that neighborhood. You would rather buy a house away from the sewage plant, and so would your friends, but you and your friends are somehow unable to coordinate your actions. This is *third-degree path dependence.*

The fact that the bad outcome was remediable is extremely important in economics. For something to be inefficient in an economic sense, there must be some better alternative. It is not enough to say that something is not as good as we would like it to be. If that were all "inefficient" meant, most everything would be inefficient all of the time. Furthermore, economic inefficiency means more than that there is some conceivable way that resources could be used, or could have been used, that would be better. For an inefficiency to be economically relevant, there must be some better alternative that is feasible in light of the information that we have at the time that we are making a decision. No economist would seriously argue, for example, that all Edison's experiments with light-bulb filaments that burned out rapidly were inefficient because, in principle, he could have selected tungsten wire first. It is easy enough to conjure up images of a world that is better than the one we have. It's fun too. But such imaginative exercises are irrelevant to the issue of economic efficiency.

Oliver Williamson (1993b: 140) introduces the term *remediability* in this context. Williamson uses the term in reference to a circumstance in which it really is possible to do better. He argues that it is necessary to establish remediability before making any claim that an allocation is inefficient. A number of other economists of note, including Harold Demsetz

(1973), Ronald Coase (1964), Guido Calabresi (1968), and Carl Dahlman (1979), have made similar points.

Assessing the Differences

The three categories of path dependence make progressively stronger claims. First-degree path dependence is a simple assertion of an intertemporal relationship, with no implied error of prediction or claim of inefficiency. Second-degree path dependence stipulates that intertemporal effects together with imperfect prediction result in actions that are regrettable, though not inefficient. Third-degree path dependence requires not only that the intertemporal effects propagate error, but also that the error is, in principle, avoidable and remediable.

Clearly, first- and second-degree path dependence are extremely common. They are a result of ordinary durability, and they have always been a part of economic thought. The conventional theories of capital and decision making under uncertainty acknowledge the considerations that give us the first- and second-degree forms of path dependence. Furthermore, first- and second-degree path dependence can be important. For example, economists recognize that people will adapt their behavior and make fixed investments in response to laws and other economic institutions. These adaptations can make it costly to change these laws and institutions later on.

But the main focus, and much of the novelty, of the current economic literature of path dependence is on third-degree path dependence, a kind of path dependence that asserts an economic inefficiency, a market failure. For example, listen to Paul David, whom we met in the previous chapter: "The accretion of technological innovations inherited from the past therefore cannot legitimately be presumed to constitute socially optimal solutions provided for us—either by heroic enterprises or herds of rational managers operating in efficient markets" (1992: 137).

It is third-degree path dependence that constitutes a new challenge to our conventional view of economic markets in which individual decisions can be regarded, with certain well-known exceptions, as leading to allocations that are, overall, the best available. Again, consider the Beta vs. VHS example: It *could* happen that we each prefer the Beta format for video tape recording, but we each buy VHS recorders in order to be compatible with each other. We each maximize privately given this expectation, and it turns out that our forecasts are correct, yet we each end up worse off than we might have. With Beta, under the assumptions here, some or all would have been better off and no one would be worse off, yet we do not choose it. And we made our choices with a full understanding of Beta's superiority.

Of course, that an economic inefficiency *could* happen does not mean that it *does* happen. Where there is economic inefficiency, there must be some feasible alternative that would have predictably been better. But where this condition is satisfied, various parties—owners, inventors, consumers, investors, someone somewhere in the economy—must be able to see a loss coming. That is to say, it must be possible for someone to have credible information that a better allocation is available. Where this is the case, someone somewhere is likely to figure out how to move to this better path and capture some of the resulting net gain. It is an empirical issue, therefore, whether we *do* get the wrong videorecorder, or more generally whether we start down or remain on inefficient paths where known, feasible, and superior alternatives exist.

Models of Lock-In

Most models of lock-in and path dependence share certain key elements. First, most of them assume some version of increasing returns, as defined in the introduction of this book. The role of increasing returns in path dependence may be readily understood using an illustration that Brian Arthur presented in a well-known paper published in 1989. For this illustration, Arthur assumes that society is faced with an opportunity to develop one of two technologies. For each technology, the greater the number of adopters of the technology, the greater the payoffs to those adopters. These increasing payoffs represent the network effect that in turn causes increasing returns in the model. If either of the technologies gets much larger than the other, it will have a tremendous advantage over the other technology in terms of consumer payoffs.

Arthur's illustration is presented in table 3.1. This table shows the payoffs to an individual based on a decision to adopt a given technology. According to the table, the first person to adopt any technology would expect a payoff of 10 if he adopts technology A, or 4 if he adopts technology B. Under these circumstances, Arthur notes, the adopter would certainly choose A. A second adopter would make the same decision, and so on, and with additional adoptions of A, the advantage of technology A over technology B only increases. This is where Arthur finds inefficiency. Notice that if the number of adopters eventually becomes large, technology B offers greater payoffs, yet we will find ourselves stuck with A. Thus, for Arthur, the table tells a story of lock-in, and lock-in to an undesirable outcome. This reasoning is at the heart of many of the models that give us lock-in.

TABLE 3.1
Payoffs to adopters of two technologies

Number of Adoptions	0	10	20	30	40	50	60	70	80	90	100
Technology A	10	11	12	13	14	15	16	17	18	19	20
Technology B	4	7	10	13	16	19	22	25	28	31	34

But there are problems with this table and the lessons that are drawn from it. First, note that the rate at which payoffs increase as adoptions increase must be greater for B than for A if this story is to unfold as presented.

Second, note that the table has no provisions to allow decision makers to anticipate or influence the outcome. But people clearly do both. If the first person faced with the opportunity to purchase a telephone had assumed that he was going to be the only user, we might still be waiting for that technology to catch on. So people making these decisions, these network-type decisions, must be somewhat forward-looking or we wouldn't get any adoptions at all.

When a technology is owned, the owner will have strong incentives to bring about its adoption. We expect the owner of a technology, like the owner of land, to capture some of the value of any special advantages that the technology (or land) offers over the alternatives. Because of that, the owner will take whatever steps are available—whatever investments are necessary—to bring about the adoption of a technology. The owner can, for example, assure early adopters that they will receive highest available payoffs by providing the technology through a lease with a cancellation option. If a different technology prevails, these early adopters can simply switch. He can publicize current and planned adoptions. He can bribe early adopters through low prices or other compensation. Of course, both technologies could be owned, and each owner could pursue these strategies. We would expect, however, that the owner of the technology that creates more wealth, technology B in this case, will be willing and able to invest more in these strategies and could therefore be expected to win such a contest.

Concluding that lock-in is inevitable requires that owners fail to pursue such strategies—and that consumers fail to take steps to protect their own interests. Lock-in is inevitable only if we assume that both consumers and entrepreneurs are passive. To conclude that lock-in follows necessarily from increasing returns requires us to assume away things like consumer and trade magazines, trade associations, guarantees, advertising, brand names, word of mouth, and so on. In short, the assertion that lock-in is a likely affliction in the modern economy assumes an economy for the information age with no information.

Must we, on the other hand, believe that markets always work perfectly in order to conclude that they can avoid the efficiency traps of increasing returns? Must we assume that every entrepreneur can perfectly appropriate the benefit of his innovation to unravel the trap that is implied by Arthur's table? And if so, doesn't our argument get to efficient outcomes just by assuming them?

The answer to all of these questions is no. The owner of the superior technology, technology B in the table, may be quite limited in his ability to capture the wealth that his technology contributes. This, in turn, would limit his ability to invest in establishing his technology. There is no reason, however, to think that the owner of a superior technology would be less able to appropriate a portion of the contribution of the technology than the owner of an inferior technology. As long as the two technology owners are equally bad or equally good at appropriating the values of their technologies, we would expect that the owner of technology B could invest more to get the technology adopted. Of course, this does not prove that technology A could never win out, but it does reveal another restriction implicit in Arthur's illustration.

If agents in the economy have the kind of information that is revealed to us in the table, they will have the motive, and some of them may have the means, of bringing about the preferred outcome. Of course, if no one has this kind of information, the incorrect choice of technology is not remediable, and therefore, by definition, is not an inefficiency in the economic sense. It is spilled milk that no one should cry over. The alternative technology does not really present us with a known feasible alternative that is an improvement; rather, it is just an alternative roll of the dice.

The Meaning of Equilibrium

Economists are interested in discovering equilibrium positions of markets. An objective in economic modeling is determining the equilibrium positions that a model implies. Because our overriding goal is to be able to explain and predict changes in market values such as prices and quantities, it is useful to have a theory that explains how an initial price arises and how the new price arises when circumstances changes. The concept of equilibrium helps us to do this.

Understanding the concept of equilibrium is made easier through a simple analogy. If we wanted to predict where a ball[3] that is used in a stickball game and accidentally hit over a fence is likely to come to rest, we use a model of equilibrium built into our subconscious, developed from everyday experience. If there is a street behind the fenced courts used for a certain type of stickball game, we would naturally look for the ball along the sides of the street and not in the middle, even if there is no traffic. This is because we know that the center of the street is elevated relative to the sides so that rain water will run off to the sewers located on the sides of a street. Anyone who has played ball in city streets knows that sewers are a prime location for balls for this very reason.

If the street is on a steep hill, we would look down the hill for our lost ball, not up the hill, since we know that balls do not roll up hills in defiance of gravity. If the hill levels off after half a block, that is where we would expect the ball to come to rest. In other words, the place we would most expect the ball to come to rest is an equilibrium position, a position where the ball will remain as long as no outside force, such as a car or a kick, moves it away.

Should our ball get picked up by a different group of stickball players, it will not achieve an equilibrium since it will be constantly moving. Balls that fail to achieve equilibrium for these reasons are usually not returned without a fight, but that is outside the realm of our models of where balls land.

An *equilibrium*, therefore, is defined as a condition such that no change will occur unless some outside event intrudes. A *stable equilibrium* is an equilibrium position such that the system will return to the equilibrium in the event of small perturbations away from the position. An *unstable equilibrium* is defined as an equilibrium to which the system will not return if there is a small perturbation. So, continuing with our stickball example, should the ball land exactly on the top of a hill after it goes over the fence, it could, in theory, remain balanced and not roll down the hill. Thus, the flat part of the top of the hill is a potential equilibrium. Any small perturbation, such as a gust of wind, however, will move the ball down the hill, so that the equilibrium on the top of the hill is unstable.

Stable equilibrium positions are, therefore, likely bets for predicting where balls will come to rest, or where prices or other economic magnitudes will come to rest. If there is only one stable equilibrium for a given set of market conditions, and if it takes only a little time for a new equilibrium to be achieved when conditions change, then the magnitudes (location of balls, prices) will almost always be near or at an equilibrium. These are some of the assumptions that underlie economic reasoning, and there is a great deal of empirical work to support conclusions based on them.

It is useful, therefore, in predicting how a variable such as price will change in response to an outside stimulus, to compare equilibrium conditions. For a soybean farmer in the United States at the outbreak of World War I, it would have been useful to be able to predict what the impact on soybean prices would be from a war that was going to disrupt European soybean production. Economists would begin their predictions by assuming that the soybean market was in equilibrium prior to the outbreak of war. Then they would determine how the large decrease of European acreage devoted to growing soybeans would influence the supply of soybeans and the equilibrium price of soybeans. The change in the two equilibrium positions would be the predicted change in price. As long as the price was initially near its equilibrium and moves fairly quickly to its new equilibrium, such an approach will be fruitful.

These economic models are generally accepted and widely used because they are so often helpful. Non-economists use them too. That is how Cal, in John Steinbeck's novel *East of Eden*, was able to make so much money betting on soybean futures.

Equilibria in Models of Network Effects

Many writers in the literature of path dependence present models that have the property of multiple equilibria.

Figure 3.1 illustrates a typical instance (see Liebowitz and Margolis 1996). Here, once again, assume that consumers must choose between two technologies, A and B. This could be the choice between Beta and VHS or between DOS and Macintosh. For a market share to be at an equilibrium position, the fraction choosing a particular alternative must equal the fraction that has recently chosen that alternative.[4] (For example, if VHS had a market share of 75 percent last period, new purchases must be at 75 percent VHS for that share to persist.) An equilibrium condition, therefore, occurs only on the upward-sloping 45-degree line (diagonal) where a format's share of new sales equals its share of the older sales.[5] The S-shaped curve reflects consumer behavior (the consumer's choice of format based on how they have been selling lately) and is consistent with positive network effects and increasing returns.[6] The curve is upward sloping because, as more consumers use technology A, technology A becomes more attractive, and the probability that a new consumer will chose A becomes larger. The S shape reflects a kind of critical-mass influence[7]: when A has very low or very high market share, small improvements in market share are assumed not to make much difference to consumers.

This chart should be interpreted as follows. At the beginning of any period (year, month, whatever) customers put their fingers to the wind to figure out which product is likely to be most popular during the period of ownership between their imminent purchase and their next purchase

FIGURE 3.1

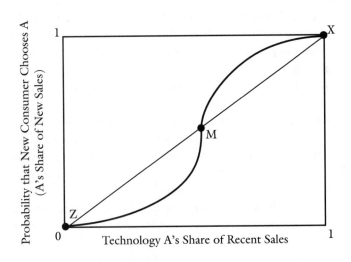

Probability that New Consumer Chooses A (A's Share of New Sales)

Technology A's Share of Recent Sales

sometime in the future. Predicting the future share of competing products is a tricky business, but we assume that consumers look at technology A's share of the recent sales and use that information (along with the quality, prices and so forth of the competing products) to determine whether to choose technology A. The S-shaped curve indicates the relationship between the recent market share of technology A and the likelihood that new consumers purchase technology A. Their choices this period determine the recent purchases at the beginning of next period, when the decision process begins again.

There are three equilibria in figure 3.1: M, Z, and X. They are all equilibria because they are on the 45-degree line, indicating that the share of new sales is equivalent to the share of recent sales, and thus that the market shares are not changing and will not change without some external change. The equilibrium at M is unstable, however. It is like the ball at the top of the hill. For any small external change leading to a displacement to the left of this intersection, the fraction of new purchasers choosing A is less than the fraction that have chosen A in the past. This will lead to a smaller recent-purchase share for A as an input to decisions made in future periods, which will lead fewer consumers to choose A, and so on. The share of A will decline eventually to zero (which is point Z). Using similar logic, we can see that to the right of M, A's share will increase until all consumers choose A (point X). Points X and Z are stable equilibria.

Such a market is sometimes said to "tip" in either direction with a small movement of the market away from M. Once such tipping begins, in these models, there is nothing in the theoretical system itself that would ever allow a movement back.

In figure 3.1, consumers respond to the recent sales. They could have been assumed to react to the installed base of a particular technology, the entire stock of commitments to a technology. VCR buyers, for example, might look at all the VCRs that have been sold. If consumers actually did base their decisions only on the stock of old commitments, markets might well show a great deal of inertia. A newcomer would always fight an uphill battle if customers decided on this basis.

If consumers behave in this way, we could expect markets to be much less agile than if prospective consumers looked only at the recent sales.[8] Much depends, therefore, on whether consumers ask, "how many Beta and VHS machines are in use?" instead of asking, "What have people been buying lately and what are they likely to buy in the future?"

The reason that markets are more agile under these latter circumstances is that it is much easier to change the flow of new commitments than it is to change all of history. That is to say, it becomes a fairly manageable matter for the owner of a technology to choose, or change, the position from which we start out on figure 3.1 if he only has to change recent market shares and not the entire installed base. The owner of a viable technology might invoke any of the strategies we discussed above, or might just simply give some products away in order to move the market from the left of M to the right of M.

Multiple-equilibria models are often invoked to argue that a particular outcome depends crucially, though perhaps perversely, on history. Under some interpretations, if we get started just slightly to the left of M, technology A will fail, regardless of the intrinsic merits of A. If we get started slightly to the right of M, A succeeds, again regardless of its merits. If A were inherently better than the alternative, a differently shaped S-shaped curve would have put M somewhere to the left of center, but without removing the possibility of a non-A equilibrium. History, perhaps some whimsical or coincidental start to things, will dictate the outcome. All of this comes to us dressed in the full rigor of mathematical proofs, supported by theorems on stochastic processes. The weak link, however, is the phrase, "if we get started."

The phrase "if we get started" buries a world of assumptions. In particular, it allows us to ignore all the things that companies do to win technological races and all of the things that consumers do to purchase well. Where we get started is a choice, not a random event. A single agent with only minimal interest in a final outcome might in fact choose whimsically or idiosyncratically, but he is not likely to have the powerful influence that is assumed in some models. Further, companies selling products will not be inclined to stand idly by watching a chance "start" to the right or left of M control their fates. They will advertise, make deals, "preannounce" a product, or cut prices, to move the market to where things will come their way. Of course, both sides of these competitions will take these steps.

Competition here takes a very different form from that found in textbook models of perfect competition. Network markets consist of contests where firms compete to be the winner in setting a standard, founding a network, or establishing a technology. For the winner, there is no inherent restriction on market share. In such competitions, all of the rivals will use all of the tools that are available to them, but the standard or network technology that has the greatest potential will have the upper hand. Winners get to control virtually the entire market, until a new winner appears.

Textbook models of competition assume that competitors are all minuscule relative to the market and that they take price and the nature of the product as given. There really is no "competing" by firms in models of perfect competition, except to keep production costs down. It is a mistake to take these models of perfect competition too literally, however. As many economists realize, in actual competition, even in traditional decreasing return industries, firms will not be passive. If there is money to be made, we can expect them to be active with respect to any attribute of the product, including price.

The Importance of Empirical Connections

Note that none of this proves that the best technology necessarily prevails. It does, however, demonstrate that economic models are merely models. They demonstrate particular results in the context of particular assumptions. Whether we consider the increasing-returns story of table 3.1, or the multiple-equilibria model of figure 3.1, we are left with an empirical question: Have the modeling choices that give us these results captured something important about the way that markets work? Or, are the influences of consumer foresight and producer entrepreneurship sufficiently important in real markets that lock-in is empirically unimportant? The next two chapters explore these modeling choices in much more detail.

NOTES TO CHAPTER 3

1. This essay is based in part on our entry for "path dependence" in *The New Palgrave Dictionary of Economics and Law* and in part on our 1995 paper in the *Journal of Law, Economics, and Organization*. We acknowledge Peter Newman and Oliver Williamson for helpful advice.

2. This was one of the main functions of our 1995 paper.

3. Properly called a "spauldeen," sometimes spelled Spaulding. Those who have no Brooklyn life experiences may wish to think of a tennis bawl (ball) without its cover.

4. An equilibrium in this instance is a condition whereby the market shares will remain constant. If all consumers are doing their best to maximize their happiness, and all producers are doing their best to maximize profits, and the market shares in new sales are equal to market shares of older sales, there would be no reason for market shares to change without some new event taking place.

5. Older sales could be the sales last period, the last few periods, or the entire installed base. We will explain later why we chose the recent period for our analysis. In other work we have also included the installed base in the analysis.

6. We will explain in detail how this curve is derived in chapter 5.

7. This is an arbitrary assumption made to ensure that there would be two serious candidate equilibria.

8. We elaborate on this in our 1996 article in the *Harvard Journal of Law and Technology*, which appears in part as chapter 4.

4

Network Markets: Pitfalls and Fixes

When the value of a good changes because the number of people using the good changes, we call this change a *network effect*.[1] An example of a product that benefits from a *positive* network effect is the telephone. A telephone becomes more valuable as the number of people who own telephones increases. The same can be said for fax machines, word processors, and metric tools. Explicit formal computer networks, such as company networks or the Internet, also exhibit network effects. Bigger is better. Accordingly, many of the arguments that have been made about increasing returns apply to network effects, and vice versa.

Network effects are intrinsic to many of the newest technologies—particularly the so-called information technologies. These technologies involve processing large amounts of information, and the agents responsible for processing this information are often separated by many things, including distance, differences in intent, differences in time, differences in industry, and so on. Agents seeking information on credit security today may be seeking information on Tibetan rugs tomorrow and on biotechnology prospects the day after that. For this reason, compatibility is important—both over national and industry boundaries, and also over time. It is also helpful today to be able to work with files that were created in the past and to have confidence that files created today will be usable in the future.

Networks, Connections, and Ownership

What most distinguishes networks from other instances of increasing returns is that the benefits of increased size come from the demand side, the willingness of consumers to pay, and not the supply side, or the costs associated with production. This increase in value as members of the network multiply comes about because people in a network are, in at least some sense, connected to one another. That connection can be literal, as in the case of a telephone system or the cable TV network, or it can be notional, as in the case of the network of Yale Law School graduates or the Shriners. Whether literal or notional, there is some expected continuing interaction among the parties involved, even if that interaction is indirect.

A second distinction is that networks can be owned, unlike economies of scale in production, which can accrue to any firm that grows in size.[2] If the network involves connections by wires or pipes or microwave towers, this ownership is inevitable. But even associations of individuals can be owned. The Boy Scouts, the Masons, a country club, and the Hair Club for Men are all networks that are owned by some entity, if only by the explicit organization of the members.[3] And even informal associations may be thought of as owned networks. Consider an informal association of drinkers at Joe's Bar. Joe has an interest in creating conditions that lead to a network, maintaining it, and assuring that it reaches an optimal size. For his efforts, he will appropriate a share of any rents, or surplus value, that are created as a result of the existence of the network.

These special properties, connectedness and ownership, are important to understanding how markets deal with the resource-allocation problems inherent in networks.

Network Effects versus Network Externalities

When network effects were first introduced to the economics literature, they were widely called "network externalities."[4] But "externality" is used in economics to refer to something very specific. An economic externality occurs only when a decision maker does not confront, or bear, the full costs or benefits of his action. In the worst case, this might lead to an economic inefficiency—a market failure. Network effects may or may not be externalities.

It would be very important if, in fact, every network effect were also a network externality—a market failure. But mechanisms exist to obviate such failures. Economists note that people and companies generally arrange their lives and organize production to exploit opportunities fully, which is to say, to avoid inefficiencies. Furthermore, it is this avoidance behavior that prevents many potential market failures.

The usual example of an externality is something like pollution. When you drive your car, you confront many of the costs, but not all of them. You pay for the gas, the oil, the wear and tear, the tires, and so on. If your insurance rates are linked to the mileage you drive, you also bear the expected accident cost. Because roads are paid for with taxes on gasoline, you pay, imperfectly, for the cost of the roads. As you drive along, you may pollute the air a bit, you may make a bit of noise, and you may slow down other drivers. Such things are also costs, but they are borne almost entirely by others. You are not charged for them, nor do they fall back on you in some other way. These are externalities. More specifically, they are negative externalities or external harms.

It used to be thought that if an activity inflicts an external harm, there is too much of that activity. In one of the most important papers in economics, Ronald Coase (1960) argues that the kinds of problems posed by external effects can be traced to impediments to bargaining among the parties involved or a lack of clearly defined property rights.

In a frictionless world, those taking an action that imposes a harm might have to pay those who have the right to be free from such harm. Alternatively, if the actor has the right to some action, those who bear the costs of that action might pay the harming actor to refrain. Let's say you have the right to burn leaves. If your neighbors don't care for your leaf burning, they might pay you to do less leaf burning. On the other hand, if it is your neighbors' right to be free from this harm, they may insist that you pay them for each bushel you burn. Either way, you will be encouraged to reduce your leaf burning. Any such voluntary transaction makes both parties better off; there is no inefficiency.

But what happens if the parties cannot transact, for one reason or another? It is often asserted that it is infeasible for consumers to transact with one another to internalize an external effect such as air pollution because consumers are many, transactions are costly, free riding is possible, and so on. Or think of all the people who are in one another's way during the morning commute. In this case, the external effect might present an inefficiency, an externality—too much driving during rush hour. For such an externality to be an inefficiency, there must be some feasible resolution that is worth more than it costs.

Not all external effects are negative. There are also positive externalities. When you are vaccinated, you not only enjoy a reduction in the probability that you will become ill, but you also reduce the probability that you will spread a disease to someone else. When you work in the yard, you improve your view, but you may also improve your neighbor's view, perhaps more than you improved your own. These are external effects and possible externalities, but they are positive externalities or external benefits.

With uncompensated external benefits, there is too little of the activity. If it were possible, your neighbors might bribe you to mow the lawn a bit more often. Most network effects are external benefits; you are better off if there are more network participants. But that does not have to be the case. Internet users who experience congestion are a bit worse off because of the increasing number Internet users. In fact, the Internet has become sufficiently congested that newer, faster, and somewhat exclusive Internets are being implemented. Internet II, for example, will serve some research and educational users, the original users of the Internet. The flight of these users to a special but smaller internet suggest that bigger isn't always better, even for high-technology networks.

It may be difficult for network participants to internalize some external effects that are not already internalized by ownership, particularly where they involve large numbers of participants. But many network effects involve direct interaction of individuals, so the number of people who affect each other may well be a reasonable few. Thus transactions to resolve an inefficiency cannot reasonably just be assumed away.

Take the example of a telephone network. It is often observed that each additional phone attached to the network enhances the value of the network to other users of the network. But most users make most of their calls to only a small number of phones. The Smith family, for example, may frequently call friends or parents on the phone. Each call is a transaction of sorts. The Smith family will derive the greatest value from those network participants they intend to call most frequently. But it is not difficult for the Smith family to transact with their parents or friends to use telephone services on a common network. This was the reasoning behind MCI's Friends and Family promotion, which attempted to enlist friends and family to expand the company's network.

A similar story applies to video recording. If Smith's parents are thinking of getting a Beta format machine, and the Smiths already have VHS, Smith might remind his parents that he can provide videotapes of the grandchildren only on VHS, and thus help to internalize the joint value in tape exchange between parents and children.

And it is not only family relationships that allow this internalization. Companies that do significant business with one another will try to standardize on similar products, in order to allow greater interaction. It is not terribly difficult to negotiate over the terms of this interaction. And because the very nature of these networks is interaction among individuals, it is unreasonable to invoke the usual condemnation of transacted solutions, which is that individuals are unable to coordinate their choices.

As we progress through the following chapters it will be important to keep these concerns in mind for two reasons. First, we will often adopt an assumption commonly made in this literature: that networks become more valuable the larger they become. In fact, if it is often only a small number of individuals that consumers care about having join their network, network size will not be important and much of the analysis based on that assumption will be misleading. Second, the internalization of network effects, which is the focus of this chapter, is easier and does not require coordination by a network owner if network participants have these types of relationships with one another.

The rest of this chapter is concerned with how networks work. Specifically, we examine how people and industries exploit network effects (internalize them) to garner the greatest possible benefits. People and industries use numerous mechanisms, many of them quite familiar, to take advantage of networks. Our claim is that although networks could, in principle, give rise to inefficiencies, this does not necessarily occur. Market institutions and other adaptations, including transactions among individuals, will avoid many potential inefficiencies. Thus, calling every network effect a "network externality" is at best an imprecise use of the economic jargon, and at worst misleading. Certainly economists should avoid giving the impression that where there's a network, there's a market failure. And policy makers should be warned against taking that impression from the economics literature.

Pecuniary Externalities

Some interactions look like externalities but actually are not. Suppose that suddenly, after a lifetime of abstaining from artichokes, the entire population of Milwaukee decides that they are crazy about artichokes. They start buying artichokes. They impose costs on the artichoke growers, of course—the cost of growing those artichokes. But they pay the artichoke growers a price for their artichokes, and the artichoke growers are happy for the business. In fact, the good citizens of Milwaukee compensate the artichoke growers for the entire cost of growing the particular artichokes that they consume. So far, there is no externality, and nothing that looks like an externality.

But what if the land that is suitable for growing artichokes is limited, and the skills required for growing artichokes are scarce? In such a situation, it could happen that Milwaukee's new culinary interest bids up the price of artichokes. The people of Santa Barbara, already big-time artichoke eaters, find that they have to pay higher prices for artichokes, and they resent it. Bitterly. This looks like an externality. But it's not a real externality, at least as economists define the term.

The reason that this externality is not real is that it operates only through price. And any increase in price is a good-news, bad-news story. A price increase that results from an increase in the demand for the good is bad for buyers, good for sellers. A price decrease that comes from a decrease in demand is bad for sellers, good for buyers. In either case, the external effects exactly balance one another: The good for the sellers is exactly offset by the bad for the buyers. This is what we call a *pecuniary externality*.[5] A pecuniary externality is an external effect that operates through price in such a way that there is no net external effect.

The distinction between regular externalities and pecuniary externalities is important. For many of the things we buy, one person's purchase decision will affect other people's opportunities. If Milwaukee's taste for artichokes means that residents of Santa Barbara will pay a higher price for them, then the satisfaction of those Santa Barbara residents is affected by the number of people who consume artichokes. This would be a network externality, as the term has been widely used. We are a network of artichoke eaters. But there is no inefficiency. The pecuniary sufferings of the Santa Barbarians is exactly offset by the windfall to the artichoke growers.

It is important to note, therefore, that the mere fact of network-type interaction does not constitute an inefficiency. There may be a network of artichoke eaters, and they may be a loyal and well-organized group.[6] But they can well be left alone to settle their differences through the market.

Tragedy of the Commons, Comedy of the Commons

Network effects are very common in the economy. Many are old and familiar and have prompted equally familiar institutional responses. Network effects constitute economic externalities only where agents do not confront, or bear, the full costs or benefits of their actions. And it is possible to escape the losses of most potential network externalities—either by coincidence or by conscious plan.

Economists have posited dozens of theoretical cases of network externalities, but on closer examination most of these cases can be called externalities only if we make very particular and peculiar assumptions about technologies, tastes, and markets. The implication is that market failure in such contexts is often a consequence not of network effects per se, but rather of conditions that economists associate (rightly or wrongly) with inefficiencies in general.

Many of the hypothetical externalities studied by economists are solved in the real world by some configuration of ownership. For example, if exterior deterioration of apartment buildings creates external costs for nearby units, common ownership of clusters of apartment buildings should solve the problem. Thus, the solution to the "externality" lies in the restructuring of property rights to the common resource. If, then, we regard a network as a common resource, we might well expect that ownership of a network would resolve network externalities. Such a conclusion would be important, because many network activities are "owned" or, in the terminology offered by Katz and Shapiro, "sponsored."

Some networks are owned by their very nature: they are literal physical networks, such as telephone or power grids that must be constructed as networks through coordinated action. Figurative networks, such as the "network" of Apple computer users or of Airstream trailer owners, can also be owned through patent, copyright, or trademark protection. Of course, some networks, such as the network of English speakers, seemingly cannot be owned.

The base problem can be likened to an old problem in economics, "the tragedy of the commons." Now, *commons* can be defined broadly as an "open-access, common-property resource." A *common-property resource* is one that is owned by a group of people who jointly own and use the property together. *Open access* means that every one of the owners can use the property whenever and however much he pleases. The problem with open access to a resource is that the resource is likely to be overused.

The Fishery Problem: The Tragedy

The classic example of the tragedy of the commons is a fishery. In fact, the whole class of problems is sometimes called the "fishery problem." Suppose there is a community that has access to a lake that is good for fishing. Suppose also that the lake has limited capacity, which means that the more fishermen that use the lake, the fewer fish each fisherman catches. Table 4.1 is an example.

TABLE 4.1

Fishermen	Fish per Fisherman	Total Catch	(Marginal) Increase in Catch
1	10	10	10
2	9	18	8
3	8	24	6
4	7	28	4
5	6	30	2
6	5	30	0

Notice that when one fisherman is on the lake, he catches ten fish. If a second fisherman is present, each of the fishermen catches nine fish. The important part of this result is that even though the second fisherman will have nine fish in his basket, his presence on the lake results in only eight additional fish for the community. We say that the marginal product of the second fisherman is eight fish. A way to think about this is that while the fisherman takes home nine fish, his presence reduced the take of the other fisherman by one fish. This reduction in the first fisherman's take is an externality.

Continuing on, we observe that a fourth fisherman catches seven fish, but the marginal product of a fisherman at that point (four fisherman working the lake) is only four. That is to say, the total take increases by four when the fourth fisherman shows up. Again there is an externality: the fourth fisherman catches seven fish but reduces by three fish the catch of the other three fishermen.

What, then, is the problem? Each of the fishermen gets the same number of fish, each can come to the lake if he wants to, and nobody is holding a gun to anyone's head. But there is a problem, and the problem is this: The fishermen might keep coming to the lake even if their energies would be better spent elsewhere. For example, imagine that if the fishermen don't work on the lake they can do things that have a value equal to that of six fish, say, carving driftwood pelicans.[7] Assume also that it does not matter how many people carve driftwood pelicans: The productivity of an individual carving a pelican is the equivalent of six fish. Under these conditions, fishing will be at least as rewarding as pelican carving until there are five fishermen on the lake. Under open access, five fishermen constitutes an equilibrium. At five fishermen on the lake, there is no reason for any of the fishermen to leave, but there is also no reason for any additional fishermen to come to the lake. Their choice is either to generate six fish on the lake or the equivalent of six fish by carving a pelican.

But this is a tragedy for the community. The tragedy is that the fourth fishermen on the lake resulted in only four additional fish and the fifth resulted in only two. If these last two individuals were to take up pelican carving, they would generate the equivalent of twelve fish. So, if all five fishermen are working the lake, the community has less wealth than it might have otherwise. Another way to see the same thing is to realize that the total take on the lake is thirty fish, exactly the value that these five fishermen could produce by pelican carving if there were no lake at all. The community ends up with nothing extra on account of the lake. The lake's entire potential contribution to the well-being of this community has been completely dissipated through overfishing. This is a serious loss, and a great cost of common property ownership.

The fishery problem is solved if the lake is owned by someone who sets out to maximize his profits from the lake. The wage for fishermen would have to equal their alternative earnings, which we've already assumed is the equivalent of six fish. So, the owner-operator of the lake would hire three fishermen, so that the marginal product of the last fisherman just equals his alternative productivity (opportunity cost). Each fisherman catches eight fish, and the owner collects some rents owing to the surplus that is now created on the lake.[8]

The lake is a network. The benefit that any user gets depends on the number of users. The difference is that the network of lake users affects one another in a negative way, whereas the networks that we have been talking about—telephones, computer users, and revelers at Joe's Bar—affect each other in a positive way. But as we will see below, the basic logic is the same.

In order to understand how this logic applies to networks, it will be helpful to look first at the fisheries problem in graphical form. Figure 4.1 shows the basic elements of the fisheries story. The horizontal axis corresponds to the number of fishermen. The vertical axis corresponds to fish caught.

The diagram illustrates all of the features of the story. With unrestricted access, fishermen come to the lake as long as the returns to fishing exceed their opportunity cost in pelican carving. This means that five fisherman come to the lake. But the ideal number of fishermen for the lake is three, where the marginal catch (or marginal product) of fishermen is six fish, their alternative earnings in the next best alternative use of their time. The profit-maximizing owner, paying a wage of six, will hire workers only as long as their marginal product exceeds what he has to pay them. This means that he hires three workers, generates a surplus of six fish, and prevents the lake's value from being diminished to zero.

Positive Network Effects: The Comedy

Okay. To be perfectly honest, this next bit is not all that funny.[9] Further, the interaction among network participants experiencing a positive network effect, if not internalized, does lead to a societal loss, another tragedy. But positive networks are, in important ways, a mirror image of the fisheries problem. Thus tragedy and comedy.

FIGURE 4.1

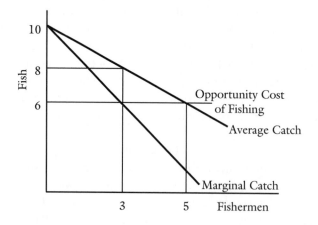

Networks that involve positive interactions can be modeled using the same kind of apparatus that we used to illustrate the fisheries problem. In figure 4.2, the horizontal axis denotes the number of participants in some network. It can be the number of telephones, computer users, or revelers at Joe's Bar. Assume that participation in the network consists of buying one unit of some basic element of the network—telephone service, a computer, a drink. As is fundamental to positive network externalities (and in contrast to our fish story), we assume that the private benefit of each network participant increases as the number of participants increases. As in the fishing example, we also assume that network participants are identical. In the fishing example, we ignored the possibility of differences in fishing ability. Such homogeneity is a fairly common assumption in the contemporary network literature. (See, for examples, Church and Gandal [1993], p. 243; Katz and Shapiro [1986], p. 826.)

Figure 4.2 shows a relationship between average benefit, AB, and the number of network participants. The height of AB is the benefit that each network participant enjoys. It is also the most that each participant would be willing to pay for one unit of network participation. Because we are now dealing with a positive network effect, average benefit rises as the number of network participants increases. (Note that absent a network effect, AB would be horizontal, at the common benefit received by all participants.) MB, the marginal network benefit, represents the change in total benefits

FIGURE 4.2

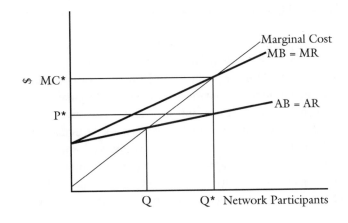

to network members when an additional member joins. MB lies above AB because an additional member not only enjoys the benefit AB himself, but also raises the benefits that all other network participants enjoy.

We assume that the marginal cost of supplying the network commodity increases with output. While there are other constructions of cost that are likely to be important in this context,[10] increasing marginal cost is a conventional assumption that has some intuitive appeal and empirical foundation. For example, literal networks such as cable television connect the closest (or otherwise easiest) customers first, and expand by connecting ever-more-distant customers at ever-increasing costs. Alfred Kahn's classic treatment of the economics of public utilities (vol. 1, p. 124; vol. 2, p. 123) provides some empirical support for this pattern. For a figurative network, such as a network of computer users, additional marketing effort may be required to reach customers less familiar with the product. Finally, network participation frequently requires the purchase of some "entry" commodity (for example, a telephone or computer), and that commodity may be subject to ordinary production conditions, which we often assume have this characteristic of increasing marginal costs.

Because AB represents the willingness of participants to pay for network participation, it is the highest price that the network owner can charge. Thus, it is the average revenue function for the network owner as well as the average benefit function for network participant.[11] The marginal revenue—the additional revenue that results from serving one more customer—captured by the network owner is equal to the price paid by the marginal participant, plus the increase in price that can be charged to all network participants. MR (= MB) accordingly lies above AR (= AB).

In this example, MB is also the marginal revenue function associated with AB. The network owner maximizes profit, equating marginal revenue with marginal cost. Q* is the profit-maximizing network size, and P* is the profit-maximizing price. P* obviously is less than marginal cost.

At first glance, this result may appear strange. The price charged to the marginal participant (which is actually any network participant) is less than the cost of serving him. That sounds like a recipe for losing money. But it is not. The network owner captures more on the marginal participant than just the price paid by that participant. He captures some of the extra value derived from each other participant when the network becomes larger. So the price paid by the marginal network participant understates the total effect on revenue of adding another network member.

When the network is not owned, network participants will arrive up to the point where their AB is equal to their MC. This is at Q. Thus, because we have a positive network effect, the network would be smaller without an owner to internalize the externalities.[12]

It is fairly trivial to relate these outcomes to the social (societal) wealth-maximizing optimum—the outcome that maximizes the net social benefit of the network. The optimum conditions are the equivalence of marginal social cost and marginal social benefits. That is to say, the quantity of any good that would yield the greatest net benefits is the one at which the cost of producing one more unit of the good is equal to the benefit that people enjoy from one more unit of the good. Because the change in benefits to society when a consumer joins the network is represented by the MB curve, the marginal social benefit thus coincides with the network owner's marginal revenue function, and Q* is the optimal network size for both society and the network owner.

The analysis of the operation of an owned network proceeds exactly like the fishery analysis. The network externality in the fishery example was negative, but the analysis is the same. Replacing common ownership of a lake with a single owner results in efficiency precisely because the owner takes into account the interactions of the fishermen in order to maximize the surplus, which, of course, he appropriates. In the fishery example, without network ownership, the network is too big; but for the case of positive network externalities, without ownership, the network is too small.

Finally, then, a punch line. The owner of a network can appropriate some or all of the value that the network creates. It is in the interest of the network owner to organize the network in such a way that the network creates the greatest possible value. This will mean that the owner has an incentive to implement a pricing structure that takes account of the contribution of the marginal participant to the network's value. The profit-maximizing price identified in figure 4.2 does that for the situation shown. There are, of course, other possible situations and many other possible pricing structures to go with them, including a network with uninternalized network effects that is, therefore, too small.

Decreasing Costs: Is Today's Future Different from Yesterday's?

We turn now from one cause of increasing returns, network effects, to another cause: decreasing average production costs. The two are tied together because many real-world network industries appear to also exhibit decreasing costs, although there need not be any such linkage.

Much of the interest in network industries has to do with a belief that a lot of contemporary production is subject to inexhaustible increasing returns to scale. "Inexhaustible increasing returns to scale" means that no matter how big output gets, average cost will continue to fall or output is increased further.

Although economists have long accepted the possibility of increasing returns, they have generally judged that, except in fairly rare instances, the economy operates in a range of decreasing returns. The literature on network effects challenges this assumption and grants a fundamental role to increasing returns. It has captured attention by choosing as its examples some new-technology products. Furthermore, writers in this field predict that as today's newest technologies take over a larger share of the economy, the share of the economy described by increasing returns will increase.

Among the most vocal proponents of this view is Brian Arthur, who trumpets the claim not only in the economics literature, but also to general audiences: "[T]he prevalent view is still that things happen in equilibrium and that there are constant or diminishing returns. . . . A high-tech, high value-added world calls for a new kind of economics" (Arthur, quoted in Wysocki, 1990).

To support his claim, Arthur approvingly cites Alfred Marshall, one of the most prominent economists of the latter part of the nineteenth century, for his early emphasis on the importance of increasing returns. But Arthur appears to be unaware of the intervening criticism of Marshall's view. Marshall's views on increasing returns were largely erroneous, a confusion of movements along cost curves with shifts in the cost curves (see Stigler, pp. 68–76; Ellis and Fellner, p. 243). Much of our criticism of the current attention to increasing returns expands on these early criticisms of Marshall.

The support for a belief in increasing returns is based largely on anecdotes and casual characterizations of technology. The past decades have evidenced a number of technologies that have experienced two correlated phenomena: first, enormous declines in price; second, tremendous growth in sales. For example, the prices of VCRs have declined remarkably and, at the same time, there has been an incredible increase in their use. The same story applies to computers, lasers, and cellular phones. One simple explanation is that these technologies are subject to increasing returns. Because bigger has been cheaper, it has been assumed that bigger causes cheaper. But an alternative explanation is that as the technology has advanced with time, the average cost at all levels of output has fallen.[13]

Consider, for example, the history of old technologies, such as refrigerators and automobiles. These industries, currently thought to exhibit conventional decreasing returns, experienced tremendous cost decreases early in their history accompanied by startling increases in output.[14] At the time they were occurring, these cost decreases may have looked like increasing returns. But as a longer view shows, once these industries settled down they began to look like traditional markets. The example should be cautionary: The currently popular association of new technology with increasing returns may well be faulty, at least for some technologies.

The casual argument for the association of new technology with increasing returns imposes a very restricted structure on production. By this argument, products are knowledge based, and the knowledge costs of a product are associated entirely with fixed costs. Computer software is sometimes argued to fit this structure: The programming costs of a new piece of software are large, and the costs of copying disks are very small and constant (they are usually assumed to be zero in theoretical models). Thus, some economists conclude that average costs of software will fall indefinitely as output increases.

There is some truth to this argument, but it is incomplete. Take a simple hypothetical example. Assume that the cost of developing Windows 95 was $500 million, an estimate that is plausibly close to reality. After the 100 millionth copy of Windows 95 was sold, the average fixed cost would be $5 per unit. The average fixed cost would fall to $4.99875 per unit if an additional 25,000 units were sold, a fall of one-eighth of a cent per unit. Assume further that there is one technical-support specialist for each 25,000 users, implying a total of 4,000 technical-support specialists for Windows 95. If the hiring of additional technical-support personnel tended to bid up their wages, this diseconomy alone could overwhelm the decreasing average fixed cost. Suppose, for example, that hiring an additional technical-support specialist (for 25,000 additional users) increased the wages of technical-support specialists by $22 per year, or an hourly wage increase of a penny.[15] This small change in wages would be sufficient to make overall average costs increase, not decrease, with output. It would put us back in the realm of decreasing returns. So it is possible (note that we are not saying necessary, or even likely) that decreasing returns can prevail even in software, when the scale of the market is large.

There are other costs beyond technical support—for instance, sales, marketing, and public relations—that may well increase at an increasing rate as output increases. Further, as in other industries, resource limitations are likely ultimately to restrain firm size. Economists have long supposed that limitations of management play a role in this. Finally, other high-technology products are less likely to exhibit increasing returns than is software. Software has an unusually large percentage of its costs in its initial fixed cost, compared to other high-technology industries such as chip production, where the costs of designing a chip might be small relative to the costs of fabrication plants. Thus, without investigation, it is unreasonable to accept that the law of diminishing returns somehow takes a vacation in new-technology industries.

Note that we do not deny the possibility that there might be important economies of scale in production in many high-technology industries. We are merely pointing out that such a result is not inevitable, and requires empirical investigation before the truth can be determined, a theme that reappears throughout the book.

There is one very important difference, however, in the production technology of software and some other contemporary goods. In these industries, it is possible for the firm to alter its scale extremely rapidly. This *instant scalability* means that firms can acquire the means to expand production with little or no lag. For software, the product-specific component of the good is largely embodied in computer code. That code can be replicated very quickly and on generic computer equipment. Contrast that with the time lags involved in adding specialized tooling in order to increase capacities in many older industries with differentiated products. This feature of the software industry contributes to the rapid turnover of its market leaders, which is discussed in chapters 7 and 8.

Finally, we do not want to give the impression that we deny the importance of progress. Quite the opposite is true. Nevertheless, we are skeptical that economic truths from the past should be ignored just because information moves more quickly and computational power has increased. Our claim is only that knowledge is always a component of goods, that the knowledge share of total cost is not necessarily greater now than it was in the past, and that the fixed-cost attribute of knowledge need not overwhelm other cost components.

Conclusions

Networks are indeed an important aspect of contemporary technologies. The Internet is the example that comes readily to mind, but any of the many communication technologies illustrate network effects. So do computers themselves and some software products. But network effects, however easy they are to find and however important they might be, are not necessarily externalities and do not necessarily lead to market imperfections. In many instances, there are obvious mechanisms for internalizing these effects and the incentives to do so.

In our time some extraordinary entrepreneurial efforts have been devoted to building networks and taking advantage of network properties. Capital markets have hardly been stingy in allocating resources to these entrepreneurial efforts. Efforts to organize, internalize, and benefit from network effects have given us Visa and MasterCard, MCI, teller machines, and Blockbuster Video. In an earlier time, they gave us railroads, Sears, telephones, and McDonald's. In any age, exploiting the potential of networks requires extraordinary creativity, but that creativity has been the cornerstone of some extraordinary fortunes.

NOTES TO CHAPTER 4

1. The material in this chapter is based largely on Liebowitz and Margolis (1994) and (1995c). We would like to thank Richard Zerbe for his assistance.

2. Of course, if the cause of the economies of scale were an innovation that was patentable, it would have at least temporary ownership.

3. Actually, we're not so sure about the Hair Club for Men. It may not be a club at all. We wouldn't know.

4. The seminal paper in this literature is Michael Katz and Carl Shapiro's "Network Externalities, Competition, and Compatibility."

5. For a concise but more complete treatment see Hirshleifer and Hirshleifer (1998).

6. Actually, this could be taken too far. In fact, if all the artichoke eaters became well organized enough, they could make themselves better off by restricting their demands and lowering price. This would be a buyer's cartel. This is what we call *monopsony*, which is an inefficiency. This is an important property of a pecuniary externality: If it were internalized, it would create an inefficiency, not remove it.

7. We assume that all fishermen have the same payoffs if they decide to engage in an activity other than fishing, or as economists would say, they have the opportunity cost of fishing. This assumption is standard in analyses of the commons tragedy, and, more important, it does not affect our results. We will, however, assume an increasing cost when we discuss the comedy later in this section. These differences do have some implications for how markets achieve stability, and we refer the interested reader to our 1995c article in *Research in Law and Economics*.

8. The lake's value is maximized with either two or three fishermen. In either instance, there are six fish caught above the opportunity cost of pelican carving. If the owner of the lake can hire fishermen for a payment of six fish each, these extra fish become profit for the owner.

9. If the reader finds the material too difficult, or insufficiently interesting, this section can be skipped, except for the final paragraph.

10. If the marginal cost is flatter than the upward-sloping benefit curves, then the number of users will tend to be either zero or the entire population of potential users, and we don't get a neat interior solution. This is because the net value generated by additional users increases only as the number of users increases. So, if it makes sense to have any users at all, it makes sense to have everyone a user. In this case, the intersection of MC with MB represents the minimum profit position, not the maximum profit position. If the MB curve eventually flattens out we could resurrect the interior solution, as pointed out to us by George Bitttingmayer. In either case, the optimal number of users will still be achieved if there is an owner, but

might not be achieved without an owner. So the result in the text is generalizable to other assumptions.

11. The typical downward-sloping demand curve is also an average revenue curve.

12. The story here is actually somewhat more complex than we are letting on. Again, the reader should consult Liebowitz and Margolis (1995c).

13. Many, if not most, of these cost decreases may be due to learning-by-doing effects, which may be related to the total volume of output, as opposed to the yearly output. See the discussion in Shughart (1990), p. 106.

14. For example, Sloan tells us that the real price of refrigeration services dropped by 77 percent from 1931 to 1955 (p. 422) and that the Frigidaire .50-caliber aircraft machine gun dropped from $689.95 in 1941, to $169 by 1944 (p. 449). Rae tells us that the price of the Model T dropped from $950 in 1909 to $360 in 1916 (p. 61).

15. If both of these changes seem so small as to be swept away, consider whether a 25 percent increase in the hiring of technical-support workers (1,000 workers) might increase their annual wages by $22,000.

5

Networks and Standards

From languages to videorecorder formats, almost all standards are also networks. But standards are an extremely important category of networks. Standards are conventions, specifications, protocols, or understandings that allow us to interact.

In chapter 2 we examined the history of one important standard, the typewriter keyboard. The keyboard arrangement is an example of an old standard originating in an old technology. Even older standards are language, measurement systems, manners, and the way we address an envelope. In the high-tech world, there are established formats (standards) for video recording, audio taping, audio compact discs, video disks, computer operating systems, spreadsheets, word processors, telecommunications protocols, and HDTV. Because standards reduce uncertainty about compatibility, they facilitate the building of networks. It is inherent in the nature of a standard that the benefits that accrue to an adopter will depend in some manner on the number of other adopters. Furthermore, it is inherent in the nature of a standard that it competes for survival with alternative standards. Even when a standard is established by fiat, its influence can wax or wane depending on its performance relative to alternatives.

Fixed and Flexible Standards

In chapter 2 we noted that standards can be fixed or flexible. There, we used orchestral tuning as an example of a flexible standard, measurement as an example of one that is fixed. Although the distinction between flexible and fixed standards is absolutely fundamental, it is often overlooked.

The model that we present in this chapter examines the competition between two standards. Implicit in our model and in many other theoretical treatments of standards is that the competing standards are fixed. They do not evolve, they do not borrow features from one another, and they are not used by their creators to form the basis of something new. But clearly, all those things can happen in the real world, and this possibility is something worth emphasizing.

An important example of a flexible standard is a language. A language stays useful because words are added to accommodate new things. No one ever has to change languages just because there are new ideas to express. Those who are slow to adopt new words may miss a few things, but they do not have to go off to learn a different language, and their communication with others is never seriously interrupted. They just add words when they need them.

Mathematical notation works the same way. A new concept might require new notation, and its originator might set out some notational conventions just to get going. If the ideas are successful, the notation may become, or at least initiate, a standard. Subsequent writers may find ways of making the new notation simpler, or easier to follow, or more compact. In time, a set of conventions becomes both handy and well known and becomes the standard. New writing no longer starts with much elaboration of notation. But mathematicians do also continue to use old notation for old things. They also choose new notation that echoes, insofar as possible, older conventions.

Computer software can be a standard, and it can be a standard that evolves. But it doesn't have to be either. Software doesn't have to be a standard at all. A firm might create specialized software for its internal operations or to be incorporated in manufactured products, with no intention of compatibility, continuity, interoperability, or any use beyond the company itself. A firm might, in fact, specifically avoid compatibility in order to preserve trade secrets or enforce product differentiation.

But many software products are standards, at least to some degree. If you use a particular version of WordPerfect, for example, you certainly expect to be able to use your document files on another computer that has the same version installed. You may even expect that you can take files created in one version of a word processor and work with them on another version. Of course, that expectation does sometimes lead to disappointment.

Some nonproprietary software has been put forward by its developers as a flexible standard. For some users, this is part of their attraction. Unix, or Apache, for example, are flexible standards. Users add features to suit their own purposes. Other users can adopt these revised versions. In this regard, such software products are much like languages. Such flexibility does, however, come at a cost: The standardization of the software may be impaired. Developers may not be able to rely on particular features of the product, and so may be frustrated in developing extensions or applications that can be widely used.

Owners of proprietary software face a choice: They can maintain a lineage of software products so that they behave as a flexible standard, or they can treat each new generation of the product as an independent product. They can adopt a program of evolution or revolution.

Much software is developed in an evolutionary way. Producers usually maintain backward compatibility, at least to some degree, so as not to alienate their installed base of users.[1] They add features, but provide users with as much consistency as possible in the interface. They design new products to read files produced by the old system. New products are presented, insofar as possible, as new versions of the old. Users can adopt the new version without losing the ability to interact with users of the old.

If an operating system can accommodate new features, or an altered interface, or increased capacity, without making older versions obsolete, or making applications software for the old versions obsolete, or making users' old skills obsolete, it is a flexible standard. It presents no real prospect of lock-in. There may, of course, be a cost to this flexibility. The standard may carry, at a cost, certain vestiges of older versions in order to allow this flexibility. That does not mean that later versions are inefficient. Such vestiges are simply a cost that is borne by anything that maintains continuity while it evolves.

Software producers often face a tradeoff: Enjoy the advantages of continuity and be bound by the resulting constraints, or make a clean break with the past but suffer the costs of discontinuity with the previous generation of products. When we look at the actual histories of some software companies later in the book, we will see that these strategic choices are among the most critical ones that these companies have made.

Choosing Standards

People do not always have opinions about alternative standards. In neutral cases, the social problem of setting a standard is not so much a matter of which one we use, as long as we have one at all. We can drive on the left side on the road or on the right—but we'd better not drive on both. On the other hand, some standards are universally appealing. A TV picture that is sharper and cheaper might suit everyone.

Sometimes there is disagreement over a standard. Some people might prefer a language that is simple but limited; others might prefer one that is more versatile, though more complicated. Some might prefer a set of building practices that is extremely durable, though expensive; others might take cheap, but less durable. It is in such circumstances that the choice of standards presents a social problem. We now look at how individuals are affected by standards, how they choose among them, and how those choices play out in the market.

The Nature of the Model

In chapter 3, as part of our discussion of path dependence, we presented a model of multiple equilibria. In this chapter we ground that model in a theory of the economics of standards. One thing that distinguishes this model from other models of standards is that it allows for consumers (or adopters) of standards to have differing preferences. That is, the standard one person prefers might be different from the standard that another person prefers. This adds a wrinkle to the technology-choice story we considered in chapter 3, where at any level of adoption, one technology was better than the other, and it was better for everyone involved.

In modeling contests between standards, we treat each standard as if it were rigid. This allows us to consider a competition between two standards that are distinct entities. But this is not an innocuous assumption. It may severely overstate, for some technologies, the either-or nature of standards battles.

In real-world competitions between standards, whether they are languages, technologies, architecture schools, governments, or even dance styles, we often see that the best features of one find their way into others. In such cases, an emphasis on a choice between standards is misplaced. Where standards are flexible, there may be no issue of whether the best standard wins. No standard wins; some standard emerges. In Part Three of this book, when we consider real-world standards competitions, we will see this process at work.

A Model of Standards Choice

We base our model[2] on a fundamental purpose of standards: Standards facilitate interaction among individuals. The term we use to refer to this effect is *synchronization*.[3] Synchronization is the benefit received by users of a standard when they interact with other individuals using the same standard. In general, synchronization effects increase with the number of people using the same standard, although sometimes the benefits are less closely tied to the total number of other users of a standard than to the number of users with whom they actually interact.

Synchronization benefits are not the same as ordinary scale effects. In our model, synchronization effects may coexist with increasing, decreasing, or constant returns to scale. We will demonstrate that neither scale economies in production nor synchronization effects are by themselves necessary or sufficient conditions for an outcome where only one standard survives.

Many commentators seem to take for granted that average production costs fall with increases in output for most high-technology, standardized goods. This is not necessarily the case. As we discussed in chapter 4, standardization is often associated, rightly or wrongly, with lower prices, but there is no reason to assume that all goods referred to as high-tech are necessarily subject to increasing returns to scale.

As we have discussed earlier, increasing returns to scale refers to a characteristic of production in which the average cost of producing a good *decreases* with an increase in the amount of production over some stated period of time. Increasing returns to scale implies that average costs fall as the rate of output increases. Increasing returns is a characteristic of a technology at a moment in time. When firms experience increasing returns to scale, the pattern over time is toward the creation of what economists call a natural monopoly, which means that there is only a single firm in the market. The inefficiency that would result from allowing several overly small firms to compete in such a market is the main economic reason offered for granting monopolies and regulating prices in the public utilities.

But technological progress presents a very different circumstance. Technological progress gives us curves that shift downward over time. If general knowledge grows, or general technical knowledge improves, we will see costs of production fall at all levels of output. This is just progress. Technological progress is perfectly compatible with markets that have many firms, with no one firm being dominant. As we noted in the previous chapter, the technical advances associated with new technologies may easily disguise actual diseconomies of scale in the production of these goods. We can observe dramatic cost decreases coupled with dramatic increases in output. But the increases in output can be the causes of cost declines, or they can be the effects. It is important not to jump to a conclusion without some evidence.

New high-technology goods are likely to be associated with unsettled formats. But an examination of correlations between time series of standardization efforts and production costs is likely to be misleading. This is because the eventual adoption of a standard, which may take several years or even decades, often occurs simultaneously with improvements in technology.

An empirical association certainly does exist between the adoption of standards and decreases in costs: IBM's personal computer became the dominant format, and computer and software prices fell, while the number of computers and programs rose; prices of fax machines and modems fell dramatically after settlement on a standard compression routine. However, a drop in costs alone cannot be taken as evidence in favor of increasing returns in the production of standardized goods, since new technologies often lead to rapid decreases in (quality adjusted) costs over time, with or without standardization. For example, although VCR prices fell after VHS won its standardization battle with Beta, VCR prices had also fallen when both formats had significant market shares.[4]

Thus, the model that follows is constructed to provide independent consideration of the impacts of synchronization effects and production-cost economies and diseconomies. While synchronization favors convergence on a single format, it does not guarantee such a result.[5]

In our model, we assume that current consumer choices are affected by the market share of each format during some time interval leading up to the point at which consumers make their choices. A consumer commits to a format, for at least a while, by purchasing a product with that particular format. This is how we commit to formats for many high-technology goods such as VCRs, cameras, computers, and software. For concreteness and familiarity in what follows, we give competing formats names, referring to the standards battle between Beta and VHS. In that battle, a commitment to a format occurs with the purchase of a VCR.

We assume that consumers make purchase decisions on the basis of market shares (percentage of market controlled by a standard) rather than on total output. We use market shares because consumer choices for one format versus another will be based on the relative, not absolute, benefit of the standard, and relative benefits are based on market shares.

The Consumer

Assumptions about consumer values that are the basic building blocks of our model are shown in figure 5.1. The horizontal axis shows the market share of recent sales of one format.[6] In our example, the horizontal axis is the market share of VHS VCRs in a recent period. We define the *autarky value* of an individual's investment in a VHS videorecorder to be its value, assuming no interaction among VHS users (that is, no other VHS users). A VCR presumably has value even if tapes are never rented or exchanged. But a positive autarky value is not required for the model. In some activities, such as communication with fax machines or modems, it is reasonable to assume an autarky value of zero.

The *synchronization value* is the additional value that results from the adoption of the same format by other consumers.[7] This value would be a kind of network effect, perhaps the kind of thing most people have in mind when they talk about network effects. We assume that the synchronization value that a consumer places on a good would be based on the consumer's estimate of the good's market share over the life of the good. We further assume that the consumer would treat market shares in today's market as the best indicator of market shares in the future. Both of these assumptions

FIGURE 5.1
A Consumer's Valuation

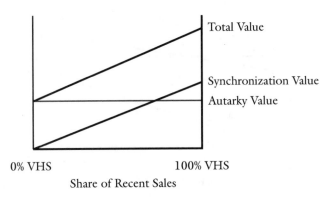

0% VHS   100% VHS

Share of Recent Sales

are somewhat arbitrary, but not unreasonable.

Thus, the synchronization value of VHS is assumed to increase with its current share of the market in the most recent period. Accordingly, total value to the consumer, defined as the autarky value plus the synchronization value, will increase as the format's market share increases.

Production

Production of VCRs could be subject to increasing, decreasing, or constant cost. For now, we assume that producers do not exercise monopoly power. For a given total quantity of VCRs sold this period, the number of machines of a particular format sold will, of course, increase directly with the share. Figure 5.2 shows the supply-price function (the price charged to consumers) under the assumption that VCR production involves increasing cost.[8] (Other specifications of cost are allowed and discussed below. Here, the figure illustrates a single possible configuration.)

From these relationships, we can derive a net-value function for video-recorder formats. The net-value function is equal to the total value (the autarky value plus the synchronization value) less supply price and is thus

FIGURE 5.2
Values for an Individual Consumer

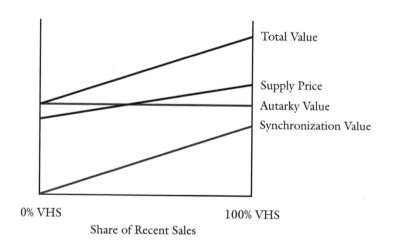

0% VHS   100% VHS

Share of Recent Sales

equivalent to consumer's surplus, the difference between a consumer's valuation of the product and the price he pays. Because the total value increases more rapidly than supply price in figure 5.2, the net value increases as VHS's share of the market grows.

Net-value functions will slope upward if the supply price function is less steeply upward sloping than the synchronization-value function.[9] In other words, if decreasing returns in production overwhelm synchronization benefits, the net-value line falls with market share. On the other hand, if synchronization benefits swamp decreasing returns in production, or if production exhibits increasing returns, then the net-value curve is upward sloping, as in figure 5.3. The net-value functions for machines with the Beta format are derived in an exactly analogous manner.

As we will see, it is only when the net-value function slopes upward that choices between standards are fundamentally different in character from choices of other goods (that is, exhibit increasing returns instead of decreasing returns). We assume throughout the analysis that the slope of the net value function for a given format has the same sign for all consumers.[10]

The net-value functions for Beta and VHS are put in a single diagram in figure 5.3. As VHS share varies from 0 percent to 100 percent, Beta share varies from 100 percent to 0 percent. If the two formats had identical costs and benefits, the Beta net-value curve would be the mirror image of the VHS net value curve.

The intersection of the two curves (if they intersect), labeled *Di*, represents the market-share equilibrium, where the consumer is indifferent

FIGURE 5.3
Choice for Individual Consumer

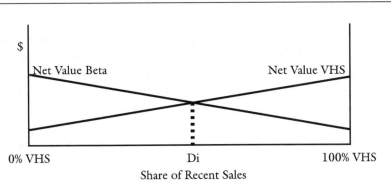

$

Net Value Beta   Net Value VHS

0% VHS   Di   100% VHS

Share of Recent Sales

between the two formats. This value plays a crucial role in our analysis. On either side of Di, the consumer will have a preference depending on the slopes of these curves. For example, if each net-value curve slopes upward with respect to its own market share, as in figure 5.3, the consumer will prefer VHS when its market share increases beyond Di (VHS has higher value, relative to Beta, as the VHS share increases beyond Di). If, however, each net-value curve slopes downward with respect to its own market share, the consumer will prefer Beta as VHS share increases beyond Di.

It is possible for owners of standards to try to change the Di for an individual consumer or for a group of consumers. If, for example, the owner of VHS desires to lower the Di for many consumers, he can lower the price of VHS machines. Lowering the price of these machines raises the VHS net-value curves for consumers, moving the Di to the left. As we will show below, lowering the Di is the key for the VHS standard owner to take the market, and raising the Di is the key for the Beta standard owner.

Note that this analysis assumes that the consumer does not take into account the impact of his decisions on other consumers (that is, he does not consider how his purchase of a videorecorder will alter the valuation to other potential purchasers of videorecorders). Therefore, the door is still left open for some sort of (network) externality.

The Market

Each customer has an individual Di, a balancing point at which the two formats are equally valuable. Accordingly, a population of customers will have a population, or distribution, of Di's. Let $G(x)$ be the fraction of VCR purchasers with $Di < x$, where x is the market share for VHS, as represented on the horizontal axis of figure 5.3. For example, suppose that 40 percent of customers have tastes such that their switching point occurs at or below a 10 percent market share. Then $G(.10)$ is 0.4. (This implies, by the way, that if VHS's market share ever were 10 percent it would not stay there very long, since 40 percent of the population would prefer and therefore purchase VHS, assuming upward-sloping, net-value functions as in figure 5.3. We consider equilibrium market shares later.) $G(x)$ is what is known as the cumulative distribution function for Di. This distribution is a key to the selection of a standard.

Perhaps the simplest distribution would be one in which all consumers had the same tastes, so that Di is the same for all consumers. Call this common value Di^*. This resulting cumulative distribution is shown in figure 5.4. The cumulative function represents the share of the population that will buy VHS this next period based on recent market shares of VHS. For recent-period market shares of VHS that are less than Di^*, all consumers will prefer to purchase Beta, and thus the market share of VHS among new purchasers will be zero. If recent sales of VHS, on the other hand, were greater than Di^*, all new purchases will be of VHS machines, and its market share of new purchases will be 100 percent. This is reflected by the bold step function in figure 5.4. We can now use figure 5.4 to look for possible market equilibria, that is, possible "rest points" in the interval of possible market shares. The candidates for equilibrium are A, B, and C, the intersection of the bold step function with the 45-degree line. Points A and C are single-format equilibria that are stable: For flows near point A (0% VHS), all consumers will choose Beta; for flows near 100 percent VHS all consumers will choose VHS. In contrast, B is an unstable equilibrium: At flows near but to the left of Di^* all consumers would choose Beta; at flows near but to the right of Di^*, all consumers would choose VHS. This is the tipping point.

So, for the case of upward-sloping net-value curves, we obtain two possible mutually exclusive stable equilibria, A or C. This winner-take-all re-

FIGURE 5.4

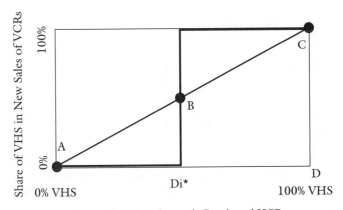

Share of VHS in Recently Purchased VCRs

sult is often argued to be the expected outcome for standards and other increasing returns markets.

This apparatus can also be used to examine the more traditional decreasing-returns case. Consider the outcome for downward-sloping, net-value curves. Remember that downward-sloping, net-value curves mean that consumers get less surplus as the market share of a product increases, and might be generated by *negative* network effects, or decreasing returns in production. (This would require relabeling the two net-value curves in figure 5.3). In this case, all consumers with Di less than Di^* choose VHS because its small market share provides greater surplus. The distribution function that helps us determine the potential equilibria is the bold line in figure 5.5. The only possible equilibrium (the only intersection with the 45-degree line) is B, a stable equilibrium. At points near but to the left of Di^*, VHS machines are more advantageous than Beta machines (through effects on supply price) and more consumers would choose VHS. Similarly, displacements of equilibrium to the right of Di^* would increase the relative advantage of Beta machines, moving the outcome back to the left.

Consumers split their purchases so that a VHS purchase and a Beta purchase have identical net values. This describes a circumstance in which the formats will coexist. This result is significant because it demonstrates that even with network effects, and even without differences in

FIGURE 5.5

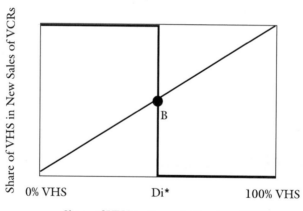

Share of VHS in Recently Purchased VCRs

taste (a factor that favors coexistence, as we will see shortly), it is still possible for a mixed-format equilibrium to exist. What is going on in this case is that diseconomies with respect to production costs are overwhelming network effects. In such cases, market forces do not move to winner-take-all solutions.

Thus, the mere existence of synchronization (network) effects is insufficient to establish the winner-take-all choice with respect to standards. That is because synchronization effects cannot, by themselves, ensure upward-sloping net-value curves. Nor are network effects required to generate an upward-sloping, net-value curve. For example, upward-sloping, net-value curves can occur when supply price falls, even when there is no synchronization effect. Synchronization effects, therefore, are neither necessary nor sufficient conditions for a winner-take-all equilibrium.

In fact, it is possible that observed winner-take-all outcomes are mostly driven by factors other than network effects. For example, if software markets were characterized by winner-take-all equilibria (which we will see later appears to be empirically true), we would have to determine whether network effects, large fixed costs, or some other factor (such as instant scalability) was responsible.[11] We will see in chapters 8 and 9 that the case for network effects causing winner-take-all solutions in software is fairly weak.

Any form of winner-take-all result has important implications for antitrust that will be more fully explored in the appendix. If a market is a natural monopoly, whether due to synchronization or production costs, there is no benefit in trying to force it into a competitive structure with many small firms each having excessively high production-cost structures and low synchronization values for consumers. The government might wish to award natural-monopoly franchises, as it does for public utilities, but the history of publicly regulated utilities does not inspire confidence that technological advancement would be promoted, or that costs would be kept down. Because high technology changes so frequently, a firm that achieves monopoly with one technology will have difficulty holding on to its lead unless it is extremely resourceful. This further argues against a regulated-utilities approach in technology markets.

Internalizing Synchronization Costs

Thus far, the model addresses only private valuations and their effects on market outcomes. But the literature of standards is also concerned with how one consumer's format choice affects the values enjoyed by others. We address this issue by examining how taking account of this extra value would affect a standards choice. We should reiterate, however, our result in the previous chapter: A single owner of a technology or standard is capable of internalizing the impact of consumer's behavior through prices. The following discussion therefore applies only to the case in which such internalization is not possible.

To this point the net-value curves have represented net private benefits. "Social" benefits are defined as before to reflect the entire set of benefits, societal benefits—not just the private benefits. Because the synchronization effect is always assumed to have a positive effect on other users of the same format, the social net-value function, which includes the synchronization value to others, will always lie above the private net-value function, regardless of the slope of the private net-value function.[12] That is to say, the total value created when someone adopts a format is not only the private benefit that accrues to the adopter, but also the creation of additional value for all other adopters of the standard. (We saw a similar effect in the previous chapter as the difference between the marginal and average benefit of network participation.)

The difference in the height of the two curves depends on the relative strength of the synchronization effects and the format's market shares. For example, at zero share of VHS, the VHS private net-value curve will be the same as the VHS social net-value curve. That is because, where there are no other users of VHS to benefit from this individual's purchase, the private and social values must coincide. Where VHS has a positive market share, the social net-value curve is everywhere above the private net-value curve. The relationship between private and social net-value curves is shown in figure 5.6. As the share of VHS increases, and the number of potential beneficiaries of this individual's VHS purchase increases, the difference between the social and private net-value curves increases. The same is true for Beta net-value curves.[13]

Depending on the relative sizes of the synchronization effects on users of the two formats, the intersection of social net-value curves can be to the right or to the left of the intersections of the private net-value curves. In the particular case where the two formats attract users with the same levels of potential interaction and where the private net-value curves are the same, internalizing the synchronization externality will have no effect on any individual's D_i, and thus no effects on the potential equilibria.

If the *Di* moves to the left or right, the cumulative distribution function moves in the same direction. In that case, internalizing the synchronization externality may lead to a different equilibrium.

On the other hand, they may not. If the values lead to a distribution as shown in figure 5.4, which in turn lead to stable equilibria that are either all VHS or all Beta, internalization will not change the outcome. For example, in figure 5.4, if the market starts out near point A, even if the *Di** moves left or right somewhat, A will remain the equilibrium. Similarly, if the market starts near point B, B will remain the equilibrium. Thus, even if internalization of the externality changes *Di*, the final market equilibrium, need not change. All that would change is the range of market shares over which each format would tend to prevail. Internalizing the synchronization effect thus might have no impact on the choice of format.

There is, however, one dimension where the internalization of the synchronization effect always has an impact. The private net-value functions consistently undervalue videorecorders. Therefore, it is not the *relative* market shares, but rather, the size of the overall market that will be affected by this difference between private and social net-value functions. Too few videorecorders of either type will be produced if the market participants do

FIGURE 5.6

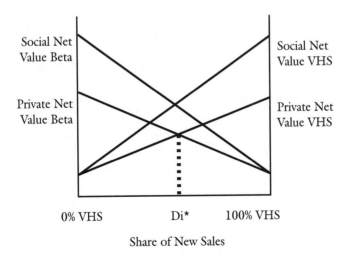

Share of New Sales

not internalize the synchronization effect.[14] Internalizing the externality enhances both VHS and Beta, causing consumption of VCRs to increase even if market shares remain constant.

This is completely compatible with the conventional literature on ordinary externalities. All this is really saying is that too little of a product will be produced if there is a positive externality (e.g., too few golf courses, or too few copies of Microsoft Excel) and too much will be produced if there is a negative externality (e.g., pollution). This is a far more likely consequence of "network externalities" than the more exotic case of winding up with the wrong standard.

Extending the Model

If you are not trained in economics but have made it this far, you deserve a pat on the back. All the effort required to understand our model of standard choice will now be put to use in a demonstration of how the market that we have modeled will change as we change the underlying tastes of consumers. Of even greater interest, we can use the model to demonstrate a theoretical instance of getting stuck with the wrong equilibrium so we can see what is taking place below the surface of simpler models.

There is one other general point that we need to make before we get going. (The equilibrium positions shown in diagrams such as figure 5.4, can be thought of as long-run, sustainable positions.) Individual standard owners can, temporarily, alter the sales in a period through short-run strategies such as pricing below cost, which would be unsustainable in the long run. We will return to this shortly.

The model provides alternative results when we change the assumptions underlying the model, which is how economists normally proceed. We assume increasing net-value curves throughout, since that is more in line with strong network effects. To start, the assumption that all consumers have the same Di can be relaxed. Allowing consumers to differ in their Di's acknowledges differences in tastes. These differences may reflect different assessments of the formats, different synchronization values, or both.

Assume that the Di's for consumers range between 20 percent and 80 percent (VHS), and that within this range the distribution of Di's are uniform, as illustrated by the bold line in figure 5.7.[15] This distribution means that some consumers would take VHS when VHS has share as low as 20 percent, but none would take it if its share fell below 20 percent. All consumers choose VHS if its share is 80 percent or higher. Between 20 percent VHS and 80 percent VHS, each percentage interval has contained within it an equivalent number of individuals with Di's in that interval.

The height of the distribution of Di's is directly related to the slope of the cumulative distribution function. To understand this, it helps to understand that a uniform distribution of Di's from 0 to 100 percent, such as the dotted line in figure 5.7, would lead to a cumulative distribution function that was equivalent to the 45-degree line market diagram of figures 5.4, 5.5, or 5.8.

A key element of distributions such as those in figure 5.7 is that the area under the function is equal to 1, since it represents the frequency of the entire population. Another way of looking at this is to think of the share of the population that has a Di in a 1 percent interval of VHS shares. For example, because 100 percent of consumers have their Di's between 20 percent and 80 percent in figure 5.7, each percentage interval between 20 percent and 80 percent has 1.67 (one and two thirds) percent of the population of new buyers.[16] The dotted-line distribution, on the other hand, has 1 percent of the population in each 1 percent interval for VHS shares. The height of the distribution in figure 5.7 depends on the number of consumers with Di's contained within, which is why the bold line is 67 percent higher than the dotted line.

The cumulative distribution function, therefore, has three straight line segments as shown in figure 5.8: between (0,0) and (20,0); between

FIGURE 5.7
Distribution of Di's

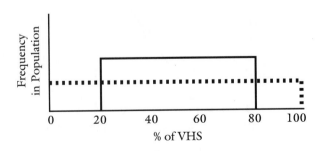

(20,0) and (80,100); between (80,100) and (100,100). [17] The cumulative distribution intersects the 45-degree diagonal at points A, B, and C. A and C are stable equilibria and B is not, as can be readily confirmed by moving slightly away from any of these points. Thus, this type of uniform distribution of Di's gives the same general result as our earlier assumption that all consumers had identical Di's: We still tend to get a winner-take-all type of equilibrium.

Strong Differences in Tastes

Up to this point, the results of the model indicate that when net-value curves slope upward, the equilibrium will be of the winner-take-all type. This need not be the case, however. Figure 5.9 shows a distribution of Di's representing the unremarkable case where each of two formats has a fairly large number of adherents who much prefer it, with the rest of the population of Di's thinly (and uniformly) distributed between 20 percent and 80 percent VHS.

The distribution of Di's in figure 5.9 results in the cumulative distribution function shown in figure 5.10. The only stable equilibrium in this case is point B, which is not a winner-take-all solution. (B is stable because if you move, say, slightly to the left of B, VHS has a larger share of

FIGURE 5.8

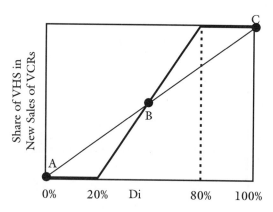

Share of VHS in Recently Purchased VCRs

new purchases than its recent share, raising VHS shares until B is achieved.) The differences in tastes allow two standards to coexist in a stable equilibrium, even where net-value curves slope upward. This is an important result. In those instances in which each format offers some advantages to different groups of customers, we should expect to find that different formats will appeal to different people. When this is so, formats can coexist in a market equilibrium, and individual consumers will not be deprived of either of the choices.

FIGURE 5.9
Distribution of Di's

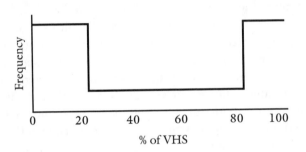

FIGURE 5.10

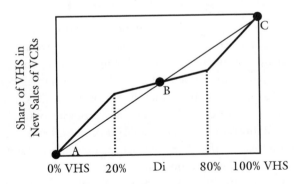

Share of VHS in Recently Purchased VCRs

It is important to point out that these sorts of differences in consumers' evaluations are things that firms might well pursue as part of their competitive strategies, where there are strong natural-monopoly elements. We would expect entrant firms to try to specialize their products to appeal strongly to particular groups of users. This is, after all, one simple way for firms to overcome any natural-monopoly advantage that an incumbent might enjoy. An incumbent, on the other hand, might do well to create products that appeal to the widest possible audience in an attempt to foreclose this possibility.

There are some straightforward implications here. First, even when there are economies of scale, network effects, or both, markets can allow more than one format to survive. The key to survival is to find a market niche and to produce a product that is as close to the preferences of that market segment as possible. Unless the established firms have much lower costs (or stronger network effects, which seems unlikely since consumers in a niche will tend to have network effects mainly with other consumers in that same niche), the superior characteristics of an entrant's product, as viewed by consumers in that niche, will provide sufficient advantage for the entrant to survive. An example might be Apple's continued existence, based in part on its strength in publishing and entertainment markets that play to its historic strengths in graphics. If each producer can produce a product that appeals strongly to some segment of the population, then the situation represented by figure 5.10 will occur. That this result is grounded in common sense does not diminish its value.

When One Product Is Superior to Another

Although it is pretty clear what "superior" would mean in one individual's assessment, it is actually rather complicated when we are considering an evaluation by a population of individuals. There is one simple case where it is easy to identify a superior format. This is the rather lopsided case of one format having higher net values than another for all consumers at all market shares. In this case, no Di occurs in the interior of 0–100 percent, and the only equilibrium is at a share of 100 percent for the superior format. Where the deck is this severely stacked, we don't usually recognize the situation as a standards battle at all.

But it generally isn't this easy to identify a superior standard. Strongly held, but divergent, preferences might lead to different views of what constitutes superiority. If some individuals prefer format A, regardless of share, and others prefer format B, regardless of share, then it is not clear that either can be said to be superior.

A weaker definition of "superior," however, might be consistent with a common-sense understanding. We can define a standard as superior if it is better than another standard under equivalent conditions. That is, define standard A to be superior if, for all consumers and any given market share the net value of A is higher than the net value of B when B has the same market share. (For example, A is superior if consumers all prefer A with 100 percent share to B with 100 percent share; and consumers all prefer A when each has a 50 percent share; and consumers all prefer A with 70 percent share to B with 70 percent share and so on.) This is the definition that we will use.

Arbitrarily, let VHS be the superior standard. The Di's will then all be less than 50 percent, because individuals would choose Beta only if it had the dominant market share. Assume that the Di's are uniformly distributed between 0 percent and 20 percent. Then the cumulative density function lies above the 45-degree line everywhere, as shown in figure 5.11. Figure 5.11 is the same as figure 5.8 except that the upward-sloping segment is displaced to the left. A and C are the only two equilibrium points, but only C is a stable equilibrium. This analysis implies that if society starts at 100 percent Beta, it could get stuck at A, but only if no one ever purchases a single VHS machine. Point A, being an unstable equilibrium, is incredibly fragile.

In this case it is almost certain that the superior format will dominate the market. If VHS is superior and both formats originate at the same time,

FIGURE 5.11

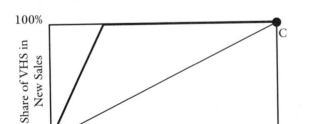

Share of VHS in Recently Purchased VCRs

VHS will win unless Beta, although inferior, can somehow capture *and keep* a market share of 100 percent. This would seem an almost impossible task.

We now turn to an instance of being locked into in an inferior format.

Getting Locked In

It is not difficult to alter the previous example so that C becomes a stable equilibrium, even though all consumers prefer VHS. One simple alteration is merely to assume some minor changes from those conditions represented in figure 5.11. For example, let the Di's range between 10 percent and 30 percent, instead of the former 0 percent and 20 percent. Because the superiority of VHS merely implies that all Di's are less than 50 percent, that condition still holds. Intuitively, creating the "hole" in Di's from 0 percent to 10 percent merely says that although VHS is superior for all consumers, there are no consumers who find VHS so overwhelming that they prefer it even when its market share is between 0 percent and 10 percent.

The market now can be represented by figure 5.12, which is very similar to figure 5.8. Because all consumers prefer Beta when the share of VHS is less than 10 percent, the cumulative distribution function is no longer always above the diagonal, and point A becomes a second stable equilibrium in addition to point C. Point B, at 12.5 percent VHS, now is an unstable equilibrium.

FIGURE 5.12

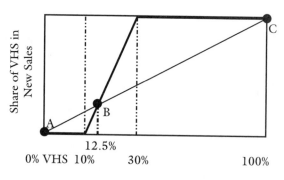

Share of VHS in Recently Purchased VCRs

Notice that the possibility of getting locked in does not require the existence of any synchronization (network) effect. Having upward-sloping, net-value curves is the necessary condition, and this can be achieved merely with old-fashioned scale economies in production.

When would the market choose A and not C, given that both are equilibrium positions? The most likely scenario would be for Beta to arrive in the market first and thus generate 100 percent of the market share. We discuss this case in more detail in the next section.

If VHS arrives first, Beta need not really show up, since it will have to generate in the current period a market share of 87.5 percent in order to move the equilibrium to A. The short-term inducements to consumers of VCRs that would be required for Beta to achieve such a large market share would be very costly. Further, since VHS owners are not likely to sit idly by, and since VHS merely needs to achieve a market share of greater than 12.5 percent of recent sales to take back the market, an attempt by Beta to take the market would seem to be doomed to failure.

Getting Unlocked

Under the conditions where Beta arrives in the market first and where the market settles at equilibrium position A, owners of the VHS format do have an incentive to temporarily alter sales through short-term inducements to consumers in order to dislodge the market from A. One method might be to dump a large number of VHS machines on the market, perhaps by lowering the price, in order to generate an immediate 12.6 percent market share, driving the equilibrium to C.[18]

Producers of VHS can also try to prime the sales pump by providing deals to the largest users, or distributors, or retailers (perhaps offering side payments) to convince them to switch to VHS.[19] If this action can produce a market share of 12.5 percent, VHS can dislodge Beta (as, of course, it did). Naturally, if the VHS format were not owned, there would have been a potential free-rider problem for the VHS producers to solve before these strategies could have been adopted.

Other mechanisms for increasing market share include advertising, publicity, and services to allow partial or total compatibility. It is important to note that the larger the difference in performance of the two formats, the easier it is for the superior format to overcome any initial lead of an inferior standard. For truly large differentials, we should expect diagrams like figure 5.11, not figure 5.12. Thus, the greater the potential error in the choice of a standard, the less likely it is that an error will be made.

Additionally, the greater the difference in performance between the two formats, the greater the difference in potential profits. This makes it more likely that the superior format can finance the pump-priming investment that would unseat an inferior incumbent. In circumstances like the ones presented above, all other things equal, the technology that creates more wealth will have an advantage over a technology that creates less. Although the owner of a technology may not be able to appropriate its value perfectly, the playing field is level: Imperfect appropriability affects both competitors. In fact, owners of a superior format can be less perfect at overcoming their appropriation problems and still win the competition.

It is important to notice here that such pump-priming measures are likely to look predatory, especially after the fact. Actions to establish a standard may appear to be actions to defeat, kill, or destroy rivals, inasmuch as the goal of achieving a contemporaneous market share large enough to push the equilibrium to a favorable position for the firm may require temporary profit-losing actions. But these seemingly predatory actions are exactly the mechanisms that prevent lock-in to inferior standards.

Further, in the example just above, the owner of VHS, the superior standard, has a much easier task than the owner of Beta has, in that the owner of VHS merely needs to get 12.5 percent of the market each period to dominate long term, whereas Beta needs 87.5 percent. Only if Beta were supported by far greater resources than VHS was would there be much likelihood of Beta dominating the market.

As we have seen, if a clearly superior technology were offered first, we would be unlikely to see a sustained attempt to dislodge the leader by the owners of inferior technologies, unless they expect that they can achieve their ends through political means, inasmuch as their expenditures in the market are likely to be futile. When the superior technology comes later than an alternative, it will have to use temporary market inducements to consumers to achieve sufficient market share to move the market to the preferred equilibrium.

If government is to do anything useful, it should help to ensure that the capital market is functioning properly so that new technologies have access to sufficient financing. The early history of Netscape, Amazon, and Yahoo, with their enormous market capitalizations, seems to indicate that such financing has been abundant in recent times.[20]

There may be more of a problem if one standard is owned and the other is not. In this case, we do not have a level playing field on which the technologies can compete. We should note, however, that ownership of a technology can take various forms, including ownership of critical inputs, patent, copyright, and industrial design. Private parties most often own literal networks such as telephones, pipelines, and computer systems. Sony licensed the Beta system; JVC-Matsushita the VHS system. Standards are often protected by patent or copyright. Resolution of these start-up problems may be an important and as yet not fully recognized function of the patent system[21] and other legal institutions.

Other Tactics for Getting Unlocked

An important method of avoiding an inefficient standard, or moving from one standard to another, is to coordinate choices. In some circumstances, the numbers of people who interact through a standard is small enough that coordination is a feasible method of resolving any externalities regarding the standard. A small group of engineers working together can certainly get together and decide to use the same CAD package. Or an extended family can coordinate the choice of camcorder format so that they can exchange tapes of grandchildren.

Another tactic is to emphasize convertibility. Suppliers of new-generation computers occasionally offer a service to convert files to new formats. Cable-television companies have offered hardware and services to adapt old televisions to new antenna systems for an interim period. For a time before and after World War II, typewriter manufacturers offered to convert QWERTY typewriters to Dvorak for a very small fee.[22] Such tactics help to unravel the apparent trap of an inefficient standard.

Furthermore, some independent conditions work on the side of the more efficient standard. An important one is the growth of the activity that uses the standard. If a market is growing rapidly, the number of users who have made a commitment to any standard is small relative to the number of future users. Although reel-to-reel and eight-track tape players were established standards, few people owned them. For buyers entering the burgeoning audiocassette market for the first time, incompatibility with the older standard was irrelevant. Similarly, incompatibility with the disks or operating systems of eight-bit computers had no effect on the purchase decisions of first-time computer buyers of sixteen-bit computers. Each of these new markets grew so much larger than the initial market that the installed base of the old standards did little to stem the tide of commitments to the new format. The same can not be said, however, for music CDs, compared to the LP records that they rapidly replaced.

Because the market provides varied and rich mechanisms to prevent instances of getting lock-in to the wrong standards, such failures should be few and far between. In the rest of this book, we look at the real world for evidence of such failures.

NOTES TO CHAPTER 5

1. We will discuss this in more detail in chapter 7.

2. This model is based on Liebowitz and Margolis (1996).

3. We have defined *synchronization* to have a meaning similar to the meaning the literature has given to the term *compatibility*.

4. It is possible that the competition between VHS and Beta enhanced the speed of innovation as the formats fought for market leadership. Increased recording time, hi-fi sound, wireless remote controls, increased picture resolution, and so on, all came about very quickly, with each format striving to keep ahead of the other. It is, however, an open question whether competition between formats might be beneficial for innovation.

5. If there were production economies at the firm level, we should see many natural and entrenched monopolies. Many early leaders of new technology industries are not those that now dominate their industries—for example, Sony's Betamax videorecorder, and Digital Research's CP/M operating system. Another example is VisiCalc's spreadsheet standard, which lost to Lotus 1-2-3, which in turn lost to Microsoft's Excel.

6. A somewhat more general mathematical model based on both stocks and flows gives the same basic results.

7. We assume that all members in the network are equally likely to interact with another user. As we have discussed earlier, this is the usual assumption, but it is probably not indicative of actual markets.

8. The assumption of non-monopoly, or competition, is equivalent to requiring firms to price their product such that it covers all costs and allows the producer a normal rate of return on their investment. This is known as *zero economic profit*, because economic profits deducts normal returns from any measured accounting magnitudes.

9. For many high-tech products it might be argued that the supply price should be flat, or falling with increases in market shares. If so, this will merely tend to make the net-value curve more upward sloping and doesn't alter anything in the analysis.

10. Of course, for any consumer, the two net-value curves need not have the same sign. Moreover, different consumers need not have the same signs on their net-value curves. In the latter case, there would be a group of customers with density functions like figure 5.4, and another group with density function like figure 5.5. The overall density function would be a mixture of these two. In the former case, if one format had an upward-sloping (with respect to market share) net-value curve, and the other a downward-sloping net-value curve, the relative size of the slopes in absolute terms would decide whether the result was a mixed-share, or an

either/or equilibrium. If the upward-sloping curve is steeper than the downward-sloping curve, the result is identical to the case in which both curves are upward sloping, and the either/or result prevails. If the upward-sloping curve is less steep, the results are the same as when both are downward sloping, and a mixed-share equilibrium would prevail.

11. Even here we shouldn't let ourselves be uncritically seduced by the natural-monopoly, production-costs story. Also, it is worth noting that the book-publishing, television, and movie industries also have large fixed costs but do not seem to engender natural-monopoly concerns. This may merely be due to variations in taste. It bears investigating why this is the case, however.

12. This discussion invokes the usual assumption that the supply function does not reflect a real or technological externality.

13. One possible consequence of internalizing the synchronization effect occurs when the sign of the slope of the social net-value function is different from the sign of the slope of the private net-value function. Because the social net-value function must have a larger slope than the private net-value function, this change in sign can only occur when the private net-value function is downward sloping, and the social net-value function upward sloping. In this case, the private net-value function implies a mixed-share equilibrium, but the social net-value function with an either/or equilibrium would result if the externality were internalized.

14. We should note that size of the market should not be taken literally here. Because the market will undervalue VCRs in the example found in the text, either too few VCRs will be produced *or* the VCRs that are produced will likely be of too low a quality, assuming that there is a quantity-quality tradeoff in consumer tastes. For some networks, such as language, there probably is not such a tradeoff. We note that the difference between private and social value is positive for any marginal consumer except the first.

15. If you are not familiar with names of distributions, such as "normal" or "uniform," feel free just to follow the diagram and ignore the name.

16. This is simply calculated as 100 percent divided by 60 percent.

17. As a matter of notation, (20,0) means 20 percent on the X axis (share of recent sales) and 80 percent on the Y axis (percentage of population about to buy VHS).

18. In fact, when VHS came to the U.S. market, largely under the RCA brand, it significantly undercut the price of Beta, although Beta almost immediately matched the price cut. See Lardner (1987), p. 164.

19. In fact, both VHS and Beta, aware of the need to generate market share, allowed other firms to put their brands on videorecorders. This was the first time

that Sony was willing to allow another firm to put its name on a Sony-produced product. See Lardner (1987), p. 159.

20. This is not to imply that a speculative bubble, which seems the proper description for Internet stocks as this book is being written (spring 1999), is required to assure sufficient financing.

21. Kitch (1977).

22. According to Foulke (1961), p. 160, it cost as little as $5 to convert a QWERTY to a Dvorak keyboard.

PART THREE

The Real World

In previous chapters we examined theories of lock-in. Although our theoretical discussion does not prove that markets must always choose the best technology, we do claim that there are good reasons to expect it to be very unusual for market participants knowingly to choose the wrong technology. This contrasts with the strong claims of path dependence that have been made by Brian Arthur, Paul David, and their compatriots. The acid test of any of these theories is whether there actually are instances of remediable lock-in, or what we have called third-degree path dependence. That test is the purpose of this part of the book.

In chapter 2 we examined the typewriter keyboard story, the archetypal case of empirical support for lock-in. Chapter 6 examines several other cases that have been used as support by proponents of lock-in theories. We conclude that none of these examples provides any support for lock-in.

In chapters 7, 8, and 9 we look at the market for computer software. This market is one that has been thought to manifest characteristics consistent with theories of lock-in and path dependence. We turn to this market for several reasons. Most notably, this is the first market where path dependence and lock-in theory has played an explicit role in public policy. We refer, of course, to the antitrust investigations and charges against Microsoft. Our examination of several software markets—word processors, spreadsheets, personal finance, desktop publishing, browsers, online services—offers no more support for strong lock-in than did the typewriter keyboard.

The difficulty of finding actual examples of lock-in strongly suggests that the claimed prevalence of deleterious lock-in is an interesting but empty conjecture. Even if such instances are found, they are likely to be anomalies. Such conjectures and anomalies may be worthy of late afternoon academic discussions over a few drinks, but hardly stuff upon which antitrust policy should be based. In the appendix we examine the role of these theories and some other antitrust concepts as they apply to software markets and Microsoft.

6

Beta, Macintosh,
and Other Fabulous Tales

Can we rely on markets to move us in the right direction, either initially or when it is time to change? If, for example, a large number of us benefit from using the same word processor, can we change word processors when it's time to change? If we can, how do we?

In the preceding chapters we presented a simple statement of a problem as it is alleged in a good deal of academic and popular writing. If everyone uses A, yet each individual regards B as better, but only when many other people also use B, then we might find ourselves stuck with A. We argued that although this trap is certainly possible, interested parties are likely to respond in ways to disable this trap if it is actually causing significant harm.

Now, the mere possibility of such a trap should not be enough to spur us to action. Before we move to correct a possible harm, we need to establish empirically that the harm actually exists. Because reliable conclusions on these issues cannot be said to follow logically from agreed-upon economic principles and unassailable assumptions and restrictions, we must look at real-world cases.

In this chapter we examine a number of the standards or technology battles that are often cited as examples of this particular type of market failure. Of course, the most prominent of these claimed failures is the QWERTY keyboard, which we discussed at length in chapter 2. In this chapter we present the VHS-Beta history at some length, then consider several other cases.

Readers familiar with scholarly empirical work in economics may find our attention to case histories a bit out of the ordinary. Economists don't usually concern themselves much with individual cases: We tend to look at time-series of aggregate data—GNP and unemployment, the money supply or consumer expenditure—or at large data sets based on hundreds, thousands, or even larger numbers of companies, individuals, and products. This is because economists are usually looking for a pattern of behavior, a test for a theory that is held to apply *in general*. But theories of path dependence are different from such generalizing theories. In contrast, theories of third-degree path dependence and lock-in do not allege that these outcomes are the norm, or even that they are particularly common. Rather, they allege only that such path dependence is possible and perhaps that it is sufficiently likely to be important. Adherents of path dependence go somewhat further than this, arguing that it is likely to be common. But this argument does not come from the theory. Given that the theoretical result is a theorem about the possibility of lock-in, the empirical support, naturally enough, is a demonstration that the possible phenomenon has occurred. And also naturally enough, the empirical counterclaim involves calling into question these alleged demonstrations.

VHS versus Beta

After the typewriter keyboard, the VHS-Beta battle is the most often mentioned of alleged path-dependent market failures.[1] In our discussions in the previous chapters, we have used the names VHS and Beta in simple hypothetical examples of how the standards traps operate and how escapes are possible.[2] We turn now to the actual history of this standards battle, a history that is significant for several reasons. First, it incorporates structural features found in some of the models discussed here: In particular, it incorporates both economies of scale and ownership. Second, the actual history of the battle fails to support the claim that an inferior format dominated as a result of technological interrelatedness and economies of scale. Finally, it is a wonderful example of the foresight of the parties involved, and the tactics and strategies used to try to establish their standards.

The Ampex Corporation publicly demonstrated the first commercially viable videorecorder in 1956. These machines were sold for several years only to professional broadcasters. Eventually, Ampex concluded that transistors would replace tubes, and, having no experience with transistors, entered into an agreement with Sony to transistorize the videorecorder. In return, Sony received the rights to use Ampex-owned patents in machines designed for the home-use (nonprofessional) market, which Ampex was willing to cede.

The Ampex-Sony relationship quickly soured, however, and Ampex decided that it needed a Japanese partner to sell its recorders to the Japanese broadcast market. This time Ampex entered a partnership agreement with

Toshiba. Other Japanese electronics producers that wanted to manufacture videorecorders then became Ampex's licensees. Eventually, various incompatible models of videorecorders coexisted in the marketplace, but none of these early machines proved successful in the home-use market.

In 1969 Sony developed a cartridge-based system called the U-matic for the home-use market. Because Matsushita, JVC (an independent subsidiary of Matsushita), Toshiba, and Hitachi all had such products in the works, Sony sought to bring in some partners to share the format in order to establish it as a standard. After Sony promised to make a few suggested changes to the machine, Matsushita, JVC, and Sony agreed to produce machines based on the U-matic specification (although Sony was to get the bulk of the eventual sales). The three companies also agreed to share technology and patents. Production of the U-matic began in 1971. Although it enjoyed some success in educational and industrial markets, high costs and excessive bulk led to its failure in the home-use market.

Attempts to break into the home-use market continued. In 1972 an American company came out with a product called Cartrivision that did many of the things that a Betamax was later to do (although it traded off picture quality for a longer playing time). Cartrivision was sold with a library of prerecorded programs. It failed when several technical problems arose, including the decomposition of the prerecorded tapes in a warehouse, which led to negative publicity. Phillips produced a home recorder in 1972, but it never achieved much success. Sanyo and Toshiba joined forces to launch a machine known as the V-Cord, which also did poorly. Matsushita produced a machine called the AutoVision—a dismal failure. Of note for our story, Matsushita's management attributed this failure to the AutoVision's short, thirty-minute tape capacity, a lesson that would later prove important. A Matsushita subsidiary, Kotobuki, introduced the VX-100 to the home-use market.

When Sony began selling Betamax in April 1975, it had a tape capacity of one hour. At the same time, JVC was also working on a machine known as the Video Home System, or VHS. As it had done earlier with the U-matic, Sony sought to cut through the clutter of competing formats and make Betamax the standard. Before introducing Betamax to the market, it once again offered its format to Matsushita and JVC, providing technical details of the Betamax, including an advance in azimuth recording that helped eliminate the problem of crosstalk. After lengthy discussions, dragging on for over a year, the three finally agreed to have a meeting to compare the Betamax, VHS, and VX machines. This meeting took place in April 1976 (a year after Sony had put Betamax on the market). Lardner (1987) describes the meeting as follows:

> The first item on the agenda was the simultaneous playing, through all three [machines], of a "Sesame Street" type of children's program. . . . The Sony contingent's eyes were on the JVC machine. . . . What they saw was a considerably smaller machine than the Betamax. . . . Mechanically, too, VHS had a notable distinction: the use of a loading system called M-loading. . . . The basic concept had been tried in some of the early U-matic prototypes. . . . In other respects, JVC's and Sony's machines were strikingly similar. Both were two-head, helical-scanning machines using half-inch tape in a U-matic type of cassette. Both—unlike the V-cord, the VX, and indeed all the color video recorders to date—used azimuth recording and countered the problem of cross talk by juggling the phase of the color signal. So the Betamax and the VHS were in a class by themselves as far as tape efficiency went.
>
> The real difference between them lay in how the two companies had chosen to exploit that advantage: Sony to make the cassette paperback size, and JVC to achieve a two-hour recording capacity. . . . Eventually one of [the Sony people] said what all of the Sony representatives were thinking: "It's a copy of Betamax." (151–152)

Needless to say, this apparent usurping of Sony's technological advances by JVC created bitterness between the one-time allies. Sony and Matsushita-JVC decided to go their separate ways.

The only real technical differences between Beta and VHS were the manner in which the tape was threaded and the size of the cassettes. The Beta format's threading offered some advantages for editing and special effects. But the larger cassette in the VHS format allowed more tape to be used, and for any given speed of tape, this implied a longer recording or playing time. For any given recording technique, slowing the tape increases recording time, but it also decreases picture quality. Because of its larger cassette size, VHS always offered an advantageous combination of picture quality and playing time. Otherwise, the differences between Beta and

VHS were fairly trivial from a technical point of view. Our current perception of the differences is likely magnified by the advertising claims of each camp, the passage of time, and possibly by the fact that Beta still survives, reincarnated as a high-end broadcasting and videophile device.

The different choices of cassette size were based on different perceptions of consumer desires: Sony's managers, perhaps as a result of problems with the bulky U-matic, perhaps as a result of their many successes with portable devices, believed that a paperback-sized cassette, allowing easy carrying, was paramount. In contrast, Matsushita's managers, responding to the failure of the thirty-minute Autovision machine, believed that a two-hour recording time, allowing the taping of full-length feature movies, was essential.

This difference was to prove crucial. Sony was first to the market and enjoyed a virtual monopoly for almost two years. In an attempt to solidify its dominance of the U.S. market, Sony allowed its Beta machines to be sold under Zenith's brand name (Zenith being one of the major U.S. television manufacturers). To counter this move, Matsushita set up a meeting with RCA, which had previously concluded and publicly stated that a two-hour recording time was essential for a successful home videorecorder. By the time the meeting between Matsushita and RCA took place, however, Sony had announced a two-hour Betamax, Beta II. RCA proposed to Matsushita that it produce a machine that could record a football game, which implied a three-hour recording time. Six weeks later Matsushita had a working four-hour machine that used the same techniques to increase recording time that Sony had used in the Beta II.

RCA began selling VHS machines in summer 1977 (two years after Sony's introduction of the Betamax), dubbing its machine SelectaVision. The advertising copy was simple: "Four hours. $1000. SelectaVision." Zenith responded by lowering the price of its Beta machine to $996. But within months VHS was outselling Beta in the United States. A Zenith marketing executive is quoted as saying, "The longer playing time turned out to be very important, and RCA's product was better styled."

The battle escalated. Sony recruited Toshiba and Sanyo to the Beta format, and Matsushita brought Hitachi, Sharp, and Mitsubishi into its camp. Any improvement in one format was soon followed by a similar improvement in the other. The similarity of the two machines made it unlikely that one format would be able to deliver a technological knockout punch. When one group lowered its price, the other soon followed. The two formats proved equally matched in almost all respects save one: VHS's longer playing time. When Beta went to two hours, VHS went to four. When Beta increased to five hours, VHS increased to eight. Of course, a consumer who wanted better picture quality could set either machine to a higher tape speed.

The market's referendum on playing time versus tape compactness was decisive and immediate, not just in the United States, but in Europe and Japan as well. By mid-1979 VHS was outselling Beta by more than two to one in the United States. By 1983 Beta's world share was down to 12 percent. By 1984 every VCR manufacturer except Sony had adopted VHS. Klopfenstein summarizes (our italics):

> Although many held the perception that the Beta VCR produced a better picture than VHS, technical experts such as Weinstein (1984) and Prentis (1981) have concluded that this was, in fact, not the case; periodic reviews in Consumers Reports found VHS picture quality superior twice, found Beta superior once, and found no difference in a fourth review. In conclusion, *the Beta format appeared to hold no advantages over VHS other than being the first on the market, and this may be a lesson for future marketers of new media products* (1989: 28).

How does this history address the theory and empiricism around path dependence? First, and most obviously, it contradicts the claim that the Beta format was better and that its demise constitutes evidence of the pernicious workings of decentralized decision making or sensitive dependence on initial conditions. Regarding the one aspect that clearly differentiated the two formats, tape length, consumers preferred VHS.

Second, even though the technical differences between the two formats were small, the advantage of longer recording times was sufficient to allow VHS to overcome Beta's initial lead. There might not have been any great harm had the market stayed with Beta, inasmuch as its recording time was up to five hours by the early 1980s. But consumers were not willing to wait those few extra years, and the market was responsive enough to make the switch to the better path.

Third, the history illustrates the role of ownership, strategy, and adopters' foresight in facilitating a change in paths. The formats were each owned, and both Sony and JVC-Matsushita expended considerable effort to establish their standards, indicating that they expected to capture some of the benefits of doing so. The ability of VHS to attract partners such as RCA and Matsushita indicates the market participants' ability to recognize the large potential gains from promoting a superior standard.

Although it is sometimes argued that the dominance of VHS resulted from the random association of VHS with a more aggressive licensing and pricing strategy, the pricing and promotion of the two formats were in fact closely matched. Sony was certainly no babe in the woods with regard to marketing consumer electronics. But consumers were apparently quick to identify a standard that they preferred and were confident that many others would do the same. Not only was the switch to VHS rapid, but it was also repeated in separate national markets. Thus, there is no evidence that the market choice was due to blunders, unlucky promotional choices, or insufficient investment by the owners of the Beta format.[3]

An additional aspect of this standards battle further illustrates the richness of market behavior. Although the Beta format's advantages in editing and special effects were apparently relatively unimportant for home users, they were important for broadcasters. And the Beta format does survive in broadcasting, where editing and special effects are relatively more important. Broadcasters and home users do interact, of course, but mostly over the airwaves or cable. Their interaction does not generally involve much exchange of the cassettes themselves, and for those occasions when it does, broadcasters can keep some VHS equipment. But the high-performance, high-cost broadcasting machines that use the Beta format are one reason that many people assume that the Beta format offers higher quality.

The importance of Beta's survival in broadcasting is that there were really two standards battles, not one, and two different outcomes. Consumers got the format that they preferred, and broadcasters got the standard they preferred. This is really a story of coexisting standards, much along the line of the possibilities discussed in the previous chapter. The broadcasters are the minority that have strong preferences for a different standard, as illustrated in figure 5.10.

The Beta-VHS standards war is a rich example of a standards battle. It is *not*, however, a story of lock-in of the first product to market. Instead, it is a story of competing formats, consumers' switching when something better for them became available, and the coexistence of a minority standard that offers special benefits to a specialized group of users.

A final postscript on the Beta-VHS rivalry: one that indicates the dangers of lock-in stories. If a standard with a better picture were to come along but not be adopted, it might be tempting to suspect a potential case of lock-in. DVD might seem to fit this description, except that DVD is still thought likely to replace VHS. But if DVD should fail, we are likely to hear choruses of lock-in from the usual places. We should be slow the accept such a conclusion, however, since the market has already rejected a system with a higher quality picture that suffers no compatibility problems with VHS.

We are talking about SuperVHS, a system that, using special tape, can record and play back a picture with much higher resolution than ordinary VHS. SuperVHS machines can be purchased for about $350, which is somewhat higher than the price of a regular VHS machine with the same set of features normally found on SuperVHS (hi-fi, cable box control, and so forth). SuperVHS machines can play back regular VHS tapes, so there is no compatibility issue, and can even record regular VHS on regular tapes. With the special tapes, however, it has a picture that has 30–40 percent greater resolution. SuperVHS has been around for most, if not all, of this decade, so it has had plenty of time to generate market share, yet it clearly has failed to catch on.

Why has it failed? It can not be due to lock-in, for there is no compatibility issue and no differential network effects. SuperVHS machines are part of the same network as regular VHS. Thus we must conclude that consumers are not willing to pay an extra $150 for SuperVHS. Improved picture quality is not, apparently, worth that difference. The difference in picture quality may be large in terms of technical specifications, but the typical consumer may not be able to see it. On ordinary television screens of twenty-seven inches or less, the fast speed of a regular VHS tape displays a picture that is about as good as the ordinary viewer can detect. Furthermore, regular VHS has a better picture than standard broadcast quality, which eliminates the value of SuperVHS for taping off the air. This is important because it tells us that even if Beta had a better picture than VHS, it might not have mattered as long as VHS's picture was good enough. After all, any difference between Beta and VHS is dwarfed by the difference between VHS and SuperVHS.

This story has implications beyond video recording. Just as the movement to a graphical operating system in computers did not take place until sufficiently powerful hardware became readily available and affordable (as we show in the next section of this chapter), the movement to a higher-quality video format (tape or broadcast HDTV) is likely to require affordable large-screen televisions that will make the enhanced picture quality worthwhile. Should DVD or HDTV, currently in their embryonic phase, fail in the market, that failure can be taken as a failure of markets or standards only if cheap large-screen televisions are readily available.

Computer Operating Systems: Mac versus IBM

Among the popular examples of economic things that go bump in the night is the success of the DOS computer operating system. Macintosh, it is alleged, was far superior to command-line DOS, and even to DOS-based Windows, at least in its earlier versions. Yet Macintosh has garnered only a small share of the computer market and appeared, until quite recently, to be on the brink of extinction.

Because users clearly prefer a graphical user interface to a command-line interface, how did the DOS command-line interface manage to dominate personal computing when it and the Macintosh graphical user interface were competing head on? The usual story is that DOS was successful because DOS was successful. DOS had a large market share because there was a lot of software available for it, and there was a lot of software available for it because there were a lot of DOS-based machines in use. But it is also possible that DOS succeeded on its own merits.

First, DOS had a cost advantage over Macintosh. A graphical user interface requires considerably more computing power to get most jobs done, which significantly increased costs when that power was hard to come by. Furthermore, although Macintosh owners could see italics and boldface on screen, to print the screen as they saw it required a PostScript printer, and such printers cost in the vicinity of $1,000 more than ordinary laser printers. Second, command-line DOS was faster than Macintosh.[4] Macintosh owners had to wait for their screen displays to change, whereas PCs owners had almost instantaneous updates.[5] Third, although the graphical user interface allowed users to access and learn programs more easily, in many business settings a computer was used for only a single application. Only one program could run at a time, and hard drives were small or nonexistent at first. Many programs were copy-protected, usually requiring that the floppy disk be kept in the drive, so it was awkward to change programs. In that environment, the operator had very little interaction with the operating system interface, and once the operator had learned the application, there were few advantages of the graphical user interface. Finally, it was easier to create software for DOS machines, which is one reason that many applications packages became available so quickly in the DOS world.

The case for DOS in the 1980s, therefore, was much stronger than it appears from the vantage of the 1990s, with our multimegabyte memories and multigigabyte hard drives. Now that we routinely use computers that run 30 times faster than the old DOS machines, with 50 times the memory and 100 times the hard-drive capacity, the requirements of a graphical operating system seem rather puny. But they were enormous back in the 1980s.

As processors became faster, memory cheaper, and hard drives larger, the advantages of command-line DOS diminished. If we were still using DOS, we would certainly have an example of being stuck with an inferior product, one that offers smaller net benefits to consumers. But we are not still using DOS. Instead we are using a Mac-like graphical user interface. If someone went to sleep in 1983 and awoke in 1999 to see a modern PC, he most likely would think that the Macintosh graphical user interface had been colorized and updated, with a second button added to the mouse.[6] This modern Rip van Winkle might be surprised to learn, however, that the owner of the graphical user interface was not Apple, but Microsoft.

Although the movement from DOS to Windows was costly, it occurred quite rapidly. As in the other examples, the evidence is quite the opposite of lock-in: It demonstrates that markets, far from getting stuck in ruts, make rapid changes when there is a clear advantage in doing so. Because Windows also ran DOS programs, it lowered the transition cost.[7]

The competition between DOS and Macintosh demonstrates the importance of the distinction between a fixed standard and flexible standard. A fixed standard at least allows for the hypothetical possibility that we get stuck—everyone would like to move but no one would like to go first. With a flexible standard, however, getting stuck is difficult to imagine. A flexible standard can evolve over time: It can add a new feature, or increase capacity, or adjust a parameter.

One important element in the success of the DOS-Windows platforms may well have been Microsoft's commitment to backward compatibility—evolution rather than revolution. In contrast, Macintosh computers were not compatible with earlier successful Apple products. This meant that the Macintosh did not have a base of carry-over users as early customers.

Whether they stayed with Apple products or moved on to DOS, Apple customers faced an inevitable task of converting or abandoning files and applications.

Furthermore, Apple's behavior signaled customers that the company would not seek continuity in its operating systems in the future. In fact, Apple implemented, in fairly short order, two generations of incompatible operating systems—first the Lisa, and then the Macintosh.[8] Computer users, particularly commercial users, who found such abrupt changes to be disruptive took note of these policies. Commodore and Atari, which also were also early adopters of graphical user interface operating systems, took approaches similar to Apple's.

The Windows system is often criticized for continuing to carry the vestiges of the dated DOS system. But, as in all interesting economic problems, benefits are usually accompanied by a cost. The benefit of continuity from DOS to the various versions of Windows was unavoidably accompanied by the cost of carrying over certain DOS features. In the remaining three chapters, we see this interplay of these costs and benefits over and over again in the applications software market.

Metric versus English Measurement

George Washington, while president, spoke against the evils of metric. Did he know something we don't?

Washington was aware that the French had gone overboard in their adoption of metric. The switch to metric time in France after the revolution is a fascinating example of a case where the costs of switching were far greater than the benefits. The reason that metric time makes no sense is that is makes obsolete all clocks and provides no particular additional value. People do not often make calculations in time units, so having a system based on decimal units is of limited value. Metric time is rather like driving on the left or right side of the street—the choice is arbitrary, with little advantage for one over the other.

The costs of switching to metric measuring systems are nontrivial, and most Americans do not think that they outweigh the benefits. Tasks for which consumers most commonly use a measuring system, such as finding out how hot or cold it is outside, purchasing meat at the supermarket, or determining the speed of your automobile, do not benefit from metric measurements. Thus, the failure to establish the metric system in the United States is a rational response to individual choices—not an indicator of a problem. This response contrasts sharply with the costly measures that have been implemented in Canada.

The metric system was adopted in Canada by government fiat in the 1970s. The change in standard happened only after considerable debate, and it is a high irony that one of the most persuasive arguments in this debate was that Canada needed to move quickly to stay on the same standard as the United States—where, at the time, there was some talk about a move to metric. In Canada, metric regulators went so far as to ban measurements in English units after the adoption of metric. Chaos in supermarkets and voter discontent quickly led regulators to allow the listing of both measurement systems, but metric continues to be the official measurement system in Canada. Nevertheless, to this day, English measurement is the de facto standard for many kinds of common measurement.

On the other hand, for many groups in the United States, such as scientists, metric is the standard. This is another example where the total number of people using a standard is less important than the particular individuals with whom one most closely interacts, and where two standards can coexist.

Bureaucracy and the Myth of MITI

All of these examples—keyboards, VCRs, computers, and the metric system—are fables that circulate as evidence of a kind of after-the-fact Murphy's law of markets. If something happened, it probably went wrong. But there is an opposite myth that may be even more costly. It is the myth that we could have avoided these "disasters" by naming an omniscient, benevolent standards-dictator as an alternative to markets. Sometimes this savior is no more omniscient than a Monday morning quarterback: When he compares actual outcomes with a hypothetical ideal, it's obvious what should have happened. Often in these discussions, the wished-for arbiter of perfection is the government.

This is not to say that people don't harbor a good deal of cynicism about politics. But discussions of industrial policy often seem to incorporate a view that government, or the experts that it might draw upon, could figure out what technologies and standards are the best, even in the circumstances in which private parties are unable to sort these things out for themselves. It seems reasonable, however, to keep things even. There's no use in comparing real markets with a hypothetical, benevolent, and perfect government. Let's at least discipline ourselves to compare real markets with real government.

Now, governments are human institutions, and they are not omniscient. They can, however, do some very important things that private parties cannot manage. Even free-market types are usually willing to concede the utility of having a government that can record and enforce property rights, adjudicate contracts, and provide for the common defense. But governments can also fail. Even liberals acknowledge waste and fraud and misdirection of some government programs. For a better understanding of technology policy, what is required is not a litany of all the things that could happen, but some discussion of what has happened. For this, we do have a very good example: the Japanese Ministry of International Trade and Industry (MITI).

Only a few years ago, when the Japanese economy seemed to be a powerhouse that never made a misstep, MITI was often held up as an example of what the U.S. government needed to do, an example of successful industrial policy. Now, with Japan in recession, and the repercussions of underpriced capital and subsidized industry being sharply felt, we do not hear so much about MITI. In fact, MITI is a story of substantial misdirection, of damaging commitments to particular technologies, and damaging restraints on entrepreneurs who were thought not to be doing the right things. MITI's gaffes are now well known—wrong on transistors, which succeeded; wrong on supercomputers, which did not; wrong on the build-up of the steel industry; wrong on synthetic fuels; wrong on Honda; and wrong on HDTV.[9] Very simply MITI, which may well have had the best shot of any government agency at steering an economy toward the best bets, was no substitute for the interplay of multitudes of profit-seeking rivals competing with each other to find the best mousetrap.

Some Other Examples

Path-dependence advocates have sometimes claimed that the continued use of FORTRAN by academics and scientists is an example of getting stuck on the wrong standard.[10] But one doesn't have to peruse too many computer magazines to realize that FORTRAN has long ago been superseded by languages such as Pascal, C, C++, and now, perhaps, Java. Individuals continuing to use FORTRAN do so not because they want to be like everyone else, but because their cost of switching is too high. This is the opposite of the typical network-effects story. Network effects, as normally modeled, should have induced them to switch to mainstream programming languages years ago. This is a story of ordinary sunk costs, not of network "externality" or other market failure. This is another story where, network effects, if of consequence, are not related to the total size of the networks as much as they are to the small group of individuals who interact in their work.

Path-dependence proponents have also sometimes claimed that the gasoline-powered engine might have been a mistake, and that steam or electricity might have been a superior choice for vehicle propulsion. They advance this argument in spite of the fact that in the century since automobiles became common, with all of the applications of motors and batteries in other endeavors, and with all the advantages of digital electronic power-management systems, the most advanced electric automobiles that anyone has been able to make do not yet equal the state of the art in internal-combustion automobiles as of the late 1920s.

A number of scholars have begun to examine other instances that have, at one time or another, been alleged to illustrate lock-in to inferior standards. For many years, economic historians argued that the small coal cars that were used in England were an example of what was called "technical backwardness." The mechanism for this backwardness was much the same as other lock-in stories. The stock of cars led to certain adaptations around the cars, which led to renewal of the stock of cars, and so on. Recently, however, Va Nee Van Vleck (1997) reconsidered this case. She found that the small coal car was in fact well suited to Britain's geography and coal-distribution systems. In a very different subject area, Larry Ribstein and Bruce Kobayashi have examined the possibility that the adoption of state laws locks in the features of the statutes that are adopted by the first states to pass legislation. They find very little persistence of these initial statutory forms.

Finally, software applications offer many instances in which one product replaces another. Those histories are presented in detail in the next three chapters.

NOTES ON CHAPTER 6

1. The example is most prominent in Arthur (1990).

2. This history draws on Lardner (1987), chapters 3, 4, and 10.

3. In the economics literature of lock-in, the Beta-VHS story, very casually told, is often used to support the lock-in claim. Here, for example, is how Brian Arthur (1990) tells the story: "The history of the videocassette recorder furnishes a simple example of positive feedback. The VCR market started out with two competing formats selling at about the same price: VHS and Beta. . . . Both systems were introduced at about the same time and so began with roughly equal market shares; those shares fluctuated early on because of external circumstance, 'luck' and corporate maneuvering. Increasing returns on early gains eventually tilted the competition toward VHS: it accumulated enough of an advantage to take virtually the entire VCR market. Yet it would have been impossible at the outset of the competition to say which system would win, which of the two possible equilibria would be selected. Furthermore, if the claim that Beta was technically superior is true, then the market's choice did not represent the best outcome" (p. 92).

4. See the discussion of a graphical spreadsheet (Excel) vis-à-vis text-based spreadsheets in chapter 7, where the speed penalty of the graphical product was rated as a fatal handicap.

5. The screen display on the PC required only 5 or 10 percent of the computer memory that was required by the Macintosh screen. Because this was constantly being updated when the screen changed, DOS screens tended to update instantaneously, whereas Macintosh screens had a noticeable lag and scrolling was much slower.

6. The original graphical user interface, developed at the Xerox PARC research center, had a mouse with three buttons. The PC has two. The use of but a single button appears to be a matter of pride in the Macintosh community and is sometimes defended as optimal. Another point that rabid Macintosh users often made when pointing to the superiority of their operating system has to do with whether menus drop down automatically, or require a mouse click. To most users, these are minor differences compared with the chasms that separated graphical and text-based operating systems.

7. If Apple had been interested in converting DOS users, they could have incorporated DOS compatibility in their operating system (purchasing or licensing a DOS clone such as DR DOS, for example) and porting their operating system to the Intel platform so as not to render obsolete a user's hardware. Apple apparently thought of themselves as a hardware company and did not actively pursue this strategy.

8. This difference still separates the two companies. Apple, when it was switching to its recent Macintosh operating system (8.0), initially announced that it would not run software applications that were made to run under its older operating system (7.x). Microsoft, on the other hand, has been very careful about making Windows NT compatible with its Windows 95/98 operating system before it begins a serious migration of users, allowing five or six years for the process to be finished (assuming that Windows 2000 is delivered on time).

9. For a general discussion of the MITI, see Zinsmeister (1993).

10. In case you think we are making this up in order to create a ridiculous straw man, see Arthur (1990). A recent Stanford economics Ph.D. dissertation (Kirsch 1998) was also devoted to examining this issue. Kirsch reports to us that he went into the project hoping to find great inefficiency in the use of the internal combustion engine, but his research forced him to conclude otherwise.

7

Using Software Markets to Test These Theories

"Build a better mousetrap and the world will beat a path to your door." This, surely, is one path to success. There's nothing mysterious or underhanded about the success of a company that provides consumers with a product that gives more bang for the buck than its competitors. It used to be taken for granted that products that succeeded usually did so because they had some superior attribute.

But the possibility of lock-in suggests that there may be other paths to market domination. The whole concept of lock-in flies in the face of quality-will-win free-market assurances. If and when there is third-degree lock-in, a product succeeds in spite of inferior quality. In such a market consumers purchase a product only because that is what everyone else is using, while in fact each consumer would have preferred to use a different product.

But enough with theoretical meanderings. Our focus here is on the real world. And to look at the real world, we must look at real-world markets. One interesting market to study is the software market, which is often alleged to exhibit network effects, lock-in, leveraging, and tipping. Software is interesting not only because it is thought to exhibit network characteristics, but also because it is the focus of the recent government antitrust action against Microsoft.

Microsoft, by any reckoning, is a tremendously successful company, but why is it so successful? Does it just build better mousetraps? Or, as some have claimed, are its products, in fact, only mediocre? Has it achieved its large market share in spite of these mediocre products, by lock-in and luck, or through the leveraging of its ownership of the operating system?

Our data provide clear answers to these questions. Good products win. Microsoft's success derives from good business decisions and superior products. When Microsoft's products are better than its competitors' they succeed. But there's an important corollary: When Microsoft's products are inferior to its competitors' they fail. This corollary throws empirical cold water on the hypothesis that Microsoft's success comes from leveraging its position in the operating systems market. Another bucket of cold water comes from our examination of pricing structures. Lock-in, we will see below, implies monopoly prices. But Microsoft does not appear to charge monopoly prices. In fact, Microsoft's prices of comparable products are lower in markets where it is dominant than they are in markets where it is not.

This chapter begins by examining the hypotheses that can be addressed by our examination of software markets. We then describe the nature of software markets and our measurement techniques. Chapter 8 goes on to apply our technique to the largest application markets: spreadsheets and word processors. Chapter 9 then applies these techniques to other software markets.

Software Markets and Tests of Network Theories

Software markets afford us the possibility of testing some of the claims that are tossed about in regard to network markets. It is widely and prominently alleged that software exhibits strong network effects. If that is so, there are implications about software markets that we can test—things that we ought to see in the real world. If these implications are contradicted, some of the most prominent claims about the consequences of networks will have to be reconsidered.

Monopoly, Natural and Serial

Strong network effects will tend to lead to monopoly. If people benefit from being connected to everyone else, or being compatible with everyone else, it is likely that one network, or one product, will dominate. Economists refer to technologies that have this characteristic as *natural monopoly*

The existence of markets where a firm has a very large market share (often casually referred to as "monopoly" or "winner-take-all") is not, however, a clear demonstration of the presence or importance of network effects.[1] As we saw in the first half of the book, network effects are not necessary to produce monopoly—it is possible to have monopoly, or natural monopoly, without network effects. Natural monopoly can result from ordinary economies of scale in production.

Domination of a market, that is to say monopoly, can also result from an attribute that we have termed *instant scalability*. Instant scalability means that a firm's output can be increased very rapidly without the usual additional costs associated with rapid increases in output. Where products are differentiated and where consumers have similar preferences about products, a product that most consumers identify as "best" can quickly be offered in sufficient quantity to satisfy the entire market.

Instant scalability is a property of the software industry and of many other industries in which products consist principally of intellectual property. In such industries, production of the good itself consists largely of reproduction of the tangible form of the intellectual property. Often, this requires only generic reproduction equipment—disk drives or Internet connections, for example—rather than specialized fixed investments. In more traditional industries, increased production capacity may require new factories, new tools, and new workers. If a new minivan is a big hit, for example, it could take years, and lots of committed capital, to expand output significantly. This is often not the case for intellectual property. The essential contrast here is not the lower (marginal) cost of increasing output in intellectual-property industries, but rather the fact that large product-specific and irreversible investments are not necessary to expand output.[2]

In industries that are subject to instant scalability, winners can rapidly win big because they can rapidly scale up, and losers leave quickly because their investments in generic capacity are reversible. Similarly, a "best" product can be scaled up to serve the entire market before other firms can imitate its winning characteristics. So industries with instant scalability will exhibit much more of this "winner-take-all" tendency than traditional markets. Of course, instant scalability is a two-edged sword. Such markets will, for all the same reasons, be "winner-take-all, but only for a while." That is, they will exhibit *serial monopoly*. In this regard, industries that embody ideas in ones and zeros are different from those that embody ideas in iron and brass.

All three of these reasons—network effects, production economies, and instant scalability—are likely to be at work, to varying degrees in software markets. Although monopoly is not necessarily a distinguishing characteristic of network markets, we observe that the software industry often is characterized by products with very large market shares.

Lock-in or Inertia

A separate question from monopoly itself is whether things get locked in. Do products, networks, standards, or technologies have difficulty overcoming entrenched incumbents? When a better product comes along, will it be adopted if there are economic advantages to its adoption? If not, we have lock-in. As we saw in chapter 5, lock-in or inertia might arise from either economies of scale or network effects.

Confirmation of lock-in requires that better products exist that are not adopted.[3] In the next two chapters, where we measure the quality of software products, we will have several direct tests for lock-in.

Testing for inertia would require that we compare the rate of change in actual market shares with the ideal rates of change. Testing for inertia therefore requires more detailed knowledge than testing for lock-in alone, and considerably more detail than our data allow. Still, it is possible to examine the speed of market-share changes in software markets and to make a casual comparison with the speed of changes in other markets.[4]

Tipping

Significant network effects ought to imply their own special dynamic of structural change. This dynamic is sometimes called *tipping*. In a network market, as a firm expands, network effects should make the firm's products progressively more attractive. Market share should grow at an increasing rate. Tipping occurs when a product subject to increasing returns generates sufficient momentum in market share that its domination of the market becomes inevitable.

Where a product dominates because of its size rather than its quality, then growth in its market share should be slow when it has achieved only small market shares and faster at larger market shares. In contrast, if a product becomes dominant because it is the best, growth will not depend on market share. Sales growth can start large and stay that way.

In markets subject to tipping, if a new product displaces an incumbent, it will grow only very slowly as it overcomes the large market share of the incumbent, but then accelerate rapidly beyond a tipping point, where the incumbent's advantage is reversed.

Price: The Neglected Implication

One implication of monopoly and lock-in brought about by network effects is rising prices. This implication is largely ignored in the literature. Because network effects flow to the market leader, the leader's products have greater value than rival products. Thus, in a world of strong network effects, the leader should appropriate some of this extra value by increasing price as his market share increases. This effect is reinforced by the tendency of network benefits, and therefore prices, to rise as the network as a whole grows. It would be further reinforced if the increase in market share led to an increase in monopoly power.

Examining prices allows us to contrast network effects with economies of scale. That is because network effects and economies of scale have the opposite impact on price. Economies of scale, by lowering the costs of the firm as the firm increases in size, will lower the price of the product for any given level of markup over cost. Network effects, on the other hand, increase the demand for the product and lead to an increase in price.[5] This should be true for individual firms as they increase their market shares and also for the market as a whole as the size of the network increases. If both network effects and economies of scale coexist, price will be influenced by the interplay of the two forces.

The Nature of Software Markets

If the concept of lock-in applies anywhere, it ought to apply to software. Network effects are likely to be stronger in software markets than in the other suspected havens of path dependence—typewriters or video recorders, for example. For some kinds of software, compatibility with other users is important. Users communicate. They send messages and exchange files. They exchange information about what can be done and they teach each other. They help each other when problems arise and they play games with each other. In addition, for software, there is less likelihood that decreasing returns in manufacturing could outweigh network effects, since software manufacturing itself may exhibit increasing returns.

Furthermore, software has several innate characteristics that encourage consumers to remain with the same vendor. One important consideration is backward compatibility—compatibility with the learned skills associated with previous versions of a program, and compatibility with file formats that were created with previous versions of the program.[6] If the adoption of a new spreadsheet or word processor negates the value of all of the consumer's old files, the consumer is much less likely to make a change. That is why almost all software products provide some degree of backward compatibility with previous versions.

Backward compatibility can also reach across product lines. Many software products are designed to be able to read files produced by other products (particularly those of the incumbent leader) or to mimic, where legal and possible, the "look and feel" of the leader. In the spreadsheet market, there were some direct clones of longtime leader Lotus 1-2-3, such as Twin, a spreadsheet that could read Lotus files and that had an interface identical to that of Lotus 1-2-3.[7] A less extreme example was Excel, which offers users the choice of using some Lotus 1-2-3 commands, but has its own distinct interface.

Ability to read files is not the only feature of backward compatibility. Other dimensions of compatibility include the idiosyncratic features of the incumbent standard. For example, an important feature of spreadsheets is their use of macros. The chances of unseating an incumbent hinges both on the ability to read the incumbent's files, and also to read the macros.[8]

Backward compatibility, of course, is consistent with the existence of some form of path dependence. Completely new adopters have an unimpeded path to whatever product they might consider to be superior. But those who have already chosen a product must consider every change or upgrade in the light of whether the advantages of the new product outweigh the costs of switching. If the costs of switching are greater than the benefits, it is rational and efficient to remain with the older product, even if it is judged to be inferior. Remaining with the old, inferior product is either first- or second-degree path dependence, depending on whether the consumer anticipated that the better product would eventually be available.

But there are indications that even the software industry manages to resist the strongest form of path dependence, pernicious lock-in. First, as we will examine in detail in chapters 8 and 9, better products consistently replace inferior products. Second, although software markets often exhibit the common network effect of drifting toward natural monopoly, there are few signs of excess inertia in leadership changes. In software markets, the speed at which serial monopolists replace one another might actually be greater than in most "ordinary" markets.

The Consumer's Choice

The logic of a software choice is pretty straightforward, whether one is changing to a completely different product or just upgrading a current one.[9] On one side of the ledger, the consumer must tally the increased value using the new software. This extra value might come from new features, increased speed, better compatibility with other users, and so forth. On the other side of the ledger go the costs of purchasing the software, the costs of the transition (presumably users will be less productive as they learn to use the new software), and the costs of file incompatibility with previous software (the cost of imperfect access to old data).

The authors of this book faced this decision a few years ago. We think our story illustrates fairly well the choices facing software users.

Late in 1991 we decided to choose Lotus's AmiPro as our word processor. The choice of AmiPro was a big change for each of us, in that we were each making a transition from another platform (Margolis from DOS and Liebowitz from an Atari ST). We wanted to be compatible with each other, since we were writing papers together, but at that time we were largely unconcerned with the fact that AmiPro had a small market share. First, we did not transfer files with very many other people. Second, the reviews indicated that AmiPro was one of the best Windows word processors, so there was reason to think that its market share would increase. Third, as indicated by Liebowitz's use of an Atari for many years, the use of esoteric products had its own charm. Finally, the leading PC word processor that happened to be used by our secretaries was WordPerfect, but our experience with this nonintuitive and nongraphical product made us reject it out of hand.

By late 1995 AmiPro was getting somewhat long in the tooth. We had found it to be very user-friendly and capable, but other word processors were beginning to incorporate features that were missing from AmiPro. It couldn't correct spelling on the fly. It couldn't create HTML (Internet) documents. It couldn't handle long file names.[10] It seemed time to move on.

We had several choices. A new version of AmiPro was coming out, called WordPro. We also considered WordPerfect and Microsoft Word (which had replaced WordPerfect as the standard). The choice seemed fairly easy. We wanted to minimize the difficulties of translating our old Ami-Pro files, because we were still using use many of these files. We also wanted a word processor that would not be costly to learn. WordPro seemed most likely to meet these criteria. Because it was an upgrade from AmiPro, we figured it would be able to translate all of our existing AmiPro files. We knew that this translation would be far from perfect on Microsoft Word. We also expected WordPro to share many features with AmiPro, minimizing the costs of the transition. It was supposed to have features that would make co-authoring and collaboration particularly easy. As a bonus, it was also inexpensive.

Notice that we didn't much care whether Word might be slightly better than WordPro. We had no reason to expect WordPro to be far inferior to Microsoft Word, and it seemed to us that adopting WordPro would be efficient. Even if we had thought WordPro "inferior" to Microsoft, our decision was not an example of third-degree lock-in because we were adopting a product with a smaller market share on the basis of our own idiosyncratic needs.

But our experience with WordPro turned out to be painful. First, it had little in common with the interface and feel of the old AmiPro. Second, it was slow. Third, it crashed with numbing frequency, particularly when importing complicated files, including many of our old AmiPro files. Before a week had passed, we were reconsidering our decision.

With the costs of switching to WordPro being as high as the costs of switching to any other product, we were put in a position of new users, and we chose the highest-rated product: Microsoft Word. We also purchased a specialized software application to convert our old AmiPro files to Word format. This story is a cautionary tale for producers of software. A software company will lose upgrade sales if it does not keep an eye on backward compatibility. As we noted in Part Two, backward compatibility involves both benefits and costs. The benefits include carryover of files and skills. The costs include the burdens of complexity, size, and functional limitations.

The WordStar word processor was famous for new versions that changed the software tremendously from previous versions. WordStar 2000 was given a different name from the original WordStar because, for all practical purposes, it was a different software product (most keystroke combinations were different). Introducing products that are very different from their predecessors is extremely dangerous for firms with large installed bases (WordStar was the leading word processor of its time) because it puts consumers in the position of selecting from the complete set of available products. It makes no sense for a firm to do this unless it is convinced that its new product is the best available or unless its old product had a trivial market share. When Samna Corporation came out with the Ami word processor it risked little in making it different from its previous product, Samna Word, inasmuch as it had a very small installed based to alienate. The same was not true for WordPerfect.

Paradigm Changes

While backward compatibility does have its advantages, it can be outweighed by other benefits. One such benefit is taking advantage of a paradigm change.

A developing industry will sometimes take a big step forward in quality, amounting to a paradigm change. At such a juncture, large numbers of current users will be willing to switch to a new product because the advantages of the new environment outweigh the costs of switching. Such a paradigm change can lead to an entire market displacement. Such changes might include a design alteration or a change in the operating environment of the product. Examples would be the removal of copy-protection, allowing the product to work in networked environments; a movement from 8-bit to 16-bit, or 16-bit to 32-bit architectures; the growth of the Internet; the invention of macros; the development of graphical screen displays; or voice recognition.

We examine here the histories of two such market displacements: the shift from DOS to Windows, and the shift to office suites.

The Shift from DOS to Windows

Microsoft Windows is now so universally accepted as the preeminent operating system, at least in terms of usage, that it is easy to overlook the fact that Windows did not have a particularly smooth path to dominance.

The origin of the modern operating system took place at the Xerox Palo Alto Research Center (PARC), which developed the idea of putting data in a resizable windowing interface controlled by a mouse. Xerox never derived much benefit from this work, but millions of computer users have.

The Apple Macintosh (1984), followed by the Atari ST (1985) and Commodore Amiga (1986) computers, all had graphical operating systems, but the vast majority of IBM-style PCs were still using the primitive (but speedy) text-based DOS. As hardware became more capable, the concept of a graphical user interface (GUI) made more and more economic sense. One of the first attempts to create such a GUI for PCs was undertaken by Digital Research,[11] which produced a system called GEM. This operating system was in fact used on the Atari ST series of computers, which had a loyal following, particularly in Germany. Ventura Publisher, the leading desktop publishing program for the PC in the 1980s, was written to work under PC GEM.

PC GEM never attracted many other leading applications, nor did it achieve much of a following. Part of the reason for its failure was that in PC GEM, only two windows could be open at one time, and those windows could not be resized. These limitations, which were not present in other versions of GEM, were Digital Research's response to legal actions by Apple over similarities in the look and feel of the two operating systems.[12] Ironically then, it may have been Apple, not Microsoft, that most hurt the Digital Research's chance to compete effectively with Microsoft's Windows.[13]

Other providers of graphical shells that operated over DOS included Quarterdeck's DeskView (introduced in 1985), a graphical version of DESQ that allowed multiple DOS Windows to operate (task switching). IBM worked on a similar product called TopView. Microsoft entered the market in 1985 with Windows 1.0.

These products were all flawed. Some were slow; some were buggy; some were memory hogs. Some were all of the above. Not surprisingly, none of these products achieved the critical goal of having large numbers of programs written to take advantage of the GUI.

And there were other problems. Many DOS users were somewhat defensive about GUIs in the first place. Most did not even own a mouse. In fact, when Microsoft eventually entered the GUI operating system market, it took the unusual step of going into the mouse business in an attempt to overcome this problem.[14]

Adding further uncertainty was the fact that Microsoft and IBM, together, were planning a new operating system, OS/2, as the "real" GUI for PC users. OS/2 was planned to be a full 32-bit multitasking operating system that would have a graphical interface and also run old DOS programs. Windows was supposed to be merely an intermediate step. OS/2, which was going to be jointly developed by IBM and Microsoft, was not going to be a mere shell over DOS, but an entirely new operating system.

Microsoft upgraded Windows 1.0 to Windows 2.0 in 1987. The new product did somewhat better than the first version, but it was not a rousing success. But by late 1990, Microsoft finally got it right with Windows 3.0. An advertisement for Windows 3.0 acknowledges the shortcomings of the previous versions: "The graphical user interface (GUI) environment on an MS-DOS PC, and subsequent demise of the 'C' prompt, is a reality today. Sure, you say. Microsoft realizes you may have heard this one before. And we agree that you have every reason to be skeptical. Well, all of this was before new Microsoft Windows version 3.0."[15]

By the time it introduced Windows 3.0, Microsoft understood that for a GUI to succeed in the DOS market, it would need a large number of applications written for it, and it would have to run old DOS applications as well. It was in Microsoft's best interest to induce as many developers as possible to write Windows applications. One way to ensure that major product categories were covered was to port its own products over, particularly in the essential categories of word processing and spreadsheets.

In retrospect we know that Windows 3.0 (and 3.1)[16] was a stunning success, eliminating DOS in a very short period of time.[17] This can be easily seen in figure 7.1, which uses spreadsheet sales to track the competition between DOS and Windows applications. The sales of DOS spreadsheets fell after the introduction of Windows 3.0 in late 1990 and became virtually insignificant by 1995.

As we will see, the decision to develop OS/2 products instead of products for the "intermediate" Windows was an important tactical mistake for many companies. Those who jumped on the Windows bandwagon early, such as Intuit and Samna, had an open field and an opportunity to score large sales gains. IDC[18] reported: "Both Lotus and Novell paid a monstrous price when Windows 3.0 shipped. Both vendors were deeply involved in OS/2 applications development—and why not? Both IBM and Bill Gates were promoting this operating system. Bill Gates in his 1988 Comdex keynote address stated that 'OS/2 is the next desktop operating system of choice.'

Consequently, 50 percent of the word processing vendors were developing for OS/2 while only 10 percent were developing for Windows. This gave Microsoft a roomy dominance of the application market."[19]

But it is not clear that being late to the party was necessarily every company's critical mistake, or even the major mistake for Lotus and Novell. Many companies were undone because of a sheer lack of experience in producing programs that used a GUI. The Windows programs created by Lotus and WordPerfect, for example, failed not so much because they were late as because they proved inferior to the competition. Poor quality was the most important element in their demise.

The Shift to Office Suites

Microsoft offered the first modern office suite in 1990, for the Macintosh. A year later Microsoft introduced the office suite to the PC market. Although sales did not really take off until 1993, they took off then with a vengeance. By 1995 unit sales of suites had eclipsed sales of stand-alone spreadsheets and word processors by a considerable margin, and by 1997 stand-alone purchases of products that were included in suites practically ceased to exist, with suites accounting for 95 percent of units sales of spreadsheets, for example. This is clearly seen in figure 7.2.

FIGURE 7.1
DOS vs. Windows: Unit Shipments of Spreadsheets

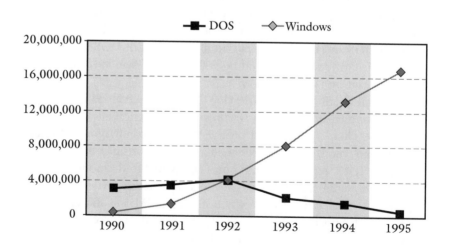

The concept of one company's selling in a single package a product that could meet the entire computing needs of a small business, home-user, or, for that matter, a large percentage of PCs used in corporations, was not new. Shortly after the success of Lotus 1-2-3, there was a flurry of activity to create all-in-one programs that could meet a majority of needs of many computer users. But programs such as Symphony, Jazz, and so forth were premature. The computers of the time were not very powerful and had limited memory. All-in-one programs usually had to strip down more powerful versions of component products. Microsoft Works and Claris Works, for example, included less powerful word processors and spreadsheets. Full-power versions took too much memory and required too much power to include in an all-in-one packages that did everything.

As hardware became more powerful and memory increased in capacity, however, all-in-one packages with full-feature component parts became more feasible. And although early suites were really little more than a packaging together of three or four stand-alone products, suite vendors now work at linking aspects of the individual programs so they work together easily.

The concept of the office suite fit well into Microsoft's strengths and needs. Microsoft's component products were generally judged better than its competitors', but they were increasing their market share less rapidly than

FIGURE 7.2
Number of Suites and Standalones (in 000s)

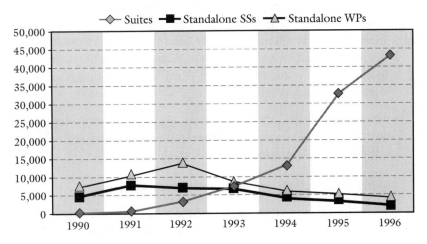

Microsoft might have wished. Microsoft wanted to convince consumers that switching to Windows would provide immediate benefits with useful products. The office suite provided this assurance, and did so at an extremely attractive price. By offering a suite at a lower price than the sum of its prices of the components, Microsoft was able to help convince consumers to make the switch. Microsoft was able to put together a Windows suite earlier and more successfully than its major competitors, WordPerfect and Lotus.

Microsoft's introduction of its office suite came shortly after its introduction of Windows 3.0. Given the tepid response to Windows 2.0, Microsoft needed to give users a reason to adopt the new operating system. The suite gave an all-in-one solution to users' applications requirements, and Windows, unlike DOS, allowed all of these applications to run at the same time. But Microsoft must always have seen the office suite as more than a strategic product for Windows, since it first brought out the suite on the Macintosh.

Microsoft's competitors had to scramble to try to keep up. Because Lotus and WordPerfect had been slow to develop products for Windows, they were not in a position to assemble Windows suites right away.[20] When they did assemble competing suites, they tended to cobble together products that had little in common. WordPerfect and Borland put together a joint suite, the Borland Office, but the complications of joint ownership interfered with developing a cohesive product strategy. Eventually, Novell purchased both WordPerfect and Borland's Quattro Pro, but that suite did little better. Here is IDC's take on Novell's strategy:

> Novell spent a majority of 1994 preparing for the shipment of its first office suite. In 1993 and 1994 the offering on the market from Novell was still the combined Borland/WordPerfect product, the Borland Office. That product languished in the market as the new ownership by Novell of WordPerfect cast uncertainty over future product releases.[21]

When Novell's new product shipped, it did not do well. Soon after, Novell sold its suite to Corel, a maker of graphics programs. This is what IDC had to say about Novell's stewardship:

What did Novell do wrong? Examine the following:

- Paid too much for the acquisition, created false expectations, perhaps based more on Ray Noorda's personal vendetta against Bill Gates than on real business opportunities

- Never created a consistent strategy between Novell and WordPerfect

- Did not understand the desktop business-applications market

- Executed a "push" marketing strategy

- Did not focus on a niche—took Microsoft head on

- Almost killed WordPerfect's historically admired support organization.[22]

It is certainly true that the paradigm shift to the office suite helped Microsoft relative to its competitors. But Microsoft succeeded in the office-suite market, as we demonstrate below, not because it was first to the market, but rather because the products that Microsoft put in its suite were better products.

Our Research Methods

Our technique for understanding the overall software market is to study individual application markets in turn. We take a disciplined look at the history of each software market: the key players, the prices of competing products, and the overall quality of each product as measured by product reviews and market shares.

Our technique is based on the examination of actual evidence, and there is a lot of actual evidence. The software industry is a huge and complicated market. To keep things manageable, we have focused on a few key software-application markets. Two of the largest markets are spreadsheets and word processors, and we devote considerable effort to uncovering the reasons for market successes and failures in each. We also examine desktop publishers, personal finance software, Internet browsers, and online services.

For the period that our analysis covers, the middle 1980s to the late 1990s, there are applications for many different operating systems. In addition to Windows/DOS and the Macintosh, competing operating systems include UNIX in all its flavors, OS/2, Commodore Amiga, Atari ST, and numerous other minor players. To keep the study manageable, we have limited our analysis to Window/DOS and, in some instances,

Macintosh products. Windows/DOS and Macintosh are clearly the two major players, with large numbers of applications in each written for a broad set of end users.

The set of applications we examine covers a fairly wide range. One reason that some people accuse Microsoft of leveraging its ownership of the operating system is the observation that Microsoft has replaced previously well-known market leaders in several major application markets. Obviously, if we wish to examine the accusation of leveraging, we will have to examine these application markets. But it is also important to look at markets where Microsoft has failed to dislodge market leaders, or markets where Microsoft has no presence. These markets serve as controls that we can then use as comparisons for the markets where Microsoft has gained dominant market shares.

Because office suites now account for such a large share of the software market (about 50 percent of Microsoft's revenue), we examine the two leading components of suites: word processors and spreadsheets. But we also examine the personal-finance software market (personal-finance software helps individuals balance their checkbooks and keep track of their expenses), a market in which Microsoft is a player but is not dominant. We examine the desktop-publishing market (desktop-publishing software facilitates the creation of newsletters and magazines) to provide some range. In desktop publishing, there were consumer and professional markets, and Macintosh and PC markets. We examine browsers primarily because of all the publicity surrounding the Microsoft case. Finally, we look at online services. Our interest here is to test the importance of instant scalability. Online services have many network features in common with software, but they are not instantly scalable.

Measuring Software Quality

The economist's usual way to measure the quality of a product is to let the market decide. In traditional markets the relevant people—the ones who will use the product—vote with their dollars, "electing" the products that best serve their purposes. But a central tenet of theories of lock-in, tipping, and the like is that under some conditions market outcomes and consumer preferences fail to coincide. The claim is that in locked-in markets, the decentralized decision making of consumers will not "elect" the best products, even from the perspective of these consumers themselves.

Thus, if we want to assess quality in markets that are allegedly subject to lock-in, we will have to measure quality in some other way. It seemed to us reasonable to look at the quality assessments of experts writing (mainly) for computer magazines.

There are, of course, many magazines that rate software products— many more than we were able to study. We are subject to the usual restrictions of time, resources, and data. But our data set, by any realistic measure, is very large. In total our database contains 158 reviews of spreadsheets, 163 reviews of word processors, 113 reviews of desktop-publishing programs, 50 reviews of personal-finance software, 67 reviews of browsers, and 23 reviews of online services.

We limited our analysis to the leading computer magazines, expanding our scope to specialist magazines when that seemed warranted. For personal-finance software, for example, we also examined specialized financial magazines such as *Money*. There are also some holes in our data sets. The holdings in the libraries visited by our research assistants were not always complete. Sometimes pages were missing, or issues were stolen, and sometimes our libraries did not have complete collections. But such holes in the data set ought to be random. There is no reason to believe that the articles that we missed would have been systematically different than the articles that we found, and this, of course, implies that our results should be unbiased.[23]

This method of analysis is not without pitfalls. Many magazines do not make quality assessments at all. Particularly during the 1980s, magazines often compared features of various products without drawing quality conclusions. Even when judgments are made, magazines often pick a "winner" or "editor's choice" without indicating the amount of quality difference between winners and losers, and without differentiating among the losers. Even magazines that do make full-scale quality comparisons do not necessarily give numerical scores to their rankings. Nevertheless, the reviews give a lot of information.

To compensate for the different formats and approaches of the various reviewers, we used several different measurement gauges.

Our first gauge is simply to score "wins." When a magazine numerically rates individual software products, a product that gets the highest numerical score scores a "win." When a magazine provides clear winners, but no overall evaluation, a "win" is defined as the product that a review identifies as the best. For any given product, the number of "wins" is the number of reviews that give the product the highest numerical score or that rate the product as the winner of the field. A weakness of this measure is that it provides no information about how close in quality the remaining products are, or even the rank order of the remaining products. It does provide, however, a relatively large number of data points.

Our second gauge is more exacting. When magazines provide scores for each product, we report these scores, normalized so that the highest-rated product always receives a 10. When they rate products by qualitative categories such as "excellent" or "poor," we convert these categories into numerical equivalents ratings (excellent = 10, good = 7.5, fair = 5, poor = 2.5). When they give no overall rating but only ratings for particular characteristics (ease of use, speed, and so forth),[24] we arrive at an overall quality rating by calculating the average value of the characteristics.[25] In many cases we leave some smaller vendors out of our charts, and occasionally the winner in a particular review may be a package from one of these vendors. In that case, the products in our charts will all have values less than 10—just as if the winner were included in the charts.[26]

Ideally, for the purpose of analysis, manufacturers would all introduce their new versions of software at the same time and we would have clear cohorts of software generations, which we could then compare. Unfortunately, things are not quite that straightforward in the real world. Nevertheless, manufacturers generally come out with new versions of software that contain many of the innovations that either are just appearing in their competitor's newest versions, or that had recently appeared their competitor's products. To allow for variations, we present our rankings as timelines showing the resulting ups and downs of relative quality positions, which can then be compared with market shares.

Measuring Market Share

We also measured market share, and here, too, we had to make some judgment calls. Market share, of course, can be measured as a share of either units or revenues. Most of the time the method of measurement makes little difference. Because revenues combine price and quantity, market share based on revenues and market share based on quantities will be highly correlated if competitors charge largely similar prices, as they often do. Unless otherwise indicated, we report shares based on revenues. Since we usually report on prices as well as market shares, readers can determine unit-based market shares for themselves.

A further complication in calculating market share arises because of the way many computers are shipped. Most original-equipment manufacturers (OEMs) ship computers with a set of software products already installed. High-end computers (particularly mail order) often include an office suite, and sometimes additional software. Market-share statistics treat these pre-installed products as though they represent actual purchase decisions and use, even though consumers may not use some or any of these products. Thus, market-share statistics may be misleading indicators of actual use. Unfortunately, however, there is no alternative measure of market share that would avoid all such problems. Furthermore, it appears that OEM sales are not likely to influence our results too strongly.

Our data indicate that OEM sales, although increasingly important, still constitute a small share of application markets. For one thing, many categories of software, such as tax, desktop-publishing, statistics, and project-management software, are rarely bundled with OEM computer sales. Office suites, of course, are a different matter. In 1996, IDC analyst Mary Wardley noted: "As the two underdogs pursue strategies to increase their market presence, OEM sales have suddenly grown to represent a significant percent of overall sales for office suites and thus spreadsheets. . . . However, OEM sales have had little to no impact on Microsoft so far, and IDC believes their impact will remain negligible throughout the forecast period." [27]

The data on OEM sales of office suites in the two years for which they are available, 1996 and 1997, reveal OEM sales to have a limited impact, as illustrated in figure 7.3. Although OEM sales are responsible for about 30 percent of unit sales in these two years, they are responsible for less than 10 percent of revenues. And for market leader Microsoft, they are responsible for only about 10 percent of sales and 7 percent of revenues. This limited impact is noteworthy in light of the role given to Microsoft's alleged attempts to control OEMs in the government's case against Microsoft.

The Data

We generated statistics on market shares and prices by using a combination of data from data-collection companies Dataquest[28] and IDC. Their estimates are the best available to us, although we cannot attest to their accuracy. There were occasional apparent errors.[29]

Where possible, we used IDC's data because IDC provides information on individual products. Dataquest, on the other hand, ordinarily reports data in terms of companies and market categories, so that if a company has more than one product in a category, the reported Dataquest value combines the products.[30] We also liked the fact that IDC provides detailed reports on the categories of software that they track whereas the Dataquest data we found provided lists of numbers without any commentary.[31]

The Role of Prices

In many of the cases that follow, we observe that the average prices of software products have declined over time. Because we do not adjust for inflation and because we do not adjust for quality increases in the products, this decline in prices is actually understated.

In many of these markets, especially those where Microsoft has become the market leader, the decline in prices is very large. Figure 7.4 shows average prices for the two largest markets, spreadsheets and word processors (in the PC, or IBM-compatible, market). The most relevant feature of this

FIGURE 7.3
Share of Sales Through OEMs (Office Suites)

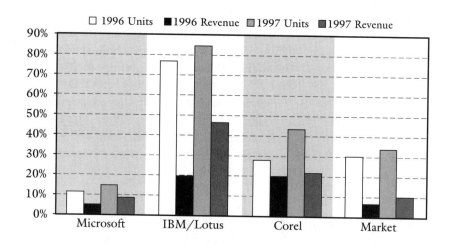

FIGURE 7.4
Average Price Received by Vendor, Word Processors, and Spreadsheets

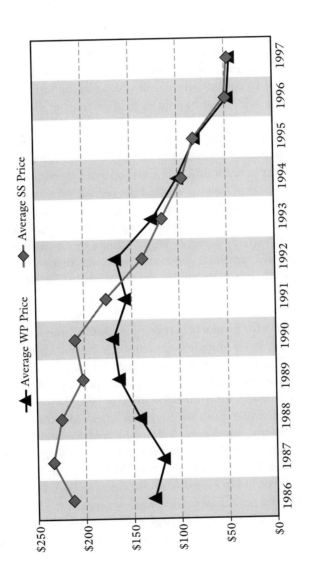

chart is the very large overall decline in prices. But this price decrease is not constant throughout the period. From 1986 until 1990, prices were either constant or slightly rising.[32] Prices did not begin to fall dramatically until after 1990, when, as we will see, Microsoft began to dominate these markets.

The most natural interpretation of these results is that Microsoft is responsible for the price declines. With all the attention that has been focused on Microsoft and its purported monopoly, however, we would be loath to form such a conclusion without additional support. Therefore, we conducted some additional examination of pricing in the industry as a whole.

To see how prices changed in all software markets, not just those we examined in detail, we performed a fairly blunt test. Dataquest provides consistent market definitions for fourteen software markets for the period 1988–1995.[33] For our analysis, we used the average price in each category for each year. This implicitly assumes that this average price actually represents changes in prices for the underlying products, even though shifts across products within a category might change the average price even if each product price remained constant. We assume that such shifts either are minimal, or that they are similar across product categories.

We then grouped the software markets into three categories: markets where Microsoft is a direct competitor; markets where Microsoft plays no role; and markets for products that compete with features in Microsoft's operating system.[34] To simplify comparisons, we normalized all prices to 1988 levels.[35] The results are shown in figure 7.5.

The results are striking. Although software prices in general have fallen over this period, prices for some software have fallen far more than prices for others. In particular, in those categories where Microsoft participates, directly or indirectly, prices have declined by approximately 60 percent, a far more dramatic drop than the 15 percent drop in markets completely devoid of Microsoft's influence. It is thus difficult not to accept the conclusion that Microsoft is responsible for the price declines. Additionally, we will discover in the next chapter additional evidence that Microsoft lowers prices in markets *after* it achieves large market shares. When we examine prices in individual markets, it will be useful to keep these overall results in mind as a benchmark.

FIGURE 7.5
Impact of Microsoft on Software Prices

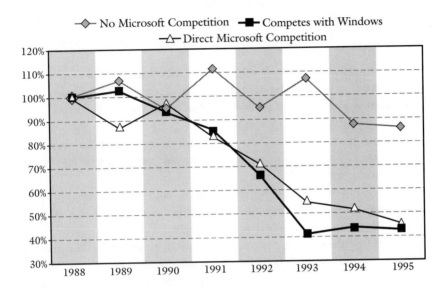

NOTES TO CHAPTER 7

1. We will use the term *monopoly* here to refer to any situation where a firm has a very large market share. This is to be distinguished from the case where a firm exerts monopoly power and harms consumers in some way, usually by raising price and lowering quantity. It is only this latter behavior that should be a focus of antitrust activity.

2. Book publishing still seems to have specialized components based on the fact that there are separate printing runs. Software also has some specialized components, such as packaging and product support, which can not be ramped up as quickly.

3. "Better" here means that the costs of switching are less than the benefits, on a social scale. Obviously, any rational consumer would switch anytime his personal benefits were greater than his costs.

4. Farrell and Saloner (1985) discuss cases of both excess inertia and excess momentum. Their excess momentum is socially inefficient and due to consumers' prematurely trying to jump to the next bandwagon.

5. The larger the network, the greater the demand by consumers. This implies a different demand curve for each level of network size. To solve this problem, we would have to create "reduced-form demand curves" that would be constructed by finding the point on each demand curve consistent with the size of the network used to construct the demand. The set of consistent points would be the reduced-form demand curve. See Liebowitz (1982) for a discussion of reduced-form demand curves.

6. It is important to note that this is not the type of compatibility normally associated with network effects, that is, compatibility with other users.

7. The Twin was so similar to Lotus 1-2-3 that it became the object of a look-and-feel lawsuit by Lotus, which ultimately led to the demise of the Twin.

8. Yet Excel was able to dethrone Lotus 1-2-3 even though its macros were not as compatible as several other competitors'.

9. We use the term *upgrade* to imply that the product has been modified but is largely the same as before in the sense that the users do not have to learn very much new to use the product. Some market upgrades are really shifts to new products that happen to use the same name, or are owned by the same company. The text provides a few examples of upgrades that do not fit our definition, such as the introduction of WordStar 2000 as an upgrade of WordStar, and AmiPro's successor, WordPro.

10. It was able to handle only the traditional DOS convention of 8.3, or eight letters followed by a three-letter extension after the period. There were add-on

products that attempted to increase the number of letters that could be used in a file name, but they didn't work very well.

11. Digital Research had produced CP/M, the leading operating system prior to DOS. According to legend, IBM was planning to use CP/M when it produced its first PC, but the behavior of the president of Digital Research was not to IBM's liking. They went looking for another operating system and wound up with Microsoft and DOS.

12. Apple, in 1987, sued both Microsoft (over Windows) and Hewlett-Packard (over New Wave, which made Windows more "Mac-like") with regard to the look and feel of their operating systems. Although HP dropped out, Microsoft successfully defended itself and won the case in 1993.

13. Interestingly, Digital Research is better known for producing a clone of DOS, DR DOS, which played an important role in the Department of Justice consent decree with Microsoft, in which it was claimed that Microsoft's pricing policies kept OEM's from installing DR DOS as opposed to Microsoft DOS.

14. Microsoft included a mouse with early copies of Windows.

15. Quote from advertisement in *PC Magazine*, October 16, 1990.

16. Windows 3.1 was introduced in April 1992 and improved 3.0 in some significant ways.

17. We realize, of course, that DOS still existed under Windows, but to the end user running Windows program, it was hidden.

18. IDC (International Data Corporation) refers to itself as "the world's leading provider of information technology data, industry analysis and strategic and tactical guidance to builders, providers and users of information technology." It can be found at http://www.idc.com. Much of our analysis in chapters 8 and 9 are based on reports from IDC. The other major source of data for our analysis comes from Dataquest, a division of GartnerGroup. Dataquest refers to itself as "a provider of market intelligence on global IT markets for semiconductors, computer systems and peripherals, document-management systems, interactive information systems and networks, multimedia, business and technical software, telecommunications, and IT services" and can be found at: http://gartner5.gartnerweb.com/dq/static/dq.html. Both companies provide detailed data reports on various aspects of the software industry.

19. Mary Loffredo, IDC, "1992 Word Processing Market: DOS, Windows, OS/2, and Macintosh," p. 13.

20. Lotus did not get a suite out the door until 1992, and WordPerfect (Borland) did not have a suite until 1993.

21. Mary Loffredo, IDC, "The Word Processing Software Market Review and Forecast, 1994–1999," p. 15.

22. David Card, IDC, "PC Office Suite, Word Processor, and Spreadsheet Markets Review and Forecast, 1995–2000," p. 37.

23. One might argue that that reviews in computer magazines will tend to focus on technical issues more than general issues and would be biased in favor of technical sophistication. Although we can not evaluate this possibility with any accuracy, our examination of the criteria used by these magazines indicates that pedestrian concerns such as usability played a large role in these reviews.

24. *PC Magazine* gives these types of evaluations.

25. We are confident that this process does pick winners consistent with magazine reviewers because in every case we found the product that produced the highest score on our constructed index also was the editor's choice.

26. For example, in the June 1998 issue of *Personal Computing Magazine*, XyWrite received the highest rating (7.3) compared to WordPerfect (7.2), WordStar (6.9) and Word (6.7). Because XyWrite was not included in many reviews after the mid-1980s, did not win many other reviews, and had a small market share, we removed it from figure 8.4 to reduce clutter. The highest score on the chart is then 9.86, WordPerfect's score normalized to XyWrite's leading score.

27 IDC, "PC Spreadsheet Market Review and Forecast, 1996–2001," p. 10.

28. For discussion of Dataquest and IDC, see note 14.

29. Sometimes we found identical numbers in two rows that were supposed to represent different vendors (Dataquest). Sometimes we would find other inconsistencies, such as identical values for sales including and excluding OEMs when it was clear that there were positive sales to OEMs (IDC). In some years we were able to compare estimates from both companies for the same data, and although usually not too far apart, in some instances they were different enough to raise concern.

30. In other words, Dataquest data for a market such as personal finance would include Intuit's Quicken. For several years, however, the category also included income tax software, so that Intuit's TurboTax was also included after Intuit merged with ChipSoft. This would make it impossible to correctly determine Quicken's market share using Dataquest data.

31. This may have led to our belief that the IDC data seemed slightly less prone to error, although we can not quantify the difference. We used IDC data when possible.

32. In the charts later in the book, spreadsheet data will only be provided beginning in 1988 because that was the earliest data we were able to find. Table 12 in IDC's 1995 spreadsheet report, however, presented data on average prices for 1986 through 1994. We thus used the prices from this table for the 1986 and 1987

values. For other years, we used our calculated values based on other reports, which were in close agreement with the numbers in table 12.

33. The categories are desktop publishing, accounting, draw and paint, forms, utilities/application, communication, personal finance, presentation graphics, spreadsheets, word processors, database, project management, integrated software. We proxied for separate desktop publishing categories by putting Microsoft into midrange and everyone else into high-end.

34. The categories where Microsoft competes are midrange desktop publishing, personal finance, presentation graphics, spreadsheets, word processors, database, project management, and integrated software. The categories where Microsoft does not have an entrant are accounting, draw and paint, high-end desktop publishing, and forms. The categories that compete with the operating system are utilities/application and communication.

35. Average prices are calculated as weighted averages, weighted by the revenues in each market. Unweighted average prices were also calculated and found to be almost identical.

8

Major Markets—
Spreadsheets and Word Processors

The Market for Spreadsheets

Today's computer programmers take it for granted that the brass ring of programming is the "killer-app," the next application that will take the market by storm. There have been a number of killer-apps in the history of the software industry—they've come and they've gone—but none has had more staying power than the oldest killer-app of them all: the spreadsheet. Spreadsheets are still one of the mainstays of computer applications.

Spreadsheets allow the manipulation of numbers and formulas, and their conversion to charts. A feature of spreadsheets that might tend to lock in consumers is their use of macros—programs within the spreadsheet that allow the spreadsheet to perform certain repetitive tasks. Many of these macros prompt the user to enter specific data, allowing even less skilled data-entry personnel to update, maintain, and make sophisticated use of data. For this reason many users, particularly business users, are loath to switch to a spreadsheet that disables their old macros. This dependence on macros makes spreadsheets, more than most other programs, very susceptible to path dependence. Of course, the cost of converting macros is a real cost that ought to weigh in any consideration of whether a switch is efficient.[1]

The Evolution of the PC Spreadsheet Market

Credit for the invention of the spreadsheet goes to Dan Bricklin and Bob Frankston, who created VisiCalc for the Apple II. VisiCalc required 32 kilobytes of memory to run. A chart from a "roundup" of spreadsheets in the 1982 *Personal Computing* magazine[2] lists eighteen spreadsheets. Most ran on either the Apple II or on machines with the CP/M operating system. VisiCalc ran on both, as well as the IBM PC, the Atari 800, the

Commodore 8032, the Radio Shack TRS-80, and various HP hand calculators. VisiCalc had a list price of $250. The most expensive spreadsheet in the roundup was M.B.A, from Context Management Systems, which combined database, graphics, word processing, and communications functions for $695.

In January 1983 Lotus introduced Lotus 1-2-3 at a price of $495. It was immediately acknowledged to be a better product than VisiCalc. In December 1982 Gregg Williams wrote in *Byte* that 1-2-3 had "many more functions and commands than VisiCalc" and that 1-2-3 was "revolutionary instead of evolutionary."[3] *PC World* called it "state of the art."

In October 1983 *PC World* reported that 1-2-3 was outselling Visi-Calc.[4] VisiCalc was removed from the market in 1985 after being purchased by Lotus. Users of VisiCalc were offered upgrades to 1-2-3.[5] Lotus would maintain a dominant market share for almost a decade. Unfortunately, we do not have detailed data on this early market. But from what we have pieced together, it is clear that in the early 1980s a superior product, Lotus 1-2-3, was able to wrest market share away from VisiCalc—and to do it very quickly.

By 1985 most spreadsheets were meant to work with the IBM PC. Lotus 1-2-3 was the market champ, with other contenders such as Computer Associates (Easy Planner, $195), Ashton-Tate (Framework, $695), Software Publishing (PFS Plan, $140), and IBM (PlannerCalc, $80, and Multiplan 1.0, $250). Microsoft had Excel for the Mac ($495) and Multiplan 2.0 ($195) for the PC. But many new spreadsheets were beginning to arrive on the scene. Some were clones of 1-2-3 at lower prices (VP Planner, The Twin, and VIP Professional). Others, such as Javelin and SuperCalc, offered improvements on 1-2-3. These alternatives elicited some praise, but the acclaim was not universal, and they did not make much of a splash in the market.

When Excel first appeared in 1985, it was offered only for the Macintosh. Jerry Pournelle, a well-known columnist for *Byte* and science-fiction author, wrote (incorrectly but nonetheless dramatically), "Excel will make the Mac into a serious business machine."[6] In late 1987 Microsoft ported Excel to the PC (running under Windows) and Borland introduced Quattro for DOS. Thus began a market struggle between Microsoft, Borland, and Lotus.

Reviews found Windows-based Excel to be the best product, with DOS-based Quattro in second place. 1-2-3's market share was unable to stand up to the assault of superior products. Excel steadily gained on 1-2-3, eventually overtaking it. It has been firmly in first place ever since.

Spreadsheet Quality

In the early and mid-1980s quality reviews rated 1-2-3's closest competitor to be SuperCalc. *PC Magazine,* in its "Best of 1986" review, had this to say: "If market dominance were based on rational criteria, Computer Associates' SuperCalc 4 would certainly replace 1-2-3 as the leading spreadsheet program. After all, it can do anything that 1-2-3 can do and adds some notable features of its own."[7]

But although various spreadsheets had attributes that were sometimes considered superior to 1-2-3's, there was no consensus that any alternative was clearly the best. For example, in October 1987 Michael Antonoff, in *Personal Computing,* wrote, "SuperCalc, VP-Planner, and Twin lack the elegance of 1-2-3 in links to applications."[8]

But the quality of the competition began to ratchet up in late 1987. In a portentous statement, *PC Magazine* remarked, "Microsoft Corp. has just unleashed a spreadsheet that makes 1-2-3 look like a rough draft."[9] This reference was to Excel 1.0 for the PC, a port of its Macintosh program.

By 1988 the spreadsheet market had developed into a three-way fight among Lotus's 1-2-3, Microsoft's Excel, and Borland's Quattro (Pro). Excel, created to run under a graphical operating system, was a late entry. It was ported from Macintosh only after an early version of Windows became available. Borland and Lotus, on the other hand, did not produce Windows versions of their programs until after Windows 3.0 had proven itself as a successful operating system.

According to reviewers, Lotus 1-2-3 was falling behind the competition in terms of functionality and usability. According to one reviewer, "Excel offers a lot in the form of tantalizing features missing from the current version of 1-2-3."[10] Another review called Quattro "a powerful spreadsheet with more features than 1-2-3 Release 2.01, yet fully compatible and at a better price."[11]

These were not isolated opinions. Reviewers in general had a very high opinion of Excel in the late 1980s, and almost as high an opinion of Quattro. In table 8.1 we give a list of review opinions for Excel. This list of reviews is not edited; it includes all the reviews in which the reviewer was willing to state an opinion. Clearly, Excel was thought to be the best spreadsheet.

TABLE 8.1
Excel Reviews

Magazine/Article
    Date   Comments

InfoWorld: John Walkenbach, "Microsoft's PC Spreadsheet Sets New Standard"
p. 41

    12/21/87   "Microsoft has a winner here." "One of the year's most innovative products, more powerful and more forward looking than any other spreadsheet on the market."

PC Magazine: Jared Taylor, "A New Face for Spreadsheets" p. 103

    12/22/87   "Feature for feature, Excel is far better than 1-2-3." p. 111 "Greater hardware demands only con."

InfoWorld: John Walkenbach, Software Review p. 55

    1/11/88   "The industry's most customizable spreadsheet." "Takes the industry standard and improves on it in the ways that matter most."

PC Magazine

    1/12/88   Award For Technical Excellence p.176

PC World: Ralph Soucie, "Excel: Should You Switch?" p. 108

    3/88   "Now a serious challenger—indeed, a better product has made its debut: Microsoft Excel." p 108 "If you're training new spreadsheet users, Excel is definitely the product of choice." p.115 for Release 2

Byte: Rich Malloy, "Excel Extraordinaire," p. 155

    3/88   New for IBM, "Rare product that combines ease of use and exceptional power." p. 157

PC Magazine: Craig Stinson, "First Looks." p. 33

    1/31/89   "For well over a year, spreadsheet users who needed to generate gorgeous printed reports from their worksheets have had one product to rely on: Microsoft Excel."

PC Magazine: Douglas Cobb and Stephen Cobb, "Spresadsheet Analysis." P. 139

    3/28/89   "Microsoft's Excel is the most powerful spreadsheet on the market today."

PC Magazine: Craig Stinson, "Spreadsheet Analysis," p. 185

    7/1/89   "About a year and a half ago, something happened. Microsoft introduced Excel, a revolutionary advance over SuperCalc, 1-2-3, and everything else in the field." "More spreadsheet than 1-2-3." "More solid product than QuattroPro."

TABLE 8.1
Excel Reviews (continued)

PC Magazine: Craig Stinson, "First Looks," p. 33.

   10/11/90   "New Macintosh spreadsheet, just introduced for Windows and OS/2 markets is the most graphical of all spreadsheets." "Least compatible of major spreadsheet programs." "Charting options unparalleled." "Comes up short in the services it provides for routine spreadsheet work." p. 35

Byte: Andrew Reinhardt, "New Extras for Excel," p. 136

   2/91   "Unassailability of vision." p. 138, Highly Recommend

---

The reviewers' main reservation about Excel was its need for powerful hardware, due to the memory requirements of its entirely graphical interface (see the December 1987 review in *PC Magazine*). Microsoft's election not to produce a DOS version of the program was something of a gamble. Windows' success was far from assured until version 3.0, which was not available until 1990. To run Excel, DOS users had to load Windows, and then return to DOS for other applications. This had a dampening effect on sales. Also, many of Excel's features worked best with a mouse, and at the time it was rare for PCs to be equipped with a mouse. Furthermore, as is the case with virtually all graphical software applications, Excel was slower at most tasks than the DOS competition, though it could show results that nongraphical (DOS) based applications could not. Some have guessed that reviewers preferred Excel only because they had modern and powerful equipment. In fact, though the reviews may have exhibited this bias to some degree, they nevertheless usually faulted Excel for its onerous hardware requirements.

The reviews for Quattro were not quite as enthusiastic as those for Excel, but were still quite positive:

TABLE 8.2
Quattro Reviews

| **Magazine/Article** | |
| **Date** | **Comments** |

Byte: Diana Gabaldon, "Double Threats to Lotus 1-2-3," p. 167

   6/88   "All of Lotus's main features and extras at a lower price." "Both have advantages over 1-2-3."

TABLE 8.2
Quattro Reviews (continued)

InfoWorld: John Walkenbach, "Spreadsheet Matches 1-2-3, Even Passes It in Some Areas," p. 50

8/22/88   "Multilevel Undo and Re-do, and background re-calculation (feature shared with Excel)."

Byte: Rich Malloy, p. 111

11/89   "Advantages of Excel with 1-2-3 compatibility." p. 112

PC Magazine: Craig Stinson, "First Looks," p. 33

12/26/89   "Noticeably slower times than competition." p. 35

PC Magazine

1/16/90   "This is the top dog spreadsheet." p. 98

Personal Computing: Joseph Devlin, p. 145

4/90   "Head and shoulders above Lotus" "requires add-ins to get Lotus to this level."

PC World: Richard Scoville, "Seven Sensible Spreadsheets," p. 116

4/90   Quattro Pro 1.0 BEST BUY "Determined to do 1-2-3 2.2 better in every critical area, and it achieves that goal in spades" p. 119

Byte: Andrew Reinhardt, p. 156

11/90   "Quattro Pro is probably your best answer." p. 157

These statements strongly imply that by the late 1980s 1-2-3 had fallen behind its major competition. This is confirmed in the opinions of magazine readers.

Figure 8.1 shows the rankings of spreadsheets by readers of *PC World*. They were asked to pick the leading spreadsheet. We expect that readers will base their ratings on their experiences, the market shares of the products, and some idea of quality as indicated in magazine articles. These rankings, therefore, are indicators of neither market share nor quality, but some combination of both.

The dominance of Lotus is clearly seen in the mid- to late 1980s, but in 1988, with the introduction of Excel and Quattro, Lotus's dominance began to erode. The introduction of Windows in 1990 accelerated this decline. By 1992 Excel had surpassed 1-2-3 and Quattro had reached parity. By the time *PC World's* reader rankings ended, in 1993, the die was cast: Lotus was doomed.

Lotus's fate is clear in figure 8.2, which gives each spreadsheet's number of annual wins (the number of times a product wins a comparison review or is declared to be the best product). Over the ten-year period shown Excel was the clear winner, although Quattro also managed a fair share of wins between 1989 and 1994. The remarkable feature of this chart, however, is that over the entire ten-year period, Lotus 1-2-3 just barely avoids a shutout, managing but a single win.[12]

Figure 8.3, which presents results from reviews that numerically score the three spreadsheets, shows the relative performance more precisely. Lotus's poor performance is easily seen, as is Excel's dominance after two initial poor showings. Note that the horizontal axis is scaled in chronological order and not by date. In other words, the distance on the axis between any two (or more) points has no meaning.[13]

One seeming inconsistency is the poor initial showing of Excel in 1988 and 1989, years when (as shown in table 8.1) Excel was garnering rave reviews. The reason for this inconsistency is buried in the two negative review of Excel that appeared in *Personal Computing*. The deciding factor in *Personal Computing*'s quality ratings was speed. Weight on this criterion was common at the time (in that background recalculation was not yet standard and the operator had to wait at the keyboard for the spreadsheet to finish calculating before entering more data). Excel, of course, was exclusively a GUI-based application. And as we noted above in our discus-

FIGURE 8.1
PC World Reader Ratings of Spreadsheets

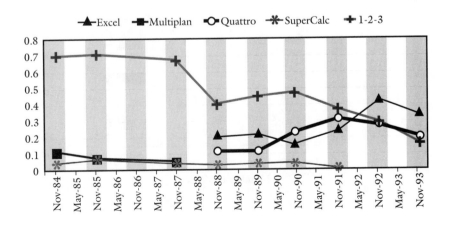

FIGURE 8.2
Spreadsheet Wins

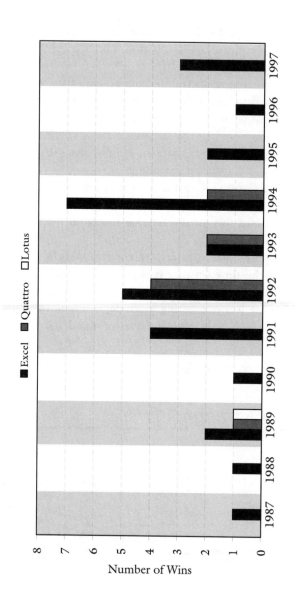

FIGURE 8.3
Comparison Spreadsheet Ratings

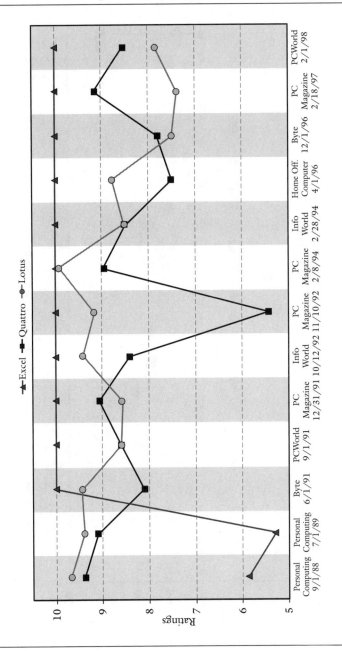

FIGURE 8.4
Spreadsheet List Prices

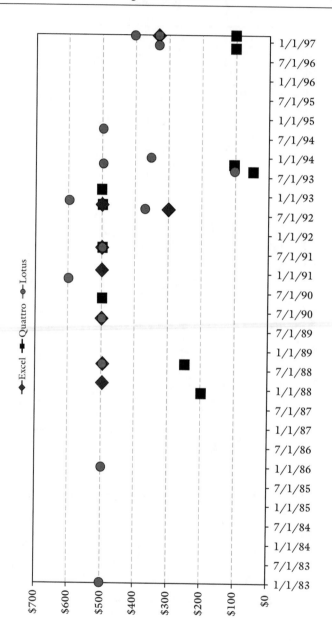

sion of the Macintosh versus the PC, graphical products are much slower than text-based products. Listen to the authors of the review (from the September 1988 issue):

> Our weighted average tended to punish Microsoft Excel for its lethargic performance; it rated only 1.3 on Overall Performance. [The others averaged about 7.] Don't forget to look at the Overall Practicality rating, where it ranked first by more than half a point at 6.6. Where features are concerned, no other spreadsheet available today can beat Excel.

> There has to be a catch—and there is. Unlike the other five spreadsheets reviewed and benchmarked here, Excel is graphics based instead of character based (it runs under Microsoft Windows). That means a lot more bits and bytes have to be processed. In five of our seven tests, Excel came in last by a wide margin.

The message is clear: Excel was clearly the leading spreadsheet in terms of capabilities. It should have been easy to predict the outcome: Once the hardware had caught up to the software (and Windows itself improved) there would be no serious challengers to Excel as long as Excel continued to outperform its competition.

The Role of Price

This brings us to another consideration: price. If there are important differences in the prices of competing products, a lower-quality and lower-priced product might have a larger market share than a higher-quality, higher-priced product. Ford sells more Tauruses and generates higher revenues than Mercedes-Benz does with its mid-sized sedan, though Mercedes would normally be considered to be of substantially higher quality.

The magazine review articles, which generally report list prices, give an account of how list prices for spreadsheets varied across time and package, but this information does not explain much about how the spreadsheet market evolved. For one thing, in any one year, the list prices for competing products don't differ by very much. As figure 8.4 shows, Lotus normally charged in the vicinity of $500 for 1-2-3, and that was about what Microsoft charged for Excel. Although Borland initially (1988, 1989) charged considerably less for its early version of Quattro, its more advanced product, Quattro Pro (introduced in 1990) was listed at just about the same price as the other two products. But the magazine review articles contain list price. And as we shall see shortly, an examination of actual prices tells quite a different story.

There are many reasons that list prices don't tell much about the market. First, list prices do not include upgrade purchases, which are less expensive than first-time purchases. Second, list prices fail to account for units sold in office suites. Third, list prices fail to account for the units sold to OEMs, which carry a far lower price.

If, then, we want to look at prices, it is far more informative to look at average prices received by the manufacturer (figure 8.5). The history of average prices clearly shows Borland's price-discount strategy, which was far less apparent looking at retail prices. It shows that Lotus kept its prices similar to Excel's even in the face of the latter's increasing market share and superior reviews. Lotus began to undercut Microsoft's price significantly only in 1996, well after it had fallen below Excel in market share.

The big story in figure 8.5, however, is the stunning decline in prices over time. By 1997 the typical price (received by the vendor) for a spreadsheet had fallen to approximately $50, a fall of over 80 percent from the typical price in 1988.

FIGURE 8.5
Prices Received by Vendor, Spreadsheets

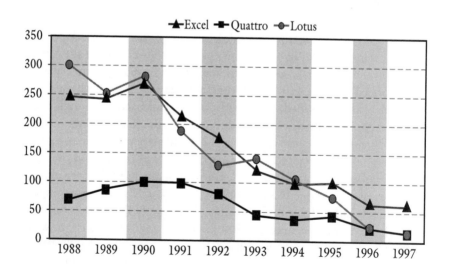

Changes in Market Share: Analysis

The history of price and quality in the spreadsheet market indicates that Lotus 1-2-3 should have lost market share and market dominance. Prices were roughly equivalent for all major competitors, but Lotus 1-2-3 lost its ranking as the top-ranked product. The winner should have been Excel. Is this what happened? Absolutely.

Figure 8.6 shows market share in the spreadsheet market based on units sold over time. It shows 1-2-3 to be decisively losing its dominant position to Excel. The evidence is even more powerful if one examines market shares based on revenues (figure 8.7).

These results support the view that markets choose better products, but it is also true that Excel's edge in quality was reinforced by several additional factors. Not only was Excel the best Windows spreadsheet, but it was also the first Windows spreadsheet. It was part of the first office suite, and it was also part of the best office suite. These reinforcing factors were strategic gambles by Microsoft. They paid off handsomely, but that doesn't mean that Microsoft was "leveraging." It means that Microsoft was smart.

FIGURE 8.6
Market Share of Spreadsheets (units)

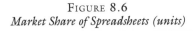

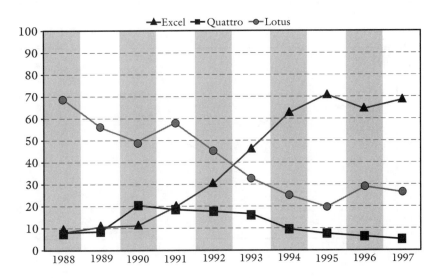

Furthermore, these results do not provide any empirical confirmation for the idea that the spreadsheet market was "tipping," a concept that has been adopted rather uncritically by many economic commentators. If network effects (or increasing returns) are important drivers in a market, then when one firm achieves a sufficiently large market share, consumers ought to flock to that firm to take advantage of network effects. We saw a theoretical illustration of this in chapter 3 in our model of multiple equilibria. In that model, any movement away from the unstable equilibrium leads to a single victorious firm. Within the limited contest of those models, when a market moves away from that equilibrium point, network effects become self-reinforcing, accelerating changes in market shares.

In a tipping market, when a product has a small market share, network effects should work against an increase in market share. But if market share does pass some break-out point, network effects should work to accelerate further market share increases.[14] This implies that we ought to see a pronounced upturn, where plots of market share against time (as in figures 8.6 and 8.7) are flatter to the left of the break-out point, and steeper to the right. Similarly, there ought to be a pronounced downturn for a product with a market share that is declining.

FIGURE 8.7
Market Share of Spreadsheets (revenues)

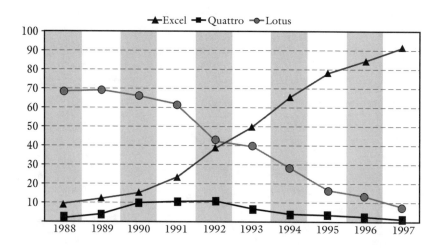

This, of course, is not at all what we find in the spreadsheet market. Instead, what we find is a fairly steady increase in Excel's market share and a fairly steady decrease in 1-2-3's. This may mean that network effects are just not a very important factor in this market, or that their impact on market share is more complex than indicated in the concept of tipping.

There are some other issues worthy of examination. In a world of instant scalability, why did it take five years, and not one or two, for Lotus to be dethroned? We can suggest a possible answer. Users know that software products often leapfrog each other in capabilities. The costs of switching are high, and it does not normally make sense for a consumer to switch products every time one product exceeds the capabilities of another. Instead, a rational consumer will bide his time, confident that the next upgrade of a product that has fallen behind, but that has a history of technological innovation, will contain the features missing from the current version—and perhaps even add a few extra features. It appears to have taken two failed generations of Lotus 1-2-3 before the market was convinced that 1-2-3 was not going to catch up to Excel any time soon.

A second question is why Quattro never surpassed 1-2-3. Most reviews rated Quattro as superior to 1-2-3, though inferior to Excel. There are two reasons, however, why Quattro might not have surpassed an inferior 1-2-3. First, if a 1-2-3 user were planning to switch, it would make more sense to switch to the number 1 product than to the number 2 product. Quattro's only advantage over Excel was its lower price, and this didn't last. Second, because of instant scalability, Microsoft could meet the demand of all defecting Lotus users without having to raise its price. In markets without instant scalability, the number two firm likely would pick up some of the slack due to constraints on production for the leading firm.

Furthermore, between 1988 and 1995, when Quattro earned better reviews than Lotus, the gap between Lotus and Quattro did diminish—from a ratio of about 7:1 in units to a ratio of 2:1. Eventually, however, Quattro came out with a product that didn't beat 1-2-3 in the reviews. Quattro for Windows never established a clear quality superiority over 1-2-3—and sometimes was rated worse. After that, not surprisingly, Quattro failed to make any further gains. And, of course, both products were losing market share to Microsoft's Excel.

One wonders whether the Lotus hegemony over spreadsheets would have ended without the advent of Windows and office suites. Certainly some GUI was going to replace DOS, and spreadsheets were going to have to take advantage of it. If Lotus couldn't produce a high-quality graphical spreadsheet, it was destined to lose the market to someone.

Microsoft would have been a strong candidate to dethrone Lotus in any graphical environment because of its experience in the Macintosh market. If the market had gone to Macintosh, where Excel was clearly the dominant product (as we demonstrate below), Lotus almost certainly would have lost. If OS/2 had predominated, there is every reason to believe that the OS/2 version of Excel would have replaced 1-2-3. And even if some third-party graphical operating system had prevailed on Intel-based machines, there is every reason to suspect that Microsoft would have produced a better product than Lotus because of its familiarity with graphical products for the Mac.

Why Did Lotus Fail?

Lotus 1-2-3 failed because competing products were judged to be superior in quality. This is not surprising. One might wonder, however, why Lotus was unable to keep up. Why didn't it manage to produce a quality product that would have allowed it to retain its market leadership?

The internal reasons that Lotus was unable to produce a product that was as good as its competitors' are beyond the strategic analyses of this book. But it's clear that Lotus made some management blunders in positioning itself in the market as a whole.

One tremendous oversight was Lotus' general disregard of the Macintosh market. Although the revenues from this market might have seemed relatively inconsequential, the experience in producing graphical spreadsheets in what was clearly the leading GUI of its time is something that Lotus should have valued.

Second, Lotus bogged itself down producing too many spreadsheet variations. Concerned that it would cede some market share in the 286 market (slower processors and smaller memory), Lotus continued to work on 2.x (text-based DOS) versions of 1-2-3, even though it was producing a quasi-graphical version (3.x) that also ran under DOS. The 3.x version of 1-2-3 was late to the market because the software engineers decided to translate it into the C language (to make it portable to other systems), which required considerable tweaking to keep it small enough to fit in the typical PC's memory.[15] Meanwhile, Lotus was slow to create a version of 1-2-3 for Windows.

Microsoft, of course, also produced multiple product lines, but it seemed better able to handle multiple versions of its products.[16]

In 1990 Lotus came out with Improv, a truly innovative spreadsheet that introduced what has come to be known as the pivot table. But Lotus squandered its innovative edge. There were two problems with Improv. First, it was introduced for the NeXT computer, a technologically overly sophisticated (for ordinary users), impractical (the hard drive was replaced by a rewriteable CD-ROM), and expensive machine that failed to survive in the market. Second, Improv was a completely separate product, not a version of 1-2-3, and for all of Improv's sophistication, it lacked some basic spreadsheet functions. If Lotus had chosen to include some of Improv's features in 1-2-3, Lotus would undoubtedly have had something of a coup. But by the time Lotus managed to incorporate Improv's innovations into 1-2-3, the competition had already caught up.

Improv's failure should have been predictable. After all, even if Lotus couldn't have been expected to know the extent to which the NeXT would flop, it should have noticed NeXT's price, which was thousands more than competing computers, would keep it from mass market appeal any time soon. If Lotus wanted to try a new market, it should have tried the Macintosh market, which did not yet have an entry from Lotus, and which would have to wait two additional years for one.

Lotus also placed a wrong bet on OS/2, creating a spreadsheet for that failed operating system.[17] More seriously, the product that Lotus created for OS/2, and then also for Windows, was merely a translation of its 3.x product for DOS (using the "portable" C code). DOS products were not similar to products designed for GUIs, and Lotus should have known that a straight port of a DOS product would not turn heads in the GUI world. And even this product was delayed.

Lotus might have been able to survive several of these mishaps if it had done one or two things right. But it seemed to choose wrong at every turn. By 1993 some reviewers were already penning obituaries:

> Unfortunately, it looks as if Lotus is internally hog-tied by an infrastructure of 1-2-3 diehards the same way Apple was nearly strangled by Apple II loyalists. . . . The company's tombstone will read "1-2-3 and out!"

Lotus was the king of spreadsheets, and was rightly the leader, as it dominated the entire market. Disregarding Improv, nobody would call Lotus a leader in the field it pioneered anymore. People would cite Excel or Quattro Pro as the leading spreadsheet program.

The long-term winner in this battle is Microsoft, which can unload Windows plus Excel for such a low site-license price that few companies can resist. [18]

Word Processors

In 1986 WordPerfect and WordStar were the two leading word processors, with moderately larger market shares than several other programs (DisplayWrite, Word, MultiMate, Samna Word). In the next few years, however, WordPerfect broke away from the pack, and by 1990 it clearly dominated the market. This history is tracked in figure 8.8, which portrays market shares of the leading word processors.

In the late 1980s Microsoft shifted its attention away from its DOS version of Word, which was then number two in the market, and began to focus on the Windows version. Microsoft Word for Windows hit the market in late 1989, and began to generate a serious market share in 1990.[19] By the time Windows became the dominant operating system, the two leading Windows word processors were Ami Professional and Microsoft Word.

After the introduction of Windows 3.0, Microsoft Word grew at an extraordinary rate. By 1994 it dominated the market more completely than WordPerfect had, even during its peak years. WordPerfect for Windows, which was introduced in late 1991, a year after its OS/2 product was introduced and almost two years after Windows 3.0 was introduced, jumped initially to a 20 percent market share, but then its market share stabilized and began to decline. AmiPro showed some good growth (in terms of units) but never achieved much of a market share in terms of revenues.

Word Processor Quality

WordStar, the original leader in the word processor market, lost its market position by failing to keep its quality at the level of its competition. The story was different with WordPerfect. Unlike WordStar, WordPerfect was always judged to be a high-quality product in its DOS incarnation. Where

FIGURE 8.8
Word Processor Market Share (revenues)

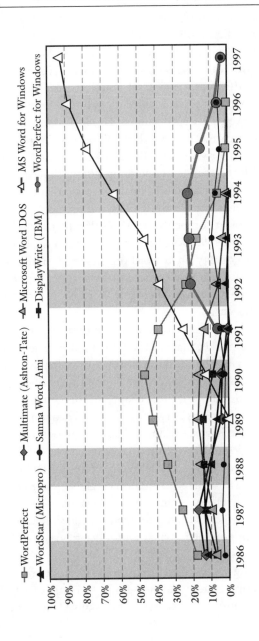

WordPerfect fell behind was in developing a high-quality product for Windows, and in incorporating its product into a high-quality office suite.

The dominance of DOS WordPerfect is clear in the reader ratings of *PC World Magazine* (figure 8.9).[20] And the story in the reader ratings accurately reflects the history of market share. In 1984 WordStar was the leading product in the reader ratings, followed by Microsoft Word (DOS) and MultiMate. WordPerfect was not yet a market leader. By 1987, however, WordPerfect was in first place. Its ascent continued until late 1991. During the 1990s, however, we see a decline in DOS word processors and a rise in Windows word processors—Word for Windows, WordPerfect for Windows, and AmiPro for Windows. In the Windows market, Word won out.

In short, with the change in operating system came a change in leadership. And once again, measures of quality explain that change. Figure 8.10 shows the number of wins in the DOS word processor market for various products. The closest competitor to DOS WordPerfect is Microsoft Word for DOS, but after 1989, WordPerfect is just about the only game in town when it comes to quality DOS word processors. A similar story is told by ratings of different DOS word processors over time (figure 8.11). The advantage of WordPerfect over Microsoft Word is, however, somewhat less discernible in this chart.

Thus, the preponderance of evidence indicates that WordPerfect deserved its leading market share in the DOS market. The scale of WordPerfect's domination may be a little surprising, given that Microsoft Word ran such a close second, but the poor showing of the number two product is a common thread throughout these chapters. This could be the result of instant scalability, or perhaps network effects and economies of scale.

WordPerfect did have an additional advantage (left out of our analysis) of offering near-legendary technical support,[21] but in this, after all, the company didn't have much choice. WordPerfect for DOS was notoriously difficult to learn, as anyone who remembers the keyboard templates for the product can attest. The program was run by using arcane combinations of the twelve function keys with the control, alt, and shift keys. Technical support was more important for such a product than for the more intuitive Windows products.

As an operating system, DOS had about run its course, but the change to a new operating system was not going to come easily. Programming for Windows required a whole new set of skills. This is evidenced by the

FIGURE **8.9**
Reader Ratings of Word Processors

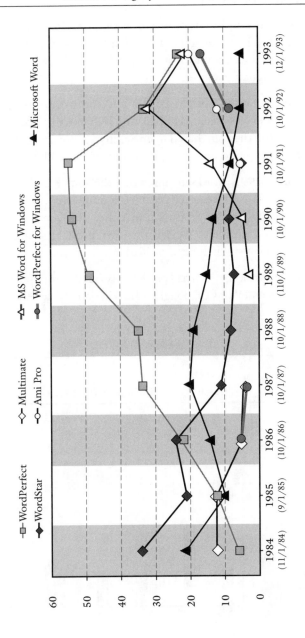

number of producers of DOS word processors that tried to buy Windows products instead of developing their own:

- IBM owned DisplayWrite, which at one time had captured 10–15 percent of the DOS market (as seen in figure 8.1). Yet in June 1990 IBM licensed technology from Xyquest for a GUI word processor, to be called Signature.

- Software Publishing produced the low-end word processors Office Writer and Professional Write, putting it in fourth place in 1989. But in early 1990 they purchased from Samna a subset of Ami on which to build its own word processor, Professional Write Plus.

- In January 1991 WordStar purchased the source code and distribution rights to NBI's Legacy product, a frames-based Windows word processor. It sold the product under the title WordStar Legacy and planned to continue to work on its own product, using the Legacy Engine, which still belonged to NBI.

- Lotus Corporation, which had produced two DOS word processors called Manuscript and Word IV, bought Samna in order to get Ami (Pro).

FIGURE 8.10
Word Processor Wins, DOS

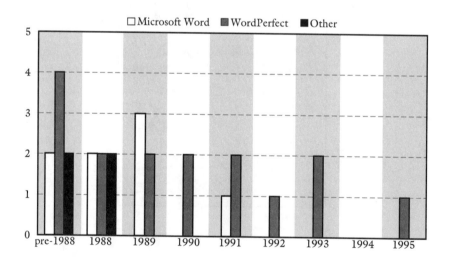

FIGURE 8.11
Word Processor Ratings, DOS

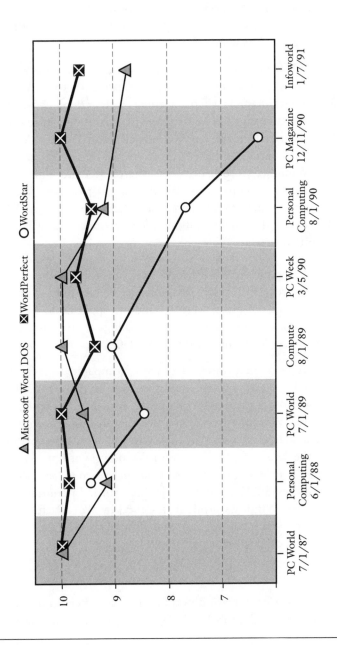

- Ashton-Tate, whose MultiMate was number two in revenues in 1987, was acquired in June 1991 by Borland. Although Ashton-Tate had been working on a Windows word processor, it never was able to get it close to market. Borland valued Ashton-Tate for its other products, and ignored its word processor.

Microsoft Word ultimately came to dominate the Windows world for pretty much the same reasons that Excel succeeded: Microsoft Word was a superior product at a time when consumers were rethinking their adoptions, and Microsoft engaged in better strategic marketing (office suites).

The quality advantage enjoyed by Microsoft Word is documented in the magazine ratings. Figure 8.12 shows the relative ratings of the three leading Windows word processors. Microsoft Word almost always won these magazine comparisons. Word's closest rival was AmiPro, which started with a much smaller market share and installed base. WordPerfect was late out of the gate with its Windows product, and when it arrived it was poorly reviewed:

> The "too much WordPerfect" criticism won't bother the DOS word processor's many fans, but believe me, folks, it keeps the program from being a great Windows application. The menus are bizarrely organized. . . . These things are the price the program pays for being faithful to the DOS version.

> Moreover, the program's rawness compared to Ami Professional 2.0 and a forthcoming version of Word for Windows points out a greater shortcoming. Ami Pro 2.0 is the fourth or fifth Windows word processor that its design team has created. While the new Word for Windows (expected by the end of the year) is only the second Windows word processor created by its team, the company has also learned from the highly successful Macintosh version of Word. In contrast, this is the first Windows product designed by WordPerfect Corporation, which has not scored well with its GUI word processors on other platforms.[22]

And:

> [WordPerfect for Windows] first release suffers from bugs and UAEs that will probably disappear from an interim release early

FIGURE 8.12
Word Processor Ratings, Windows

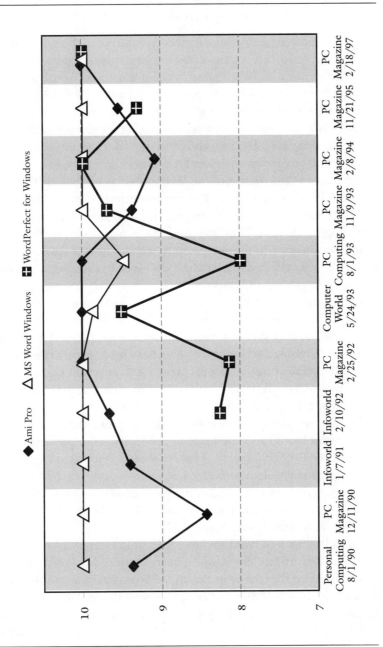

> in 1992. . . . WordPerfect for Windows doesn't feel fully at
> home in its GUI environment. . . . Its limitations derive from
> the DOS version and won't bother users of the DOS version.[23]

The large installed base of WordPerfect customers had their allegiance test-ed, first, by WordPerfect's late entry into this market, and second, by the poor performance of WordPerfect when it did enter. WordPerfect didn't produce a reasonable Windows product until the end of 1993. This delay set the stage for WordPerfect's fall.

If the Windows versions of word-processing programs had shared char-acteristics with earlier DOS versions from the same vendor—or at least had greater ability to import the older DOS files—this backward compatibility might have enticed owners of the DOS products to upgrade to the same vendors' Windows products. But the producers of many leading DOS word processors were not able to produce their own Windows products; they simply purchased Windows products from outside providers and at-tached their names. In the process, they sacrificed backward compatibility, which certainly affected the purchase decisions of their former customers who were upgrading to Windows.

Sacrificing sales to former customers was not always a bad idea. Consid-er, for example, the history of AmiPro. The installed base of SamnaWord customers was very small—a clear hindrance to its success if it were to re-main tied to its installed base.[24] It would have made sense to the owners of Ami to design the best product they could and ignore the consequences to their installed base. As it was, AmiPro (for Windows) achieved a far greater market share than its previous DOS incarnations.

Of the producers of Windows word processors, only the creators of AmiPro and Word had experience in producing word processors that fit well into GUI environments. Thus, it should come as no surprise that these two products dominated the magazine reviews.

Figure 8.13, which illustrates the number of wins for Windows word processors, is almost completely dominated by Word for Windows and Ami Pro, as was the case in figure 8.12.[25]

The advantages of Word are less apparent in figure 8.13 than in figure 8.12, however. In fact, the relative quality between MS Word and AmiPro is very similar to the relative quality of MS Word for DOS and WordPerfect for DOS in the late 1980s. But even if we were to conclude that Word and AmiPro were exactly equal in quality, which is inconsistent with the results in figure 8.12, there are several reasons why Word would be expected to do better in the marketplace than AmiPro. First, as already noted, Microsoft Word for DOS had a much larger installed base. Second, AmiPro went through several owners (Samna, Lotus, and IBM) in a fairly short period of time. Third, Microsoft had its office suite on the market first, at a lower price and, as we have seen, Excel was a more powerful companion spreadsheet than 1-2-3.

Word Processor Prices

As in the spreadsheet market, price differences among the major programs did not play a very important role in the evolution of the word processor market. Price was used strategically, but competitors ordinarily matched each other's prices.

Figure 8.14 shows prices (received by vendors) for the major word processors.[26] As in the spreadsheet market, the most important trend is the decline in prices that began when Windows 3.0 was introduced in 1990. The resulting competitive jockeying led to price wars. It is important to note, however, that there is no evidence of price declines until Microsoft Word began its assault on WordPerfect's position.

FIGURE 8.13
Word Processor Wins, Windows

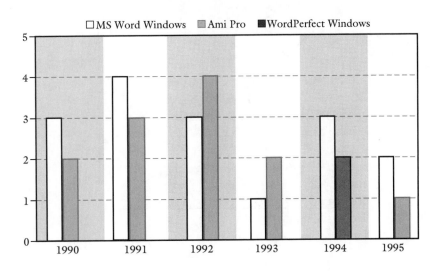

FIGURE 8.14
Word Processor Prices

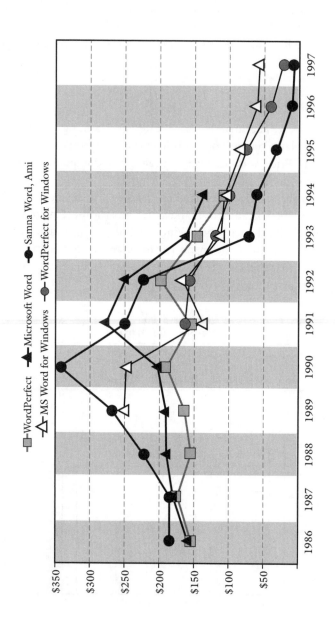

In 1990, 1991, and 1992, AmiPro was more expensive than Word for Windows. These were important transition years, yet Lotus provided no economic incentive for users to pick AmiPro over Microsoft Word. Both were ranked higher than WordPerfect, but Word had a slight edge in quality, a larger installed base, a lower price, and was part of a superior office suite. AmiPro did not lower its prices until Lotus was purchased by IBM. By the time AmiPro became price competitive (1993), Microsoft had 40 percent of the market and the reviews were about to start concluding that AmiPro was no longer competitive with Microsoft Word.

As for WordPerfect, the price for its late and inferior Windows product was virtually identical to that of Microsoft Word through 1995. After that, it was priced below Word, but the price cut was a case of too little, too late.

Analysis

The transition from DOS to Windows presented a golden opportunity for ratcheting up market share in the word processor market, and Microsoft was positioned perfectly to take advantage of this opportunity. Microsoft offered a Windows-based word processor that was clearly better than the incumbent market leader and as good as or better than any other challengers. Microsoft Word for Windows was a much better product than WordPerfect for Windows, and it was available much sooner. AmiPro was close in quality to Word, but Microsoft had a larger installed base and a superior and more stable market plan. Furthermore, Microsoft had a top-flight spreadsheet, Excel, which it was able to bundle with Word into a very attractive office suite. This combination of factors proved irresistible.

In each market, the highest-ranked product racked up the largest market share. Whether the shift from WordPerfect to Microsoft Word was "too" slow, "too" fast, or just right, we don't know. Certainly the market-share changes in the word processor market—first WordPerfect's growth, and then its replacement by Microsoft Word, all within a decade—are more rapid than we find in many markets. But the history of the word processor market certainly doesn't provide any support for the claim that a market will standardize on an inferior product, or that consumers lock in to products.

Another important feature of this market is the smoothness of the changes in market share. There are no sudden accelerations or decelerations that might be consistent with tipping. After WordPerfect had grown to almost 50 percent of the market, a position that might have been thought consistent with the market having tipped in its favor, it actually began to *lose* market share in favor of a product with a much smaller market share. Once again, the empirical evidence fails to support the theoretical construct of tipping.

Macintosh Spreadsheets and Word Processors

We have decided to group the spreadsheet and word processor analysis for the Macintosh market into one section because of certain similarities and comparisons to one another that we wish to make.

In both markets, the Microsoft product was the market leader as well as the highest-quality product.

In the spreadsheet market, Microsoft Excel was clearly the leading spreadsheet in terms of quality. As figure 8.15 indicates, Excel won every numerical review that we found. For all reviews that rated products, Excel won in ten of twelve instances. In *MacUser Magazine*'s ratings of spread-sheets, Microsoft Excel scored an average of 4.79, Lotus 1-2-3 averaged 4.2, Resolve scored 4.5, and Full Impact scored 3.33 (out of 5 points).[27] The small number of reviews might be a cause for some concern, but this small number may be due in part to the fact that this market settled early on a single product—Microsoft Excel.

The degree to which sales of Excel have dominated the Macintosh spreadsheet market is quite remarkable. In fact, it would be fair to say that it is rare to find a market where one product is as dominant as Excel has been in the Macintosh spreadsheet market since 1988. Figure 8.16 displays the market shares of Excel and several other spreadsheets. One has to look hard even to see the market shares of Excel's "major" competitors on this diagram.[28]

A similar story can be told for the word processor market. Microsoft Word was the leading word processor for the Mac from the time of our earliest data (1988). Alternative products included MacWrite, WordPerfect, WriteNow, Full Write, and Nisus Writer. Figure 8.17 shows trends in the market shares of the leading products.[29]

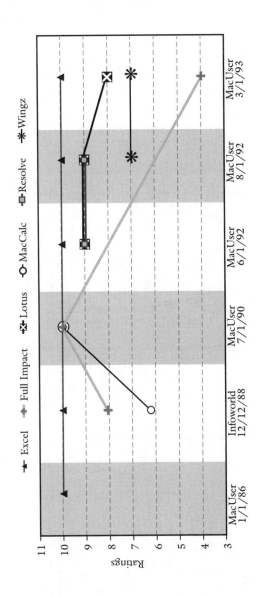

FIGURE 8.15
Macintosh Spreadsheet Ratings

Although the number of available reviews is small, Word won 59 percent of them (ten of seventeen).[30] In *MacUser Magazine*'s ratings of word processors over several years, Microsoft Word scored an average of 4.21, MacWrite scored 4.0, WordPerfect scored 3.7, and Nisus Writer scored 3.88 (out of 5 points).[31] Word was clearly the highest-rated word processor in the Macintosh market.

We can conclude, therefore, that Microsoft's two entries in this market, Word and Excel, were the best of breed.

FIGURE 8.16
Macintosh Spreadsheet Market Shares

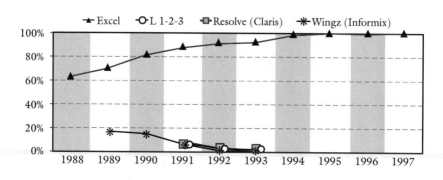

FIGURE 8.17
Macintosh Word Processor Market Shares

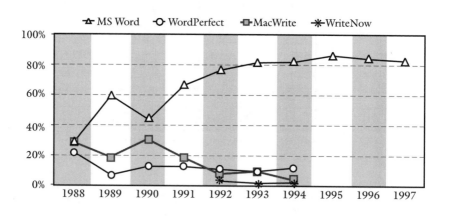

Comparing PC and Macintosh Markets

Some particularly revealing evidence has to do with a comparison of Excel and Word in the PC and Macintosh markets. First, note that Microsoft achieved dominance in the Macintosh market considerably earlier than in the PC market. This is clearly seen in figure 8.18.

Examination of figure 8.18 reveals that Microsoft achieved very high market shares in the Macintosh market even while it was still struggling in the PC market. On average, Microsoft's market share was about 40 to 60 percentage points higher in the Macintosh market than in the PC market in the 1988–90 period.[32] It wasn't until 1996 that Microsoft was able to equal in the PC market its success in the Macintosh market. These facts can be used to discredit a claim sometime heard that Microsoft achieved success in applications only because it owned the operating system. Apple, not Microsoft, owned the Macintosh operating system and Microsoft actually competed with Apple in the Macintosh markets.

Our main interest here, however, is in comparing the Macintosh price to the PC price for the same product sold in the two markets, one market

FIGURE 8.18
Market Shares for Excel and Word in Macintosh and PC Markets

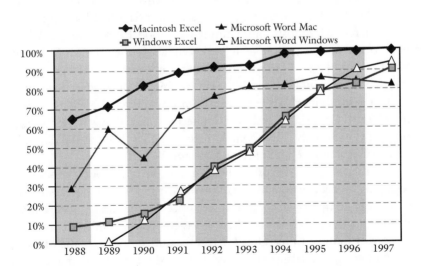

where the seller has a dominant market share and another market where the seller's market share is relatively small. This will allow us to test the structuralist theory of monopoly and whether Microsoft acted like a monopoly.

Economists have historically been of two views with regard to the relationship between market share and monopoly behavior. Market structuralists, following in the footsteps of Joe Bain, argue that high market share almost always leads to monopoly behavior. Critics of this theory, collectively known as the Chicago School, disagree. They argue that even if one firm dominates a market, in the absence of barriers to entry, potential competition will cause the market to behave competitively.[33]

The behavior of Microsoft in these markets supports the Chicago School view and also supports Microsoft's contention that it has neither harmed consumers nor acted like a monopolist.

Excel's Macintosh market share of 70 percent in 1989 would indicate monopoly to a structuralist. In the PC market, on the other hand, Excel was just getting off the ground. In 1990, when Microsoft Word for Windows was first being launched, Microsoft Word for the Macintosh had a market share of almost 60 percent. Again, Word's Macintosh market share would appear monopolistic to a structuralist.

Those holding a structural view of monopoly would expect Microsoft to charge a monopoly price in the Macintosh market and a competitive price in the PC market.

Price comparisons suggest the opposite of what a structuralist would expect.[34] PC-Excel, far from being cheaper, in fact averaged 13 percent higher prices than its Macintosh cousin during the period 1988–1992. PC Word's price, on average, was more than 80 percent above the price for Macintosh Word prior to 1993. Both pairs of prices became virtually the same later in the decade. To double-check this result we went to price advertisements in computer magazines. We used data from a single retailer selling to both markets (PC Connection and Mac Connection) and compared prices. Excel on the PC was consistently about 33 percent higher than for the Macintosh version.[35] A similar result holds for Microsoft Word.

In other words, Microsoft did not act like a textbook monopolist (charging higher prices) in the market where it appeared to have a structural monopoly. In fact, it charged lower prices in the market where it was dominant than in the market where it was competing. Furthermore, as we saw earlier in the chapter, after Microsoft came to dominate the PC word processing and spreadsheet markets, it lowered prices again—dramatically.

What might be going on then?

One answer is potential competition—that is, Microsoft worries about competitors even when it has a very large market share. Potential competition is capable of causing a monopolist to behave like a competitive firm. In an industry where entrenched incumbents such as Lotus and WordPerfect were eclipsed in relatively rapid fashion, this might seem to be a very real concern. Microsoft's concern about losing its markets might also explain why Microsoft has not lost any markets it has gained. The decline of Lotus and WordPerfect might have been due to an erroneous lack of such concern.

Falling prices, of course, don't have to last. A firm might initially lower prices (as Microsoft did as it was conquering the PC spreadsheet market) as a predatory strategy intended to drive out competitors. The facts, however, do not support any rational predation story. If Microsoft were using predation to achieve victory in the PC market, it would be irrational to charge equivalently low prices, to say nothing of lower prices, in the Macintosh market. Furthermore, predation requires low prices now (to destroy a rival) and high prices later (after the rival is gone). But the pricing story here is prices that fall, and then fall further. It's hard to make a case for predation in that.

Notes to Chapter 8

1. Several programs created macro readers that were completely compatible with that of Lotus 1-2-3. Lotus sued several of these companies over the look and feel of their software. It won its cases against Paperback Software and Mosaic Software, and forced Borland to remove its 100 percent-compatible macro reader.

2. *Personal Computing* (April 1982), p. 62.

3. Williams (1982), p. 182.

4. *PC World* (October 1983), p. 120.

5. *PC World* (December 1985), p. 221.

6. Review of Excel demo at Comdex, *Byte Magazine* (September 1985), p. 347.

7. *PC Magazine* (January 13, 1987), p. 115.

8. Personal Computing (October 1987), p. 101.

9. *PC Magazine* (November 10, 1987), p. 33.

10. *Personal Computing* (December 1987), p. 102.

11. *PC Magazine* (December 12, 1987), p. 33.

12. We exclude the November '93 issue of *InfoWorld*, which gave Lotus the highest marks, because Excel was not included in the comparison.

13. Beginning with the October 1992 *InfoWorld* review, all reviewed programs are of Windows versions. Prior to that review, all are of DOS versions, except Excel.

14. We are using recent market shares to check for tipping, which is consistent with our view that consumers update their forecasts based on what has happened lately. Alternatively, it is possible to use installed base as a measure of network effect, which would be more consistent with much of the previous literature. We will examine that issue in future research.

15. ICD, "PC Spreadsheet Software." From page 9: "The production of Lotus's upgrade to 1-2-3 Release 2.1 proved to be a difficult undertaking for the company. In the end, Lotus shipped two products as possible upgrades to 2.1. . . . Release 3.0's production schedule stretched out as Lotus attempted to fit the product within reasonable memory restraints. . . . Finally, Lotus went to an outside source, Rational Systems, and purchased DOS extender technology."

16. Microsoft also had several product lines: Excel for Macintosh, Excel for Windows, Excel for OS/2 (released in October 89), and Multiplan for DOS. Multiplan had been a significant product, placing number two among DOS spreadsheet in 1988 and fifth in 1989. Microsoft wisely let it go in favor of Excel.

17. This was Lotus 1-2-3 3.0g, where the *g* stood for graphical. It was essentially the same as Lotus 3.0 for DOS, as was the initial version of 1-2-3 for Windows.

18. John C. Dvorak, "Lotus, move forward or die!" *PC Magazine* (March 16, 1993), p. 93.

19. IDC reports that Microsoft Word sold 15,000 units in 1989, but most magazine reviews indicate that Word did not actually appear until 1990. An advertisement for PC Connection in the June 1989 issue of *PC Magazine*, however, provides a price of $329 for Microsoft Word for Windows.

20. We remind the readers that this information represents readers' opinions regarding the leading product, not actual market shares. These opinions likely reflect a mixture of market share, brand name, and experience.

21. As discussed on p. 37 of David Card's "PC Office Suite, Word Processor, and Spreadsheet Markets Review and Forecast," 1995–2000.

22. Paul Bonner, "Is It a Great Windows Application, Though?" *PC Computing* (November 1991), p. 38.

23. Edward Mendelson, "WordPerfect for Windows: A Character-Based Powerhouse All Dressed Up for Windows," *PC Magazine* (January 14, 1992), p. 37.

24. In 1991 AmiPro had an installed DOS base to draw on of fewer than 50,000 users, whereas WordPerfect had an installed DOS base of 5.7 million and Word had an installed DOS base of 1.7 million. (See Table 28 in Mary Loffredo, IDC, July 1992.)

25. In 1991 there were at least seven vendors of Windows word processors.

26. This table is a mixture of IDC and Dataquest data. IDC is somewhat unclear how they handle office suites until 1994, and thus we use Dataquest data for the years 1991 through 1995. This is one instance where the choice of data sets makes some difference, as the raw IDC data indicate higher prices for Word for Windows relative to WordPerfect in 1991–93.

27. Excel had seven observations, 1-2-3 five, and Resolve and Full Impact three each.

28. This is due, in part, to the fact that those spreadsheets in the "other" category were often not "major" spreadsheets, and thus not listed individually in the Dataquest data that was used to create most of these market shares.

29. After 1995, IDC kept detailed information only for Microsoft Word, and not for any other individual word processors.

30. Note, however, that in two cases, Microsoft Word tied with another product.

31. Word had seven observations, WordPerfect five, and Nisus Writer and MacWrite four each.

32. This chart examines only Word for Windows, and ignores Word for DOS. The latter had a 13 percent and 16 percent market share in 1988 and 1989, respectively.

33. The conflict in the profession reached its peak in the early 1970s and is well illustrated by Goldschmid, Mann, and Weston (1974). The economics profession

largely adopted the view that market share did not necessarily lead to the exercise of monopoly power, thanks in large part to the work of Demsetz.

34. We were forced to use Dataquest data for the late 1980s even though the price values are too variable to generate much confidence. That is why we looked for alternative sources.

35. In June 1990 Excel and Microsoft Word for Windows were both $329, whereas both products for the Macintosh were $245. In 1989 Macintosh Word and Excel were both $255 whereas Excel was $319. In 1988 both products were $249 in the Macintosh market, but Excel was $319 in the PC market.

9

Other Software Markets

Personal Finance Software

Personal finance software allows individuals to balance their checkbooks, track their investments, and plan for the future. The software has become inexpensive and easy to use. The major players are Quicken by Intuit, Microsoft Money, and Managing Your Money by Meca. This market is particularly interesting because Microsoft is a major player in the market but not the leader.

Network effects should be of less consequence in the personal finance software market than in many other software markets. Consumers of personal finance products are generally not interested in being able to exchange files with other individuals although some may wish to exchange files with their accountants. This may change in the future, however, as banks and other financial institutions begin to offer Internet products that require compatibility.

Personal finance products were introduced in the early 1980s. During the 1980s Andrew Tobias's Managing Your Money was generally considered the best program of its kind. When Quicken was introduced in the mid-1980s, early reviews found it to be less powerful than Managing Your Money. Quicken had limited capabilities (basically checkbook balancing and budgeting), but it performed these functions quite well,[1] and it was one-third the price of Managing Your Money.[2]

Over time Intuit improved Quicken, adding more sophisticated features. By the early 1990s, it was considered at least the equal of Managing Your Money, as reflected in figure 9.1, which indicates the wins for the various products in this market. Managing Your Money still appealed to those more interested in power, for example, tracking sophisticated investments as opposed to just ordinary stocks and bonds. Microsoft Money, a new offering, appealed to those interested in ease of use.[3] By the mid-1990s, Quicken was generally ranked first.

The results of reviews that provided quality ratings of each program are shown in figure 9.2. Managing Your Money remained relatively competitive until the mid-1990s. It beat Quicken for DOS on two early occasions and Quicken for Windows on another early test. But the Quicken products were always at least a close second, and in the early nineties, Managing Your Money had no clear quality advantage over Quicken—and it was more expensive. By the mid-1990s, Quicken for Windows dominated the numerical quality reviews.

Figure 9.3 tracks the market shares of the three leading products. As the figure shows, the personal finance software market is another case of serial monopoly. A market leader (with 60 percent of the market) is displaced within three years by another firm (which then achieves a market share of greater than 60 percent). The rapidity with which Quicken overtook Managing Your Money is astonishing. Although we have some reservations about the exact values, owing to the source of the data,[4] the general story that the figure tells is certainly correct: Managing Your Money lost out to Quicken, which has ever since successfully defended its market share.

Once again, the history of this market flies in the face of the concept of tipping. The change in market share is dramatic and abrupt, with no evidence of an acceleration beyond some tipping point. There's no hint of

FIGURE 9.1
Personal Finance Wins

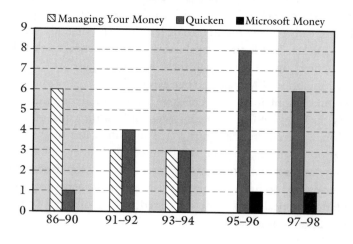

inertia in this market. Consumers simply switched to a product that was widely regarded as better.

The personal finance software market developed slightly differently from the markets for word processors and spreadsheets. Quicken became the leading product in the market when it had merely matched the quality of Managing Your Money. In the word processor and spreadsheet markets, products did not take over leadership positions until they had actually surpassed the quality ratings of the incumbent.

Figure 9.4, which presents the prices for the leading products, provides a possible explanation for Quicken's ascendancy: It was cheaper. The retail price of Managing Your Money was three times the price of Quicken. Unlike the market for spreadsheets and word processors, the personal finance software market caters mainly to individuals rather than to businesses. This can explain why price was more effective in this market than in the markets

FIGURE 9.2
Ratings of Personal Finance Software

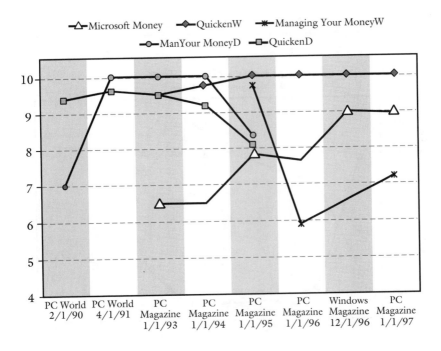

examined in the last chapter. Once the two products were similar in quality, price-conscious consumers made a rational choice. By the time Managing Your Money finally lowered its price to match the competition in 1992, it had lost its quality advantage.

Managing Your Money was also hurt by its inability to provide a timely Windows version of the product; there was no Windows version of Managing Your Money until 1994. Both Microsoft and Intuit introduced products for the Windows market in 1991. Quicken for Windows, Intuit's early Windows product, was well positioned in the early Windows market; it had a 70 to 80 percent market share, which was some 10 to 20 points higher than Quicken's DOS market share. Part of the reason for this success may have been Intuit's experience in the Macintosh market, where Quicken was also the leading program. Experience in the Macintosh market gave Intuit a clear edge in understanding how to write a successful GUI application.[5] This is a theme that we have found over and over again—success in the Windows market is presaged by success in the Macintosh market.

FIGURE 9.3
Market Share PC Personal Finance

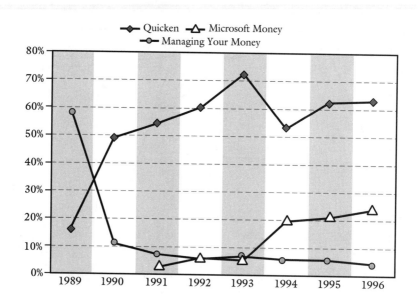

Microsoft gained market share throughout 1990s, but not from Quicken. Instead, it replaced other products, particularly products in the DOS market and most particularly Managing Your Money. Microsoft's share of the Windows market has remained nearly unchanged, and has actually fallen slightly since 1991. Since 1992 Microsoft has had a lower price than its competitors, perhaps taking its cue from some reviewers who argued that since it was less powerful it should have a lower price.

Quicken's retention of its market leadership is not surprising given that it has consistently been ranked as highest in quality. It is apparent that in the personal finance software market, where it offers a lower-rated product, any "leverage" that Microsoft might have as a consequence of its ownership of the operating system has had little effect.

This market continues to change, of course, and Microsoft appears to be making a run at Quicken's quality superiority, although only the beginnings of this run show up in figure 9.2. In November 1997, *Money Magazine* said, [6] "Microsoft is finally giving Quicken a run with its Money, but Quicken remains our top choice for personal finance software." In

FIGURE 9.4
Prices of Personal Finance Software

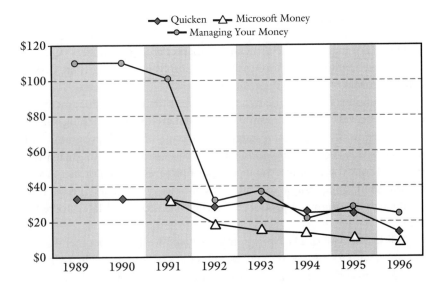

February 1998, *PC Magazine* said,[7] "For the first time the two-horse race between Money and Quicken is a photo-finish." The October 1998 issue of *Windows Magazine* declared that Money 99 was better than Quicken. If Microsoft can manage to produce a better product than Intuit (something it has been unable to do in the past), Quicken is likely to lose market share.

As we write this book, however, all we can say is that the personal finance software market is another case where an incumbent was quickly replaced after it lost its quality advantage. Furthermore, this market proves that Microsoft cannot leverage its ownership of the operating system at will. Microsoft Money, a lower-quality, less powerful product, has not managed to dislodge Quicken as the market leader—and this is in spite of the fact that Microsoft Money is offered at a considerably lower price. This history of this market reinforces our theory that achieving product quality parity or superiority is a requirement for increasing market share.

Desktop Publishing Software

Desktop publishing (DTP) software is used to create magazines, books, brochures, newsletters, and other printed materials. The market has bifurcated into professional (high-end) and amateur (mid-range) segments.

High-End DTP Products

The major players in the professional market are QuarkXPress (Quark), PageMaker (Aldus, then Adobe), Ventura Publisher (Xerox, then Corel), and FrameMaker (Frame, then Adobe).

High-end products are of two types: page oriented and document oriented. PageMaker, the program usually given credit for launching the entire genre, was, as its name suggests, a page-oriented program. This program specialized in the placement of pictures and text, with great attention paid to text attributes, the insertion of pictures, and color use. A similar program, appearing a year after PageMaker, was QuarkXPress. Both products were originally produced for the Macintosh and later ported to Windows.

A different type of DTP program is targeted for long documents, such as books, with footnotes, references, and tables of contents. The two leading programs of this type are Ventura Publisher and FrameMaker.

Professional desktop publishing has long been a Macintosh stronghold, though the advent of Windows gave the PC a similar graphics strength upon which to compete. The reviews of these programs often cover both the Macintosh and PC markets, treating the Macintosh and PC versions of the same program as two separate programs with two separate scores. Surprisingly, the scores for the Macintosh and PC versions of the same program are often quite different.

Because Macintosh is where DTP originated, it is the market of choice for many DTP professionals.[8] Quark and PageMaker dominate the Macintosh market.[9] The numerical evidence from magazine reviews (figure 9.5) reveals that although PageMaker, the product that was first to market, might have had a quality lead early on, Quark surpassed PageMaker in quality in 1990 and kept that edge from 1990 onward. Not all of the results are shown in the chart. Three post-1990 reviews chose a winner but did not give a score. In all three, Quark was found to be superior to PageMaker.[10] We did not find many reviews after 1993—probably because Quark 3.3, which was introduced in 1993, was not upgraded to version 4.0 until late 1997. PageMaker closed the quality gap somewhat while Quark was failing to innovate, but it never surpassed Quark, and it fell further behind after Quark 4.0 was introduced.[11]

FIGURE 9.5
High-End DTP Ratings, Macintosh

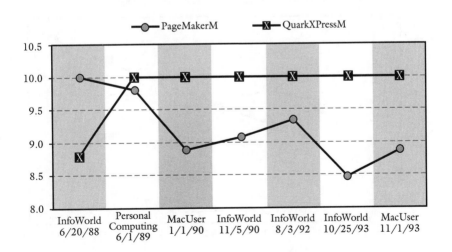

Figure 9.6, which shows the market shares of the two Macintosh products, is another portrait of a serial monopoly. PageMaker entered the decade with a dominant market share, but by 1995 Quark replaced PageMaker as the dominant firm.[12] Note that in six years Quark's market share rose from about 25 percent to over 70 percent. Although such a leap is not unusual by the standards of the software industry, such a dramatic change is practically unheard of in most other industries.

Once more we see no evidence of tipping, although the lack of data for 1993 and 1994 could hinder that effort. Nor does inertia seem to be playing much of a role in this market. Again we have what appears to be a simple switch, with no indication of an influence coming from prior market share.

In the PC market, the leading products are Ventura Publisher by Xerox, later to be bought by Corel, and PageMaker from Aldus, later to be bought by Adobe. Ventura Publisher first ran under Digital Research's GEM graphical operating system and did not run under Windows until 1990. PageMaker was ported over from the Macintosh to (pre-3.0) Windows in 1987. QuarkXPress was ported to Windows in late 1992.

FIGURE 9.6
Market Shares, High-End Macintosh DTP

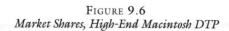

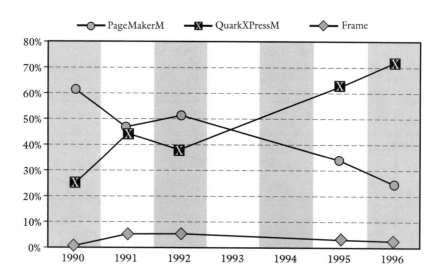

The greatest difficulty in assessing the PC DTP market is the incorporation of the previously stand-alone Ventura Publisher into the Corel Draw suite in 1995, which will be described in more detail later.

In the PC DTP market there is no single clear quality winner after 1990. figure 9.7 provides the magazine ratings for these products. In all but one case, Ventura wins the comparison reviews through 1990 (four of five), after which it loses out fairly consistently and very badly to Quark, FrameMaker, and PageMaker until May 1996, when it becomes competitive again. figure 9.8 shows the wins for each product. This chart, too, shows Ventura as the clear leader through 1990. After 1990, the winner is more uncertain with PageMaker appearing to have the quality edge, but Ventura clearly is no longer one of the leaders.

Figure 9.9 provides details on market share.[13] There are some surprises. First, Ventura is not the leading product in terms of market share in 1990; the leading product is PageMaker. Second, Quark's entry in 1992 led fairly quickly to a sizable market share, although the lack of data in 1993 and 1994 hamper our ability to know just how quickly this occurred.[14] Third, Ventura practically disappears from the market, which seems somewhat too strong a response to a decline in relative quality, even in a world without lock-in.

An explanation that might be given for PageMaker's leading position in the PC market is its position in the Macintosh market. It seems conceivable that network effects in the DTP market were sufficiently strong that PageMaker's leading position in the Macintosh market caused its success in the PC market. But there are flaws in this hypothesis. For one thing, the high-end PC DTP market in 1990 was actually larger than the corresponding Macintosh market, with sales of $77 million compared to $61 million. The installed base of high-end DTP in the PC market was 713,000 units compared to 427,000 in the Macintosh market. Thus, even if we want to postulate network effects, they should have run the other way.

An alternative explanation might be that the two types of programs, page-oriented and document-oriented, are not very good substitutes. In other words, maybe these two types of products aren't really in the same market. If a consumer needs a page-oriented program (for newsletters and magazines), even the best document-oriented program (for books) will not suit his needs. So it may not be all that significant that PageMaker outsold Ventura in spite of Ventura's superior reviews.[15]

FIGURE 9.7
Market Shares, High-End PC DTP

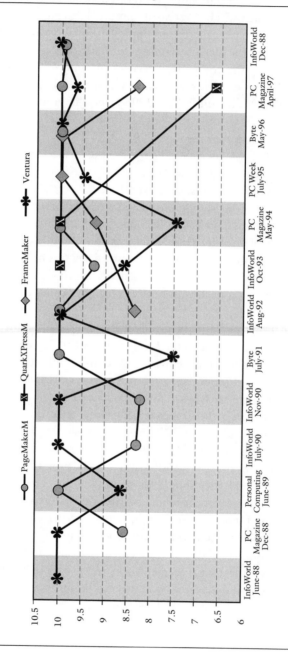

FIGURE 9.8
High-End DTP Wins, PC

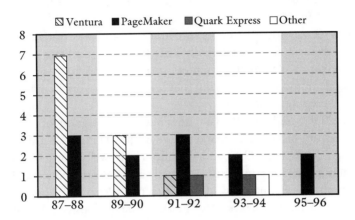

FIGURE 9.9
Market Share, High-End PC DTP

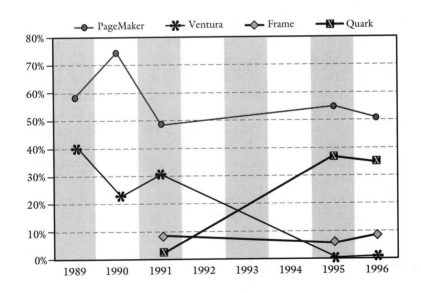

Quark, on the other hand, was a page-oriented program. The explanation for Quark's success in the PC market might have something to do with its reputation in the Macintosh market (which is *not* a network effect), but notice that it was also considered the best PC product in several reviews shortly after its introduction and was not included in some later reviews, making it difficult for us to estimate its quality. FrameMaker, a document-oriented program, was less successful—a predictable outcome considering that it had no network benefits and its reviews were unexceptional.

Figure 9.9, based on IDC data, does not do a very good job of explaining the history of Ventura's market share in the DTP market. After Corel purchased Ventura in 1993 it added Ventura to its well-known Corel Draw Suite, and in 1995 it temporarily stopped selling Ventura as a stand-alone product entirely. Because IDC does not record sales of DTP products unless they are stand-alone products, the IDC data obviously understate sales of Ventura.[16]

It is not possible to know precisely what the sales of Ventura would have been if it had not been made a part of Corel Draw, but we can calculate a rough estimate that indicates that its 1995 share would have been well above the near-zero level reported—though below its 1992 level. The list price of Corel 5 (with Ventura) was $695 compared to $545 for Corel 4 (without Ventura), and the upgrade for Corel 5 was $200 or $300, depending on what the base product had been, compared to an upgrade price of $250 for Corel 4.[17] This gives differences of $150 for new users and a maximum of $50 for upgrades, which we assume measures the value of Ventura. The prices to the vendors are approximately half of the list price. Thus, the revenues that might be expected, given the figures in note 16, are $14.6 million, which would create a market share of 12.1 percent. Corel's revenues from Draw 5 and Draw 6 in 1995 were $51.6 million.[18] The $14.6 million figure would imply that Ventura was responsible for 28 percent of the revenues of the suite, a figure that seems more likely to be too high than too low.

Whatever we think about the data, it is pretty clear that Ventura suffered a serious fall in market share from 1990 to 1995. And once again we find that that market share is linked to perceived product quality.

Finally, note that Microsoft has no entry in this market at all. And as figure 9.10 shows, the pattern of prices shows no overall decline.

Mid-Range DTP Products

Mid-range DTP products are less expensive products aimed at users who occasionally produce a newsletter or brochure. These products are generally for nonprofessionals, have low prices, and sometimes are just watered-down versions of the more expensive professional products. Some of the more successful early products were Publish It, First Publisher, and Express Publisher, but none of these managed a sustained dominance of the market. The most successful mid-range DTP product has been Microsoft Publisher, which was introduced in late 1991.

The earliest mid-range DTP programs filled a void created by the non-graphical nature of most word processors then available for the PC. The Macintosh market, with word processors that offered the ability to include graphics and different fonts on the same page, never had much of a mid-range DTP market and will be ignored in this section.[19]

FIGURE 9.10
High-End DTP Prices

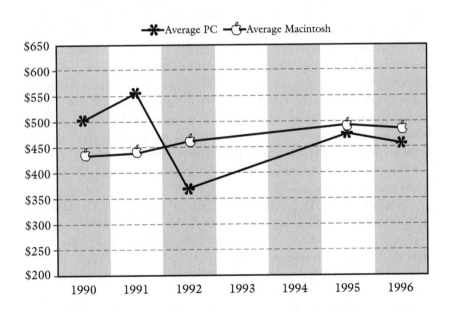

After the introduction of Windows, the mid-range DTP market for PCs should have been threatened by increasingly graphical word processors. But Microsoft Publisher grabbed hold of the industry and turned the mid-range PC DTP market from a weak also-ran into a fast-growing market with revenues at about half the level of the high-end PC DTP market. In 1992 revenues were 2.5 times as large as the 1991 revenues. By 1996 revenues had increased to over 4.5 times the 1991 revenues. Contrast this with the high-end DTP market, where 1996 revenues were a mere 1.5 times their 1991 values.

In terms of product quality, there was no clear market leader until the introduction of Microsoft Publisher. As figure 9.11 shows, however, Microsoft Publisher, after its introduction, completely dominated the magazine reviews. A look at wins (figure 9.12) also indicates that Publisher was the compelling winner among mid-range products. We would expect, therefore, that Microsoft Publisher's market share would grow and that the product would come to dominate the market. And that is exactly what happened.

Figure 9.13 shows the market shares of the leading mid-range DTP products. Before the introduction of Microsoft Publisher, various products jockeyed for the lead. The leading product in 1990, First Publisher, had a market share of 40 percent in 1990, but it fell to third place in 1991, behind Express Publisher, which had a market share of only 15 percent in 1991. Again, we must note that a market share of 40 percent would, in many other markets, be considered a very considerable presence. Yet a mere two years later First Publisher's market share was down to 5 percent. Meanwhile, Microsoft Publisher's market share was growing very rapidly.[20] It is worth noting that Microsoft Publisher managed this coup in spite of the fact that it entered the market with a price approximately 25 percent above the industry mean.

These are enormous changes in very short periods of time. Certainly, we do not find evidence of lock-in or inertia in this market. Nor is there any evidence of tipping, although the market changed so rapidly that yearly data would mask any tipping effect.

Finally, how did mid-range DTP prices change over time? figure 9.14 shows that, unlike the high-end DTP market, the mid-range market experienced considerable price declines. The average price in the industry fell by over 40 percent from 1990 to 1996, in spite of the fact that average industry prices actually rose in 1991 and 1992 as the relatively expensive

FIGURE 9.11
Mid-Range DTP Ratings

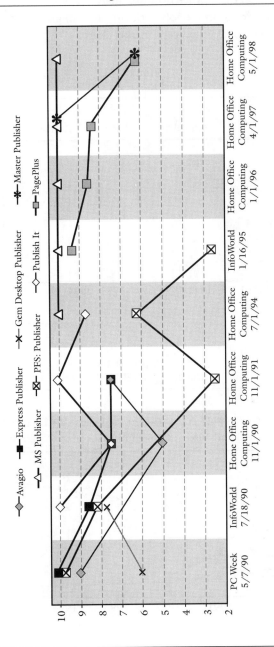

Microsoft product entered the market. Once again we find sharp price declines in a market that Microsoft dominates. There is no evidence of consumer harm from monopoly pricing that might be associated with Microsoft's eventual 70 percent market share.

FIGURE 9.12
Mid-Range DTP Wins

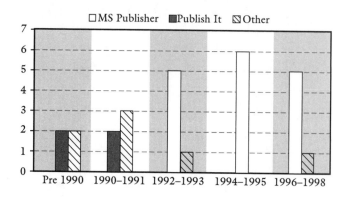

FIGURE 9.13
Mid-Range DTP Market Shares

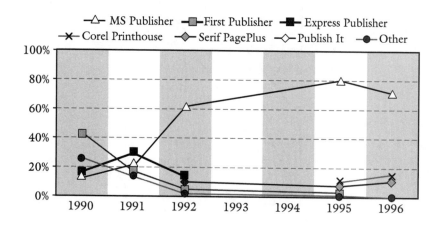

FIGURE 9.14
Mid-Range DTP Prices

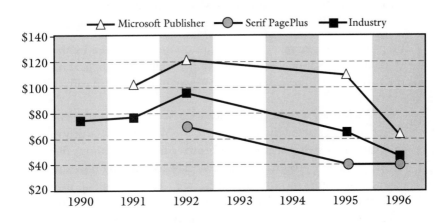

Browsers

Browsers are products that allow PC users to access the World Wide Web (WWW). Because the WWW is a relatively recent phenomenon, browsers are a relatively new product. As late as October 1994, the browser market was still largely unformed. Listen to the following quote from *PC Magazine*:

> Why so volatile, this market? In part, because no one knows quite how connections to the Net will be made in a year or so . . . . Microsoft . . . is now building both TCP/IP and PPP support into Chicago [i.e., Windows 95] and Windows NT 3.5 and has assigned at least one person to work directly with Internet service providers. Not to be outdone, both Novell and IBM are rumored to be including World-Wide-Web browsers in upcoming versions of LAN WorkPlace and OS/2 for Windows.

> Mosaic . . . has been licensed far and wide to commercial companies, and NCSA continues to develop the program in conjunction with Spyglass.

> Expect other, non-Mosaic World-Wide-Web browsers to make
> waves soon. Jim Clark's new company, Mosaic Communications
> [to become Netscape], is a likely source, and it's thought that
> Novell's WWW browser will not be particularly Mosaic-like.[21]

The product Mosaic mentioned in this quote was created by the University of Illinois' National Center for Supercomputing Applications and was the first successful browser. As *PC Magazine* reported in early 1995:

> NCSA's Mosaic was the first Windows-based Web browser—the
> killer app that started the stampede to the Web. Today, largely as
> a result of its stellar success, the browser field is in furious fer-
> ment, with new products released weekly and existing ones up-
> dated sometimes hourly. Browsers are even making it into
> operating-systems: IBM includes a browser with OS/2 Warp,
> Version 3, and Microsoft plans one for Windows 95.[22]

The first magazine reviews of browsers appeared in mid-1994. Netscape, which was formed by some former Mosaic programmers, introduced Navigator in late 1994. The magazine reviews considered Navigator to be a better product than Mosaic from the day it was introduced. Both products were free. There were and continue to be various other shareware/freeware browsers available.[23] Microsoft introduced its entry in this market, Internet Explorer, in 1995.

Because the browsers were initially offered as freeware and largely continue to be distributed that way, there are no direct revenues. Like over-the-air television, browsers generate revenue by selling a related product.[24] Browser revenues can come from the sale of servers, which send out the information retrieved by browsers, or by selling advertising from the sites that browsers go to initially.[25] Although consumers can easily change the starting location on their browsers, continued patronage at the starting point initially specified for the browser (which is likely to occur) can provide considerable advertising revenues to browser providers.[26]

The public and academic interest in the browser competition has been heightened considerably by its role in the antitrust proceedings of the U.S. Department of Justice against Microsoft. The Department of Justice claims that Microsoft's addition of its browser to its operating system has increased its browser's market share and threatened Netscape's share, independent of the quality of the browsers. The Department of Justice presented email evidence that some of Microsoft's top executives doubted whether browser quality by itself was sufficient to wrest control of the market away from Netscape, although at the time of this writing, Microsoft has not yet had a chance to give its interpretation of these email messages. Nevertheless, given the prominence of concepts such as lock-in in high-tech circles, business executives might be forgiven for questioning the strength of the link and the speed of adjustment between product quality and market share.

In other software markets, we have consistently found that market share is strongly related to product quality, and that market share responds quickly to quality differentials. We would expect a similar relationship to hold in the browser market. In addition, the relationship between market share and browser quality should be strong because price can not be a differentiating variable when virtually all browsers have the same price (zero). [27]

Figure 9.15 shows the wins in the browser market since 1995. Because this market is so new, the time span is compressed, with intervals of six months as opposed to the one- or two-year intervals we used in our analysis of other markets. Still, the trend is very clear. Netscape Navigator was clearly considered the highest-quality product until the second half of 1996, when Internet Explorer became the superior product.[28] We should note that Internet Explorer was not introduced until well into the second half of 1995, so that the time period where Netscape Navigator was superior to Internet Explorer is approximately one year.

FIGURE 9.15
Browser Wins

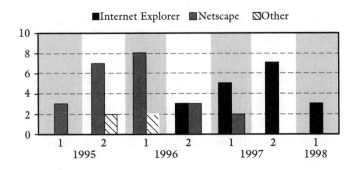

Figure 9.16 shows the relative scores of Internet Explorer and Netscape Navigator. Unlike figure 9.15, figure 9.16 presents data only for the period after Internet Explorer became available as an alternative to Navigator, thus truncating the period where Netscape ruled the market in terms of quality. Although the number of observations is smaller than we might like, Internet Explorer's superiority at the end of the period still shows up, although not as clearly as in figure 9.15.

How have market shares changed as the products' quality rankings have changed?[29] Clearly, as seen in figure 9.17, Internet Explorer has increased its market share relative to Netscape Navigator.[30] This increased market share, not surprisingly, correlates strongly with the data on Internet Explorer's increase in quality.

Internet Explorer's market share barely grew at all until July 1996, when it was first rated as equal in quality to Netscape. By 1997 Internet Explorer was rapidly gaining market share, but it was also rated as superior in quality in the reviews. Thus, quality superiority in the browser market, as in the other markets we have examined, is highly correlated with increased market share.

The browser market is still another market that does not seem to exhibit either inertia, lock-in, or tipping. This, however, might not be the best test of lock-in in that, as we will explain, network effects would not be expected to play much of a role in this market.

The reason for Internet Explorer's increased market share is central to the Microsoft case. The government's case is based largely on the claim that Internet Explorer's increased market share is due to monopolistic behavior by Microsoft, and *not* any quality advantage held by Internet Explorer. Because Internet Explorer's quality has surpassed Netscape Navigator's, it is not surprising that Explorer's market share is increasing. The question becomes, however, whether the *size* of the market share change can be attributed to the quality differentials.

Does the size of the change in market shares in the browser market seem out of place with our findings in other markets? We think not.

To begin, we have seen two other markets where market shares changed by 40 or 60 percentage points within two years (personal finance and midrange desktop publishing software). In the browser market we find a change in market share of approximately 40 points within a two-year interval from July 1996 to July 1998.

In addition, there are several reasons why we might expect more rapid changes in market share in the browser market than in a typical software

FIGURE 9.16
Browser Ratings

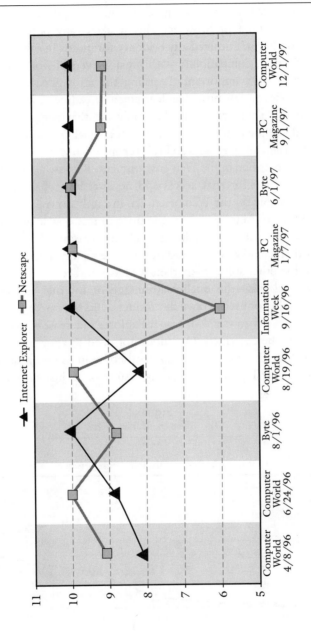

market. First, as already mentioned, network effects are likely to be small in this market. Browsers are products used by individuals, and those individuals don't usually interact in ways that might cause them to care who else is using their brand of browser. This weakens any potential for inertia, though we haven't noticed any evidence for inertia in other software markets.[31] Second, compatibility with previous versions of a browser is not likely to be very important. Learning the idiosyncrasies of a particular browser takes far less time than learning a spreadsheet, word processor, or desktop-publishing program. The only file that needs to be backward compatible is the user's list of favorite sites, which is relatively easy to transport. This enhances a user's ability to change browsers. Third, instant scalability is intensified in the Web environment. Because all browser users, by definition, have Internet access and new versions of these browsers are readily available on the Web, users can instantly download a new product from the Web. And, of course, the price of this download is zero. This is virtually pure instant scalability. For all these reasons, therefore, we should expect that a market shift could occur more rapidly in the browser market than in the other software markets we have studied.

Given all this—the quality advantage of Internet Explorer, the enhanced ability of users to switch products, and the ease of providing additional copies of browsers—Internet Explorer's increase in market share can quite easily be explained. One does not need to appeal to other factors, such as those the government has focused on in its case against Microsoft (that is, ownership of the operating system or exclusionary contracts), to

FIGURE 9.17
Browser Market Shares

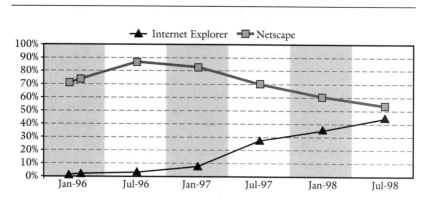

explain Microsoft's increasing share of the market. Still, we do not want to overstate this conclusion—Internet Explorer's gain on Netscape can be explained by quality differentials, but that doesn't prove that quality differentials are responsible for the entire gain.

Internet Explorer's increasing market share is a problem for proponents of lock-in and market inertia. Netscape's browser had an early lead, established itself as something of a standard, and captured overwhelming market share. That it now seems to be losing out to Internet Explorer might well be taken as another defeat for lock-in theories. Some lock-in proponents have chosen to attribute the apparent anomaly to monopoly power. The data, however, support the interpretation that the most important factor is Microsoft's quality advantage.

At the time of this writing, early in 1999, Netscape has retained its edge in market share over Internet Explorer. But if Internet Explorer retains its advantage in quality, we are confident that it will dethrone Netscape in fairly short order—whether or not it is included in the Windows operating system.

Online Services

Online services provide modem access to specialized data and communications facilities. Consumers can use online services to download software, participate in discussion and newsgroups, or retrieve information on a host of topics. Since the mid-1990s, these kinds of services have been widely available through the Internet. Online services have since transmuted into services that allow access to the Internet, but they continue to provide the above-mentioned services.

The online services market is unlike the other markets examined in this chapter because it is not primarily a software market. Instant scalability is not an attribute of this market, nor is compatibility with old files.[32] Network effects, on the other hand, have been important because much of the value of a closed online service depends on how many others use the service. For example, the size of the service increases the value of e-mail and newsgroups within the service.[33] With the growth of the Internet, however, the importance of such provider-specific network effects has diminished. The Internet versions of such functions as e-mail and newsgroups are much larger than the capabilities of any particular online service.

Online services have complexities that make them hard to analyze. The nature and pricing of online services have changed dramatically over the past few years. Specifically, online services were deeply affected by the growth of the Internet and now serve a dual function: They provide both specialized content and a portal to the Internet. Furthermore, the pricing of these services can be a complicated maze, making comparisons difficult. Some online services charge different prices by time of day and the type of service used by the consumer. CompuServe, for example, for a time imposed a special surcharge for users who accessed particular areas (such as its extensive database of newspaper articles) and charged different prices depending on the speed of the modem connection, and Genie (a service excluded from our charts) charged lower prices at night than during the day. In the last few years, however, pricing schemes have simplified. Most services now charging a fixed monthly fee for unlimited access of all of the company's services (although other price plans are also available).

The data are less complete for the online services market than for the other markets we have examined, but these data are broadly consistent with the pattern we have found in other markets.

In 1991, when our data begin, Prodigy was the leading product in terms of market share (figure 9.18). But as figure 9.19 shows, Prodigy was not the leading online service based on quality. The quality leader (in terms of such innovations as access to the Internet, the ability to download files, and the ability to handle attachments to e-mail) was CompuServe, with AOL almost as far behind as Prodigy.

FIGURE 9.18
Online Service Market Shares

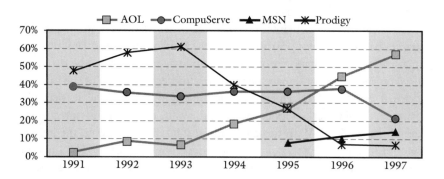

FIGURE 9.19
Online Service Ratings

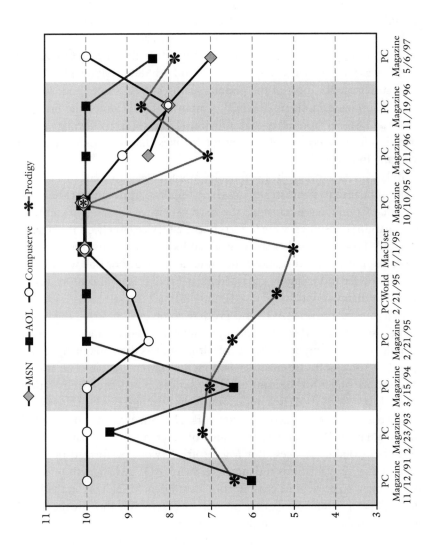

As an aside, it is interesting to note that Prodigy, a creation of IBM and Sears, appeared to be ahead of its time and suffered for it. It had advertising long before advertising was understood to be the model on which the Internet would be based. It had graphics and an easy-to-use interface. The graphics and advertising, however, were criticized as being annoying and ugly.

It had a fixed monthly fee years before it was adopted by other online services, which was its main advantage.[34] Its 1993 flat rate of $14.95 per month was far less than CompuServe's standard $8 fee with a $12.80 per hour surcharge for most of the popular features ($22.80 per hour for the faster 9600 baud modems), or AOL's monthly fee of $8 for the first two hours and $6 per hour after that. Obviously, the choice of Prodigy could save significant amounts of money for families that used online services with any frequency.

In late 1994 Prodigy dropped its flat monthly fee and went to a pricing policy similar to its competitors'. With no important price differentials (except that CompuServe remained the most expensive service by a considerable margin) consumers were left to choose a service largely on the basis of quality.[35] Prodigy's market share dropped like a stone. Customers largely chose AOL, which had at about the same time, as luck or skill would have it, become far more highly regarded than Prodigy and also more highly regarded than CompuServe.

In a four-year period, AOL and Prodigy completely reversed their positions, a swing in market share of approximately 50 percentage points for each firm. This swing in market share, although less dramatic than we have found in some software markets, is nonetheless remarkable. The market shares, once prices had become relatively similar, reflect the quality ratings quite closely, with AOL first and CompuServe second.

Microsoft's entry, Microsoft Network (MSN), was introduced with much fanfare in 1995, and was the cause of much public trepidation by the incumbent online services. But Microsoft Network performed poorly—both in quality evaluations and in market share. AOL, which petitioned the government to prevent Microsoft from including a MSN icon on the Windows desktop, went on to ever greater success—even though the MSN icon was, in fact, included on the desktop.

As we found in the personal finance and browser markets, Microsoft's ownership of the operating system did not seem to provide any leverage at all when all it had to offer was a product that was not up to par. And furthermore, Microsoft Network shows no sign of closing the quality gap with its rivals.

Despite the importance of network effects in this market (particularly before the rise of the Internet), we find no evidence here of either inertia or tipping: Market share changes have been rapid, and yearly changes have been relatively constant.

Conclusions

To our knowledge, this material is the first systematic examination of real-world data from software applications markets, and our results are surprising—perhaps even startling. What we have found runs counter to much of what passes for conventional wisdom.

Our most important finding is the close relationship between market-share change and product quality.[36] We find this relationship in market after market. Market-share swings in software markets are large and rapid, a phenomenon that runs counter to the suspicion that a dominant firm might become locked in. Time after time, we find examples of dominant products that fade away (Lotus 1-2-3, WordPerfect, Managing Your Money, PageMaker, First Publisher, and Prodigy).[37] Sometimes the product that replaces the one-time leader is a product from Microsoft; sometimes it is a product from some other company. In each case, however, the product that replaces the incumbent is of far higher quality, or is cheaper, or is more advanced in some other way.

When you combine the empirical evidence from the software market with the empirical evidence from the earlier chapters, the verdict on third-degree path dependence is clear. If it exists at all, it is so rare that it hasn't been found in over ten years of searching. Of course, we cannot rule out the theoretical possibility of pernicious lock-in. But if anyone ever does find a real-world example, it will be an extraordinary exception to an important rule: Consumers do not get locked in to inferior products.

When a market leader loses its dominance in a software market, the most important factor in its decline is that another firm has a better product. Price can play a role as well, but less than one might think (perhaps because a price change is often matched by competitors). Sometimes getting a jump on market conditions (such as producing a Windows product, or being part of a suite) has an impact on market share. But such an edge is insufficient if the product is not of high quality.

The conventional wisdom, of course, is the claim to the contrary: Winning a market has little to do with quality. But like so much conventional wisdom, this claim is completely without foundation.

Another important finding—a byproduct of our analysis—is the explanation our data give for the success of Microsoft. It's really pretty simple: Microsoft produces good products at low prices. Some, including the Department of Justice, have suggested that Microsoft did not earn its large market shares in applications. Our data are at complete variance with this claim. Our data show that when Microsoft moved from a low to a high market share, its products were always of higher quality than the market leader's. When its products were not superior, it did not make inroads against the market leader.

Our data also disprove the claim that Microsoft has used its monopoly position to keep prices high. As a matter of fact, we found that after Microsoft becomes dominant in a product category, prices in that market begin to fall.

We studied three different market patterns that might be viewed as tests of the Microsoft-as-monopolist hypothesis. Here's what we found. First, in markets where Microsoft participated, prices declined faster and farther than in markets where Microsoft did not participate. Second, in markets where Microsoft became dominant, prices fell after Microsoft achieved that dominance. Third, in markets where Microsoft was dominant, it charged lower prices than it did for the same product in markets where some other firm was dominant.

In short, Microsoft's effect on the software markets has been to lower prices and improve product quality. Such outcomes benefit consumers—though, of course, they hurt Microsoft's competitors. The Department of Justice's antitrust campaign against Microsoft may or may not help Microsoft's competitors, but it certainly doesn't seem to be in the interest of software consumers.

Our findings should also interest theorists and policymakers. For one thing, we find no evidence of market inertia or tipping. This should raise red flags for those who have treated these untested claims as established facts. It seems clear to us that if we are going to talk about market inertia (or momentum), we need to start out by establishing clear benchmarks. We had no such measures when we looked at these data, but our results are clear even without them: Changes in market share were fast and rational, always linked to perceived quality measures of products. This result should give pause to believers in inertia.

Our data also provide no support for the concept of tipping, however reasonable it may seem in principle. To test for tipping in software markets we looked for accelerated rates of change that were caused by self-reinforcing mechanisms. We are well aware that some will claim that this is the wrong test, but we challenge such critics to come up with a test of their own. Tipping is supposed to mean more than market domination by natural monopolists. If we're going to talk about it, it's going to need some empirical content and testable implications. We do not expect ours to be the final word on this subject, but we hope that our work will lead to some dialogue about what tipping might mean that would warrant a term at all, and how one might test for its existence.

Notes to Chapter 9

1. For example, in the September 1987 issue of *PC Magazine* we find the quote, "Quicken, the checkbook manager, does one thing and does it well" (p. 482).

2. The list price for Managing Your Money in the late 1980s was $220, and for Quicken was $60. According to Dataquest figures, the average price received by the vendor for Quicken in 1989 was $33, and for Managing Your Money was $110 (tables 22 and 23 in "Market Statistics 1994, Personal Computing software Vendor Shipment and Revenue Data," June 6, 1994).

3. For example: "But it's what Managing Your Money offers beyond basic banking that truly sets it apart from the rest. . . . The package provides the most comprehensive tax and financial planning and portfolio management of any product reviewed here. . . . This package is also the only real choice for active investors." *PC Magazine* (January 12, 1993), p. 258. Also: "If your needs are simple, you'll be especially happy with Money. Individuals who track investments or want to pay bills electronically should get one of the Quickens. . . .Those who want more than checkwriting—a total personal finance package—should consider Managing Your Money" *PC Magazine* (January 14, 1992).

4. Because of the large price differential, market shares based on revenues can give quite different results than those based on units sold, making it unclear exactly when Quicken began to dominate Managing Your Money. IDC has Quicken outselling Managing Your Money 8:1 in revenues and 25:1 in unit shipments by 1991. Dataquest reports almost identical unit sales for the two products in 1989 (a 10 percent edge to Managing Your Money), providing Managing Your Money a 3.5:1 edge in revenues. For 1990, however, Dataquest gives Quicken a 15:1 edge in sales and 4:1 edge in revenues in 1990. The November 1988 issue of *Money Magazine* states that Quicken "does only check-writing and budgeting, but outsells the rest." By 1990 Quicken was clearly outselling Managing Your Money in unit sales and most likely in revenues.

5. Intuit had the Macintosh program with the leading market share as early as 1988, when our data on this market begin.

6. *Money Magazine* (November 1997), p. 194.

7. *Personal Computing* (November 1998), p. 103.

8. Interestingly, our data indicate that the PC DTP market was larger than the Macintosh market from 1989 through 1991, and that the Macintosh market surpassed it from 1992 onward (our data end in 1996). Part of this, however, is due to the treatment of Ventura Publisher in the data, which will be discussed in more detail later.

9. For a short period of time there was a Macintosh version of Ventura, but it never achieved much market share and was allowed to die.

10. See *MacUser* (November 1990), *InfoWorld* (May 4, 1992), and *MacWorld* (December 1997).

11. For example: "Although slow to upgrade its software, Quark has had the advantage of being ahead of PageMaker for many years and watching first Aldus's and then Adobe's frequent but haphazard upgrades. PageMaker 6.5 achieved rough parity with QuarkXPress 3.3, but now QuarkXPress 4 is ready to go. Its significant new features pull the program back into the lead." See Galen Gruman "QuarkXPress versus PageMaker: The Battle Intensifies," *MacWorld*, December 1997.

12. Unfortunately, we do not have data for 1993 and 1994, and have interpolated the values for those two years based on 1992 and 1995. This will be the case for all the charts in this section.

13. Again, the lack of data in 1993 and 1994 forced us to interpolate the results for those years.

14. Quark entered very late in 1992 and so the 1992 figure severely understates what its share would be in a full year.

15. It should also be noted that if PC reviewers were more interested in document creation than page creation Ventura would tend to receive better grades.

16. IDC reports (Edward Buckingham and Nicole Miller, "The Windows and Macintosh based DTP Software Markets, 1996–2001," p. 8) that Corel sold 113,000 new units and 245,000 upgrades of its Draw suite in 1995.

17. These are prices for the version on CD.

18. Joan-Carol Brigham, IDC, "The Drawing/Diagramming and Illustration Software Markets 1995–2000," table 6, p. 19.

19. According to IDC: "This segment on the Macintosh faces more competition than its parallel segment on PC/MS-DOS. The strength of the Macintosh graphics, architecture, and word processing products leaves little room for midrange desktop publishing." IDC, "The Desktop Publishing Software Market 1989–1995," p. 4.

20. Microsoft Publisher was introduced in October 1991. Therefore, the 1991 market share indicated in the chart is likely to be considerably lower than a full-year market share would have been.

21. "Internet Front Ends to Watch For," *PC Magazine* (October 11, 1994).

22. "Web Browsers: The Web Untangled," *PC Magazine* (February 7, 1995).

23. There are at least nine other browsers that were available in 1995 and 1996 that can still be downloaded from Stroud's Web page (www.stroud.com). There are

four other browsers that have been upgraded in 1998 that are available from Stroud's Web page besides Microsoft's and Netscape's. Most of these browsers are free.

24. Similarly, newspapers lose money on circulation, but make up for it by charging advertisers for the ability to reach their newspaper's readers

25. When a browser is first activated it goes to a preordained location (e.g., Netscape's or Microsoft's home page) just as a television or radio tuner, when turned on, will be set for some frequency that may contain a station. The difference is that the browser is set to receive information from a Web page that exists, whereas radio and television frequencies vary by city and, thus, may or may not be tuned to an actual station when first turned on.

26. According to a survey in *Family PC Magazine*: "About 38 percent set their start-up page to a site they found surfing, while 15 percent made their own start page. Most people grow so accustomed to their start-up page they never change it." The survey also examined where readers obtained their browsers, an issue of some importance given the Department of Justice claim that inclusion on the opening screen was crucial: "When asked where they got their browser, 42 percent said they downloaded it, 32 percent got it from their ISP, and 12 percent said it came with their computer." "Browsers" (October 1, 1998).

27. Netscape originally gave its Navigator browser away but later charged for it. After Microsoft's Internet Explorer, which was free, began making serious inroads into Netscape's market share, Netscape again began to give its browser away.

28. James Barksdale, in his testimony at the Microsoft trial, admitted that Internet Explorer had caught up to Netscape Navigator in quality, but although he got the direction right, he clearly understated the degree to which Internet Explorer moved relative to Netscape Navigator.

29. We must note that market share has a different meaning when the price of the product is zero and the product is given away to many users. Market shares, as we use them, are defined as the share of usage, based on surveys.

30. These data come from Zona Research, which conducts periodic surveys.

31. The various browsers have at times tried to create proprietary "extensions" to the language used to create Web pages. If a browser can create proprietary extensions, then certain Web locations created with those extensions will be better translated with that browser, and network effects then would become important. This has not happened to any serious extent, however.

32. If online services wish to expand, they must increase their computing power and also increase the number of access lines and modems that consumers call.

33. Network effects could be negative at some levels of network participation, at least in the short run. That is, bigger networks could bring congestion, a nega-

tive network effect, as the network providers approached their capacity. The congestion problems experienced by America Online when it started its unlimited-use, $19.95 pricing would be an example of this.

34. It had a fixed monthly fee of $14.95 for unlimited service, but this was not complete. There was, for example, a limitation of thirty email messages a month, and extra messages would raise the cost of the service.

35. AOL and Prodigy both charged $9.95 for the first five hours and $2.95 for each additional hour. CompuServe charged $10 per month and hourly fees that were as high as $4.80 per hour for some services.

36. One might question our use of magazine reviews as a measure of quality, but if such reviews were irrelevant, there should be no relationship at all between market share and reviews. But the relationship is in fact pronounced.

37. This excludes products such as VisiCalc and WordStar, which had similar fates, but which were replaced prior to the period of our data.

10

The Moral

Our message is simple: Good products win. Whether they are lowly mousetraps or high-tech networks, better products prevail in the marketplace. People choose what they want, and what they want survives, at least for a while. Surviving products are imitated and become the norm. They may be improved upon—sometimes by their original provider, and sometimes by someone else. Eventually, when something decidedly better comes along, there is a transition to the new product.

There are, of course, circumstances in which the simple logic of "people choose what they want" is not quite adequate. Some economists have conjectured that when certain kinds of complications intervene, in certain kinds of markets, consumers may be kept from choosing what they want. This conjecture is reasonable enough, and it is important enough. But it is not correct enough.

The most common conjecture is that in those circumstances in which we care not only about the products themselves, but also about other people's decisions regarding those products, we may—all of us—choose the wrong things—things that we would rather not have. We may all choose to use the most popular word processor, but we may all wish the most popular word processor were a different one.

This conjecture raises the possibility of an economic problem. And this possibility can be explored in complicated ways. It can be proven that under particular conditions, bad choices are possible; bad products can prevail. Such proofs do not, of course, establish that the problem does occur—only that it could occur. And as a matter of fact, the proofs don't even establish that the problem could occur in any real world that we live in—only that it is possible to conjure up a situation in which the problem is a logical possibility.

In Part Two, we discussed some of the economic theories that imply the possibility of this particular market failure: the social choice of inferior products, technologies, standards, networks, or what have you. We presented these theories in order to show that they rely on a very restricted conception of how markets work. In these theories, increasing returns appears to lead, almost inevitably, to social choices of products that depend on almost anything but the inherent quality of the products. Our answer to such theories is that they exclude, almost by necessity, the myriad actions that people take to avoid such problems. We cannot, of course, prove that these myriad actions do save the day, every day. We can only suggest that they might save the day, especially when saving the day matters a lot, and especially when saving the day can pay very well.

As consumers, can we figure out what we want? Do we anticipate that others will do the same? If we all really do want to switch to a different word processor, isn't it very likely that we will switch to it? Do people develop habits in their shopping, their planning, and their responses to new things that help them avoid lock-in-style traps? Do companies profit by putting together winning programs of products, prices, contracts, and strategies that overcome the inertia that might otherwise occur? If the answers to these questions are affirmative, then the logical possibility of an economic problem is not enough. We need to be concerned with what really happens.

And thus the claim of market failure becomes, as economists are inclined to say, an empirical issue. (This terminology suggests that some issues are not empirical, a questionable position.) Part Three and chapter 2 of this volume address this empirical issue.

In chapter 2, we present the evidence that the QWERTY keyboard is a good product that succeeded in the marketplace. The claim that QWERTY is an example of lock-in is, or should have been, an issue of serious importance to those who have built a substantial theoretical edifice on top of it. Yet, the claim has prompted surprisingly little investigative effort.

A study purportedly performed by the U.S. Navy has been used as the major evidence to support the claim of QWERTY's inferiority. In an academic paper making the case against QWERTY, a leading economic historian discusses the study but does not provide a citation. As we now know, that economic historian never read the Navy study, which is probably why he doesn't provide a full cite to it. Nor did he attempt to discover whether there were other studies that might have tested keyboard designs. Had he been a little more curious—a little more skeptical—he would have discovered that the author of the Navy study was Dr. August Dvorak, the patent holder and creator of the alternative keyboard. He also would have discovered that a G.S.A. study concluded that the QWERTY design was as good as any of the available substitutes.

What is most unfortunate in this sad bit of academic history is that at this late date, almost a decade after we published our results, the keyboard story is still used by some writers to illustrate and substantiate the lock-in paradigm. The facts become subservient to the theory. That's their story, and they're sticking to it. The facts be damned.

Market-failure theory is a set of possibility theorems: These theorems demonstrate merely that it is possible that the market might fail. The empirical standing of a possibility theorem is unusual in science. For the most part, those who present such theorems acknowledge no obligation to submit to an empirical test. They simply prove that in the world they have assumed, the possibility is there. If they acknowledge an obligation to submit this theory to a test at all, the test is very modest. Since the theory claims only the possibility of something occurring, the theory is endorsed, or validated, if that something can be shown to have happened even once. Of course, one instance might not demonstrate that the phenomenon is important, only that it is possible.

Debunking the keyboard fable—or the stories that have been told about VCRs, operating systems, or other standards—is important because it demonstrates that the market-failure possibility theorems in this literature fail to meet even the most modest of tests. If the theory of market failure is to be taken seriously, and especially if the market-failure claim is to be recognized in public-policy actions, we ought to be able to find at least one clear instance of a lock-in type of market failure. In case after case, however, careful examination shows that there has been no failure. In the real world, good products have won.

Even in the relatively new computer-software markets, in instance after instance, we find corroboration for our simple observation that good products win. The products that have prevailed have always been the products that were regarded as best by software consumers and by the reviewers in specialist magazines. It hasn't mattered whether the producer is Microsoft or somebody else; whether the producer owns the operating system or not. Good products have won. And in particular, Microsoft's products have won when they were good—and have lost when they were not.

Rating quality, of course, is not always easy. Our empirical studies reflect certain methodological choices. First, we argue that the best, for the purposes relevant to economics, does not mean technically best, or thermody-namically most efficient, or artistically most noble. It means economically best. That, in turn, means that the product offers the greatest net value—benefit minus cost—to the consumer, measured in terms of the consumer's own willingness to pay. An automobile engine that costs an extra hundred thousand dollars to return a fuel savings worth a few dollars a year might be more efficient in an engineering sense, but it is not more efficient in an economic sense. Similarly, a piece of software that may be regarded as particularly intriguing or elegant by computer scientists but does not offer useful advantages to users cannot be called "best" in the economic sense. Our claim, therefore, that the best things win might seem preposterous to some scientists, engineers, clergy, artists, or environmentalists—all for different reasons. Our claim may also seem wrong to some economists, but most of them will at least see the claim from the same frame of reference that we do.

In considering computer-software quality, we used published results of magazine reviews and consumer polls as the indicators of quality. This inevitably involves certain maintained hypotheses. First, it gives credit to the reviewers for knowing what they are doing. Second, it assumes, if we are to be consistent with our perspective, that the reviewers' concerns correlate with consumers' concerns. We expect that these assumptions will hold, if only imperfectly, or consumers will cease to purchase magazines that contain these reviews, and publishers will find they can do just as well printing advertising alone.

Whatever the quality of these reviews, they probably do represent the best information available to consumers—and from the lock-in perspective this is highly relevant. Any reasonable definition of economic efficiency requires only that society chooses the best product given the best available information at the time the choice is made. That is to say, using the terminology that we explained in chapter 3, there is no third-degree lock-in if a choice is the best that we can make, given what we can reasonably know when we commit, or renew our commitment, to a product, technology, or standard.

Having assembled our data on performance and market share, we were also able to look at pricing in software markets. Because computer technologies offer what we have termed *instant scalability,* we have witnessed market-share shifts in some software markets that would be quite unusual in any other industry. In software markets, however, a large market share, even an extraordinarily large market share, is not a good predictor of a price increase. On the contrary, where companies have accumulated extraordinarily large market share, prices have often fallen. Specifically, for closely comparable products, Microsoft's prices have been lower in markets where its market shares are higher. Further, in those markets where Microsoft has become the dominant firm, prices have fallen more rapidly than they have in markets where Microsoft is absent or less important. This is strong evidence against the structuralist view of market performance, which holds that monopoly behavior—price elevation—can reliably be predicted from market structure.

Instant scalability creates the opportunity for the best software products to dominate their markets more completely than would be the case in markets where capacity adjusts more slowly and where capacity adjustments are costly and difficult to reverse. This domination, however, appears to be quite fragile. When we looked at the real world, we saw instances in which a firm dominated a market, only to disappear from view. Whatever this may be, it certainly is not lock-in.

Market domination through the action of networks or other increasing returns influences should lead to some other phenomena that are strongly associated with lock-in, tipping, and inertia. But our data show that where a software product was regarded as the best one available, its market share did not build gradually, increasing at an increasing rate; but rather it grew rapidly, increasing quite steadily. This is not tipping or inertia. It is just consumers choosing what they have found to be better.

So we come back to our simple point: Good products win. Bad paths are not chosen, or if they are chosen and they truly are bad, they are overcome. Our finding is that deleterious lock-in, if it exists at all, is not a common occurrence.

Notwithstanding all the economic elaboration that we have presented, there is a simple economic explanation for that finding: An inefficiency is a profit opportunity. By definition, an inefficiency means that there is some feasible change for which the benefits outweigh the costs. That is to say, there exists a potential surplus. The person who can figure out a way to bring about the necessary reallocation and capture some of the net benefit will enjoy a profit. Where property rights are clear and freedom of contract is broad and secure, inefficiencies will face assault from profit-seeking entrepreneurs. For that reason, proofs of existence of inefficiency can never rely on the mechanics of production and consumption alone. Increasing returns are not enough. Networks are not enough. Standards or paths or tipping or inertia are not enough.

Sometimes entrepreneurs will lose in their assaults on unexploited opportunities. When they do, there exists the possibility that there is a feasible improvement to economic allocation that uses some form of collective action, perhaps action that uses the power of government. But market failure ought to be a very specific and very worldly claim. Policymakers shouldn't go about correcting markets until they have concrete proof that markets have failed. The abstract possibility of market failure is an inadequate basis for the making of real-world policy.

The history, both of the economy and of economic thought, that we have presented in this volume offers insights about what economists do and about how many grains of salt should be taken with economists' claims. Economists teach their students, beginning with the first principles of economics classes, that the goal of economics is to figure out the logic behind what consumers and producers do—not to pass judgment on whether consumers and producers are handling their private affairs correctly and to correct them when we find them to be in error. Economists learn that when marketplace actions seem like errors at first pass, it is probably the observers, and not the actors, who are confused. Behaviors that persist for a long time are given some deference. Those that persist for a long time probably do so for a reason

Which is to say that economists are not entirely without humility. We respect the consumer in his realm and the producer in his. But when we add up all the pieces and look at social organizations, we tend to be less restrained, less respectful. At the aggregate level—markets, countries, governments—economists have little trouble finding fault with things and proposing improvements.

There is a long history of economists and biologists learning from each other. Models of natural selection and models of optimization work back and forth between the disciplines. But biologists manage to regard their subject matter with a good bit more humility than economists do. It would be surprising to learn of an anatomist examining a human eye, for example, and declaring, "What a stupid design," or possibly, "I could have done much better."

Many of the social systems that economists study and attempt to reform are institutions that have long histories. They have stood the test of time; they have withstood competition from alternatives. This isn't to say that they are perfect, but only that they deserve thorough and thoughtful study before we declare them lacking. We should spend more than an afternoon shaping a stylized version of an institution before we head off into theorem proving. We should keep in mind that institutions do adapt, that actors do act, to exploit an unrealized opportunity.

Networks are among those long enduring social institutions. In this volume, we, like many others, have emphasized the connection of networks to our newest technologies. But networks are actually quite old—older, perhaps, than some of the economic institutions that we think are most fundamental. Older, say, than money or prices. The earliest human social structures—families, clans, tribes, and kingdoms—are all networks of sorts. The leader of the tribe figured out how to internalize the externalities of hunting and lived the life of Riley, relatively speaking. His modern counterpart assembles patent pools. Both work because they capture potential gains from cooperation.

Our job as economists, or at least our first order of business, is not to figure out how wrong our social institutions are. Instead, our charge is to figure out exactly how these institutions work, to recognize, if we can, the richness of the systems that time and humanity have developed. In short, economists ought to give institutions, which are the product of individuals' actions, some of the same deference they give to individuals themselves.

Sure enough, we will "discover" problems with networks if we pretend that they work according to economists' most stylized version of a market: Many actors selling homogeneous products at fixed prices; no false trading; no advertising; no give-aways; and no refunds. On that stage, there are many tragedies. We will find many theoretical inefficiencies if our theory assumes away all of the things that people do to overcome the problems they encounter in the real world. In that context it is easy to prove an inefficiency—a market failure. "What a stupid design," we say. "I could have done much better." Such a claim is personally rewarding. It inflates the ego, it empowers the bureaucracy, it discredits the successful, and best of all, it leads to tenure. The public has a right to be wary.

In this volume, we describe the complications that are introduced by networks, standards, and increasing returns. These complications, we note, are likely to give rise to adaptive institutions and strategies that fall outside the economists' textbook model of perfect competition. We have taken a stab at explaining some of the adaptations and strategies that have emerged in this environment. We look forward to others' stabs.

Certainly the adaptive institutions and strategies that have emerged do look strange indeed from a worldview that is taken a bit too literally from an intermediate microeconomics textbook. In the real world, information is not perfect; the future is not known with certainty; products are not perfectly homogeneous; and sometimes what we like is influenced by what others like. Constructive behavior in such a world will be different from constructive behavior in a textbook world. Some will find such behavior puzzling; others will be sure it is illegal. Or ought to be.[1] More advanced texts and more advanced models may bring some of these complications into the analysis, but often these advanced models differ only in the level of mathematical sophistication brought into the analysis, and often the economics is subservient to the limitations of the mathematical tools. We can only begin to have confidence that any of these models are correct after they have been tested and found to have predictive power, a step that has been forgotten in much of the current literature.

Problems are inevitable when a policymaker looks to such untested abstract models as benchmarks for what he ought to see in the real world. When he looks at the real world, he's going to see many behaviors that are absent in these models. He will, for example, see advertising. Advertising, of course, has no place in the simple textbook model of the competitive economy. In that textbook world, people know what they want, where to find it, and what it costs. Resources spent on advertising, judged against that textbook benchmark, are wasteful at best, manipulative at worst. A policymaker who was just a bit too proud of his textbook knowledge might therefore decide that things could be better if advertising were outlawed. When our policymaker looks at the real world, he's going to see decision makers puzzling over what prices to charge. In the simple textbook model of the competitive economy, price is obvious, no one needs to puzzle over it. Our policymaker may therefore take such calculation to be a symptom of monopoly. It may even be taken as proof. Such leaps to conclusions are not as unlikely as they might seem. Not too long ago, the courts, acting as policymakers, looked at a number of real-world industries that were, by today's standards, mildly concentrated. Taking their cue from the economics of that time, the courts concluded that those industries should be restructured.

Today, economic policymaking falls into the same trap. Textbook versions of perfect competition do not accommodate increasing returns, networks, or standards. The models that examine these issues have often done so in the same rarified world as the textbooks, where entrepreneurs play no role and consumers have very restricted foresight. These models do not contemplate that there are differences in product quality that matter to people. They do not contemplate actions that people take to facilitate co-ordination. They do not contemplate the sort of instant scalability that allows a best product to capture a market quickly—and subsequently to be replaced by a better one. They do not contemplate that the public might be well served by efforts, perhaps costly and extensive efforts, to articulate, establish, advance, and maintain a common standard.

Against the backdrop of these models, many market behaviors that we see today might well seem out of place. They may seem anticompetitive, inefficient, and even unfair. From the perspective offered by that textbook model of the ideal economy, we might well be confused by strategic alliances, by technology-sharing agreements, by long-term guarantees, or by the continuous addition of functionality to a product. From that perspective, we might well suspect that the sorts of market shares that we see in many high-technology markets will lead only to trouble. From that perspective, the creation of families of products might well look like monopoly extension.

All this calls for economists to recognize the limitations of their models and to work at understanding the world a little better. For policymakers the implications ought to be quite sobering. They must be careful not to enshrine our imperfect understanding of markets in something as real-world as public policy.

Our claim is that good products win. The rival claim of some economic models is that good products might not win. Instead, bad products, high prices, burdensome bundling might all be "protected" by network and other effects. There is a world of evidence to support our view. There is not a single clear documented example to support the rival claim.

The policy implication of the rival claim is that winners might more appropriately be chosen by policymakers than by people making choices in the free market. But that implication is as flawed as the theory behind it. We return to our simple truth: In the market, good products win. And we can add a corollary: When good products win, the public wins. The policy implication of all this is that governments can help ensure that consumers get the best products by keeping government impediments out of the way of entrepreneurs competing to establish their mousetraps in the marketplace.

NOTES TO CHAPTER 10

1. Several economists have observed that the competitive model is somewhat distant from perfect competitions. Hayek makes this point in a number of his writings. Our argument here, however, is most closely related to the argument in Demsetz (1982)

Appendix A
Networks, Antitrust Economics, and the Case Against Microsoft

Revolutions in science and technology, while bringing benefits to large numbers of people, also bring stresses of various sorts.[1] New technologies can alter the scale of business activities, the geographic distribution of these activities, the types of firms that are involved in production and distribution, and the distribution of wealth. The benefits are many: Consumers may enjoy cheaper goods and new products; firms that implement the new technology may make very substantial profits; and workers may enjoy higher wages, new types of careers, and generally expanded opportunities. At the same time, some businesses and workers will lose as new skills and methods of commerce supplant old ones.

In these circumstances, interested parties have often enlisted legislation or regulation to preserve old interests or defend new ones. The historical motivations for U.S. antitrust law have been at least in part an attempt by various parties to defend their stakes in the economy. The antitrust debates over new computer technologies in general, and Microsoft in particular, are consistent with this pattern. In particular, today, as in the past, there are calls for restrictions on the leading firms in new technology industries. Although the focus for scrutiny is Microsoft, the effects are likely to reach much further. As with past generations of antitrust law, the precedent and enforcement practice reached in the current debate are likely to have a wide and long-lasting influence.

In the policy debates surrounding the antitrust campaign against Microsoft, both the Justice Department and various parties that have aligned against Microsoft have invoked some of the theories of networks and lock-in that we discussed in the body of the book. For example, as we noted in chapter 1, Franklin Fisher, the government's economic expert in the Microsoft case, argues that network effects "protect" Microsoft against competition.

245

Widespread acceptance of the theories that we have presented and criticized in this volume would necessitate a radical rethinking of antitrust policy. It also appears that these theories are holding considerable sway in today's antitrust debates. For example, *Business Week* reports:

> Instead of basing his attack against Microsoft on outdated economic theories that demonize bigness, Assistant Attorney General Joel I. Klein is relying on a developing body of antitrust thinking that warns that the threat of anticompetitive behavior could be even greater in high technology than in traditional industries. This research on "network externalities" deserves to be taken seriously. . . . The Microsoft case is one of the first ever in which Justice has made use of network theory.[2]

A writer at the *Wall Street Journal*, a publication not known for embracing radical expansions of antitrust law, has fallen for lock-in theory. Alan Murray recently opined, on that paper's front page, that:

> [H]igh-tech industries might be more susceptible to antitrust problems than their low-tech brethren. That's because consumers often feel a need to buy the product that everyone else is using, even if it isn't the best, so their equipment is compatible. Economists call this "network externalities."
>
> It's why most people use a keyboard that begins clumsily with the letters QWERTY; why most videos are now available only in VHS format; and why Windows has become the dominant operating system.[3]

These new theories provide a convenient solution for those who would bring antitrust claims to bear against market leaders such as Microsoft. Those "outdated economic theories," so cavalierly dismissed in *Business Week*, might fail to support antitrust enforcement against the current generation of high-tech market leaders. Standard theories of monopoly, which have long provided what economic foundation there was for antitrust, hold that monopoly restricts output in order to elevate prices. This, from the perspective of those "outdated theories," is the social harm of monopoly. What we seem to see in high-technology markets, however, are falling prices and increased quantities, even as market shares of the market leaders become extremely large.[4] Absent an allegation of high prices, antitrust authorities need to rely on these new lock-in theories in order to provide some economic support for their actions against such high-technology firms.

In the following, we first present some of the history of the conflict between Microsoft and the U.S. Department of Justice. Following that, we consider the economics of the allegations and doctrines that make up the case against Microsoft, with particular reference to the economics that we have discussed in the body of this book.

Microsoft's Dispute with the Justice Department

Historically, new antitrust doctrines have developed in connection with the big cases of the times. These big cases most often involved the biggest and most successful companies. The pattern of attacking success is being repeated today.

Microsoft's antitrust problems began with a government investigation of Microsoft's pricing of software sold to original equipment manufacturers (OEMs). Microsoft agreed to end the disputed practices in a highly publicized 1994 consent decree with the Department of Justice (DoJ). Whether these practices were anticompetitive or not, there can be little doubt that these practices had little to do with Microsoft's successes in the market.[5]

The consent decree did little, however, to end Microsoft's legal problems with the DoJ. When Microsoft attempted to purchase Intuit, a maker of financial software, the DoJ opposed the deal. In a highly publicized decision, the consent decree itself was temporarily overturned by Judge Stanley Sporkin's decision, which itself was later overturned. Sporkin's decision rejecting the consent decree appears to be the first time that path-dependence theory had such an explicit influence on policy.

There were other skirmishes between Microsoft and the DoJ as well. The DoJ examined Microsoft's inclusion of the Microsoft Network icon on the Windows 95 desktop, claiming that consumers would be unwittingly forced into acceptance of this product to the detriment of competition in the online service industry.

A later twist in the DoJ's continuing investigation was its interest in Microsoft's channel partners on its "active desktop."[6] The antitrust theory behind this investigation is still unclear, but appears to be related to the exclusionary claims being made against Microsoft with regard to Internet Explorer.

Many of the DoJ's allegations against Microsoft concern the competition between Netscape and Microsoft that began in 1996. This investigation erupted into litigation in 1998 when the DoJ accused Microsoft of an antitrust violation, apparently because of Microsoft's inclusion of its Web browser in the operating system. We use the term *apparently* in the last sentence because it is not clear to us that the DoJ has a simple consistent theme in its case. Many other issues and claims have been raised in the trial, such as potential splitting of markets by ersatz competitors, predatory behavior, exclusionary agreements, and so forth.

Newspaper accounts and public statements by Department of Justice officials and other participants prior to the trial indicated that the economics behind these investigations were either partly or completely based on the theories of path dependence. The government's expert economist, Franklin Fisher, considers network effects to be a very important element in his analysis and testimony. Perhaps deserving the credit or blame for promoting network effects into the antitrust arena is a series of briefs prepared by Gary Reback, a lawyer working for several of Microsoft's competitors, along with two economists who have played prominent roles in this literature: Brian Arthur and Garth Saloner.

These briefs actually went much farther than the economics literature has gone. Reback does not stop with the traditional path-dependence claim that a market-based economy is likely to choose all sorts of wrong products. Nor does he stop with the claim that innovation might be eliminated in the computing industry. Instead, Reback portrays Microsoft as an evil empire intent on nothing less than world domination. To hear him tell it, the American Way of Life will be imperiled if the government does not rein in Microsoft. Lest you think we exaggerate, consider this from the amicus brief: "It is difficult to imagine that in an open society such as this one with multiple information sources, a single company could seize sufficient control of information transmission so as to constitute a threat to the underpinnings of a free society. But such a scenario is a realistic (and perhaps probable) outcome."[7]

These are fantastic claims indeed. They were repeated at the conference on Microsoft held by Ralph Nader before the start of the Microsoft trial.[8] Brian Arthur, Gary Reback, and Garth Saloner all made presentations. Although these claims do not appear in the government's case, they seem to be just under the surface.

Antitrust Doctrines and Network Technologies

Both the Justice Department and some of Microsoft's private competitors have used theories of lock-in to support a call for heightened antitrust scrutiny of Microsoft. By itself, lock-in would seem not to constitute an antitrust offense. There is nothing in the law that makes it a crime to have technologies that are less than the best available or less than the best imaginable.[9] Instead, lock-in theories offer an alternative way to claim harm in the absence of the usual monopoly problem of elevated prices and restricted outputs. Also lock-in stories offer new life and a contemporary spin on old antitrust doctrines.

The following two subsections consider some of the antitrust issues that have been raised in the software industry. The first subsection describes why monopoly leverage requires special conditions that make it nearly impossible to increase profits. The second describes why no smart monopolist would try predatory bundling.

Monopoly Leverage, Tie-ins, and Bundling

In theory, monopoly leverage occurs when a firm uses its monopoly in one industry to win a monopoly in another industry. Tie-in sales and bundling are contractual practices that are sometimes alleged to facilitate monopoly leverage, but tie-ins and bundling do not have to create new monopoly to be profitable. Nor do tie-ins necessarily harm consumers.[10] In fact, as this subsection explains, the theory of monopoly leverage requires so many special conditions that it seems certain to remain just that: a theoretical problem.

Economists have long been skeptical that monopoly leverage is either feasible or profitable. In most circumstances, forcing consumers to purchase some other product so as to create a second monopoly will not add to a firm's profits. A monopolist can instead simply extract the value of its monopoly through the pricing of the good in the market where it has its first monopoly.

Suppose, for example, that a firm held a monopoly on oil furnaces. Such a monopoly might be quite profitable; oil furnaces are useful things that offer some advantages over other kinds of furnaces. The monopolist's ability to maximize profits would face some limits, of course, such as the availability of substitutes like propane and electric heating.[11] Still, the monopolist could devise a pricing system that captures the extra value of using an oil furnace rather than a competing source of heat. The lower the price of heating oil relative to the price of propane or electricity, the greater that value would be. If the furnace monopolist were to become the oil monopolist too, he might raise the price of heating oil, but that would only reduce what he could extract through the furnace price.

Consider this analogy: Regardless of whether or not it worries you that someone has a key to the front door of your house, it would not worry you more if that person also has a key to your back door. Nevertheless, the idea that the second monopoly could be used for something has intuitive appeal. Even if the monopoly in furnaces could be used to extract everything that can be extracted from the furnace users, could not a monopoly in heating oil be used to extract something from people who use heating oil for another purpose? It turns out that, yes, there is a circumstance in which a second monopoly is worth something. That circumstance is a very limited one, however. If the furnace monopolist could also monopolize the heating oil industry, he could extract additional monopoly rents from heating-oil users who were not also his furnace customers.

The question then arises whether one monopoly could ever be extended to capture customers of solely another market. The answer again is yes, it is possible—but, again, only under very special circumstances. *If* there were economies of scale in the heating oil industry and *if* too few customers bought heating oil for non-furnace uses to support a separate supply of heating oil, then the furnace seller could lever his monopoly in furnaces into a monopoly in heating oil by preventing furnace customers from buying heating oil from other sources. By assumption, the non-furnace customers would not offer a large enough market to support any independent oil supplier and the furnace monopolist could then extract new monopoly rents in this other market. This explanation of leverage is sometimes referred to as *market foreclosure*.[12] Ironically, the larger the furnace monopolist relative to the heating oil industry, the less likely it will benefit from monopolizing heating oil because it will already have nearly all the potential customers.[13]

This explanation shows that there is a theoretical possibility of harmful monopoly leverage, but that it requires very special conditions. The levered market must be big enough to matter, but not so big as to allow competitive independent suppliers to survive. There must be some economies of scale in the levered market, but not enough to have caused prior monopolization of the market. In short, leveraging can be viewed as the

Goldilocks theory of monopoly extension—everything has to be just the right size.

Do the facts of the Microsoft case fit within the leverage story at all? If Microsoft requires each customer to buy one copy of some other Microsoft product, this would, in and of itself, add nothing to its profits. That sort of tie-in sale with fixed proportions has long been understood to offer no advantage to the monopolist.[14, 15] This is because the fixed proportions imply that the products can only be used together, as would be the case for left and right shoes. In that case, where consumers really are buying *pairs* of shoes, it is fairly easy to show that a monopolistic seller of left-only or right-only shoes can capture all the profit that there is to be captured as long as the other shoe type is sold competitively. So the issue must revolve around some variable proportion story, whether Microsoft could crowd out any rivals that sell to customers who do not use Microsoft's own operating system.

Here the application to Microsoft of the market foreclosure theory runs into trouble. If the products that are allegedly crowded out by Microsoft's bundling are products that run only under the Windows operating system, then monopoly leverage offers Microsoft no advantage.

To illustrate this point, consider a hypothetical example of successful tying-foreclosure using personal software products, such as Quicken and Microsoft Money. Both are sold in the Macintosh market and the Windows market. *If* Microsoft were to build Microsoft Money into the Windows operating system, *and if* this eliminated Quicken in the Windows market, *and if* the Macintosh market were too small to allow a product like Quicken to be produced at reasonable average cost in that market alone, *and if* Microsoft continued to sell the product separately in the Macintosh market (now at a monopoly price), *and if* there were few additional costs for Microsoft in creating a Macintosh version, *then and only then*, would Microsoft benefit from leveraging monopoly.

Has this occurred? Does Microsoft sell in the Macintosh market disk compression, backup, fax software, or any other program that is included in the Windows operating system? The only product that comes to mind is a Macintosh version of Internet Explorer. But Microsoft *gives away* this product in the Macintosh market, and promises a permanent price of zero. If Microsoft sticks to its promise, it cannot profit from including the browser in the operating system. Even then, the other required conditions for market foreclosure (the Macintosh market being too small to support

Navigator and the costs of Microsoft creating a Macintosh version not being too large) may very well fail to obtain.

A simple rule that would prevent this type of foreclosure would be to prevent Microsoft from including in its operating system any program that it sells separately in another market. But although such a rule might remove the risk of this sort of market leverage, it also would penalize customers in other markets, who would be excluded from the benefits of these programs in cases where no market leverage was contemplated. Given all the special conditions required for successful leveraging, it would be unwise to implement such a rule without further investigation of the potential harm of denying Microsoft products to consumers in tied markets.

Predatory Bundling

The current allegation against Microsoft concerns predatory use of its ownership of the Windows operating system. The specific allegation is that Microsoft's integration of its browser into the operating system is largely predatory, aimed at forcing other firms (Netscape) out of the browser market. The implications of this issue, however, extend well beyond the browser market, and extend to the very concept of what an operating system can be, and the nature of progress in the software industry.

Antitrust law defines as predatory those actions that are inconsistent with profit-maximizing behavior except when they succeed in driving a competitor out of business. In predatory pricing, for example, a would-be monopolist allegedly charges a price that is so low that other firms cannot sell their outputs at prices that will cover even their variable costs. These other firms are then forced either into bankruptcy or to exit the industry because they have become unprofitable. Upon completing the predatory episode, the predator then gets to enjoy the benefits of monopoly pricing. It should be noted that during the predatory episode, consumers benefit greatly from the low prices, so it is only the later monopoly pricing that causes harm to consumers.

Economists are generally skeptical of claims that price cuts or other actions have predatory intent because they have determined, both in theory and practice, that predatory campaigns are unlikely to have profitable endings. First, the predatory action is likely to be more expensive for the predator than for the prey. The predator cannot just cut price; it must also meet market demand at the lower price. Otherwise, customers will be forced to patronize the prey, even if at higher prices. If the predator is a large firm, it stands to lose money at a faster rate than the prey. Second, even if the predation succeeds in bankrupting the prey, there is no guarantee that a reestablished firm will not just reenter the industry once the predator has established monopoly pricing. If there are fixed investments in the industry, such as durable specialized equipment, the predator cannot establish monopoly prices as long as these durable assets can return to the market. If there are no durable assets, then the prey can cheaply exit the industry and re-enter when monopoly prices return. Either way, the predatory episode drains the predator while imposing uncertain burdens on the prey.

Another problem with predation is that almost any action that a firm takes to become more attractive to consumers can be alleged to be predatory. If customers like something a firm is doing, its competitors will not. In the most elementary case, a price cut or product improvement will damage the prospects for some competitor. It bears noting that most of the alleged cases of predation have been demonstrated to be false.[16]

Predatory bundling, like predatory pricing, is a simple idea that ultimately has the same failings as pure predation. If a firm with a controlling share of one product bundles in some other product, competitors who sell the bundled-in product will have to compete with a product that, to the consumer, has a zero cost. If Microsoft includes in its operating system a piece of software that competes with other vendors in what had been a separate market, Microsoft ensures that virtually all purchasers of computers then have a copy of the new software.

Suppose Microsoft bundles a fax program into Windows 98. If Microsoft's fax program, relative to its cost, is better than other fax products, then the bundling cannot really be predatory. The Microsoft product would win in the marketplace anyway, and adding it to the operating system costs less than its value to consumers. If the product is worth more to consumers than the costs of creating it, then bundling will also be profitable without any exclusionary consequences. In contrast, if Microsoft's fax program, again considering its cost, is inferior to alternatives or provides less value than its cost, then Microsoft would profit only if bundling caused other firms to exit the market and Microsoft were able to raise the price of the operating system by the now higher implicit monopoly price for its fax product.

As a strategy, however, predatory bundling has the same liabilities as predatory pricing. As in predatory pricing, Microsoft stands to lose money (relative to not including the fax software) faster than its rivals do if its fax program costs more to produce than its value to consumers. Moreover, a rival with a superior fax program could keep the product on the market for a price that reflects the advantages that it offers over the bundled product. The rival could not charge more than that because the Windows consumer would already have the inferior fax program. The rival could still capture the extra value that its own intellectual property contributes, however, especially since it would enjoy low marginal costs of "producing" (that is, copying) its software and the marketing edge of an installed customer base. Although it may lose profits or market share, the rival will retire its fax program only if it is inferior to Microsoft's.

From a social or consumer welfare perspective, then, Microsoft's bundling action would do no harm. The rival software is a fixed asset in the industry; it does not wear out. In the extreme case, a bankrupt producer might put its fax program on the Web, making it freely available to all. This would limit what consumers would be willing to pay for the program bundled into Windows 98 to its extra value, which is zero. Thus Microsoft would be unable to charge a higher price for the bundled software despite having incurred the costs of creating the fax program. Microsoft would lose money and fail to monopolize the market. Furthermore, the creative talents used to make the rival fax program still exist, ready for some other firm to hire should Microsoft ever achieve a monopoly price on the fax program.

Of course, an antitrust enforcer might reply that the operating system producer has distribution or coordination advantages that an independent rival lacks. But, if these are real advantages that outweigh any quality advantages of the rival, then it is efficient for the operating system producer to bundle its fax program.

All this suggests that bundling, as a predatory action, is unlikely to succeed. Furthermore, the software industry has very important nonpredatory reasons to bundle functions into operating systems and other software products. As we explain below, new sales of software will require continual additions to functionality.

In the case of Netscape, antitrust enforcers allege that Microsoft is not interested in defeating the Netscape browser so much as destroying Netscape as a company. Industry pundits have often theorized that Web browsers might constitute a means of establishing a new operating system. Netscape, in this scenario, constitutes a threat to Microsoft's position in the operating system market. Regardless of the technical reasonableness of this claim, however, it runs into the same problems as other allegations of predation.

Here, as elsewhere, predation would not destroy the durable assets of the prey. Netscape's software will hardly disappear if Microsoft bundles a browser into Windows. Indeed, Netscape has already made the source code for its Navigator program publicly available. Even if Microsoft still tried to destroy Netscape in order to protect Windows' market share, it would ultimately fail. Any of Microsoft's several large and vigorous competitors, such as IBM or Sun, would happily purchase Netscape, or hire its engineers, if they thought that by so doing they could share some of Microsoft's enviable profits. In fact, AOL in combination with Sun, has done just that.

The Rate of Innovation

Putative Dangers

One concern that has been raised by the Justice Department, in the Judiciary Committee hearings, by some journalists, and by several path-dependence theorists, is that Microsoft's dominant position in the market will somehow inhibit innovation. The suggestion is that Microsoft will be able to so dominate the software market that no small firms will dare compete with it. Firms will be unwilling to create new products in any market that is likely to attract Microsoft's attention, especially in products that are possible additions to the operating system. It is not clear that current antitrust law addresses such concerns. If valid, however, and if not addressed by antitrust law, they might encourage new legislation. Of course, the impact of such legislation would probably reach beyond the computer industry.

Concerns about lock-in drive the accusations against Microsoft. Consumers are viewed as being so locked in to Microsoft's products that even if the Wintel platform fell far behind the cutting edge of computer technology, no other combination of an operating system, applications, and support could displace it. Obviously, no one can empirically disprove the claim that products that might have been created would have been better than currently existing products. Instead, the analysis here focuses on whether lock-in theory correctly concludes that Microsoft will stifle innovation in the computer industry.

Certainly there are instances where Microsoft has incorporated programs into the operating system where the former providers of such programs have gone on to other things. Disk compression and memory management programs are two examples. Fax programs, backup programs, and disk-defragmenting programs are counterexamples, where the inclusion of such programs in the operating system has not eliminated the separate market. The difference appears to be in whether the programs Microsoft includes in its operating system are as good as the separate programs or not. When Microsoft produces a product as good or better than the competition, the separate market usually does disappear. It is difficult, however to conceive of consumer harm in this case.

The general claim that innovation will suffer if Microsoft is allowed to grow and add programs to the operating system has several shortcomings. For one thing, it wrongly assumes that programmers hired by Microsoft lack or lose creativity. It proves nothing to observe that small startup companies generate creative ideas more frequently than Microsoft does. There are fifteen times as many outside programmers developing programs for Windows as there are programmers working for Microsoft. Instead, it assumes that Microsoft could not, or would not, use these programmers to produce as much creative activity as they would produce if they continued to work for smaller companies.

Firms benefit from good new ideas. Profits will increase when these new products are brought to market. Monopolists benefit just as much from an extra dollar of profit as do competitive firms. The argument that large firms might innovate less than small firms do usually relies on some variation of the view that large firms are fat and lazy. That is, that they do not innovate because they do not have to. Still, a dollar is a dollar. Most investors are just as eager for their large-firm stocks to perform well as they are for their small-firm stocks to perform well. For the fat-and-lazy condition to hold, it must be that large firms with dispersed ownership of their stock do not have the same incentives to maximize shareholder value and profits as do small firms, which are usually closely held. This real possibility is known as the problem of separation of ownership and control.

Although it is conceivable that large firms produce less innovation than small firms do (adjusting for size) this has been investigated at length in the economics literature with no clear consensus.[17] If there were a reason to believe that the software industry would be different from most other industries in this regard, it would tend to support a view that large software firms will continue to innovate, in large part because of the entrepreneurial character of these firms and the hands-on activity of the largest stockholders who usually still work within the firm.[18] The ownership of Microsoft and most other high-tech firms is not widely disbursed. For example, Bill Gates owns almost 25 percent of Microsoft and several other early Microsoft investors own very substantial stakes. This may in fact explain why Microsoft is still considered such an intense competitor.

Alternatively, it is vaguely suggested that Microsoft stifles innovation because it copies software ideas from others, leaving these other firms no reward for their efforts. If there were any truth to this claim, the problem would appear to lie in intellectual property law, not in any potential monopoly power on the part of Microsoft. After all, if Microsoft could copy the ideas of its rivals, so could a host of other large (or small) firms in the industry, in each instance lowering the profits of the innovator, large or small.[19]

It would be a serious problem if innovators in software were not being properly rewarded for their efforts. The purpose of intellectual property laws is to allow innovators to collect economic rewards for their efforts. Without such laws, imitators could take a free ride off the efforts of innovators and produce similar products at lower cost, driving true innovators out of business. So, while deserving investigation, these problems do not seem fundamental in any way to Microsoft, or its ownership of the operating system. Perhaps a reevaluation of intellectual property laws would be in order. But this claim seems to have little to do with antitrust.

There are some factual matters that do not seem consistent with the claim that Microsoft reduces innovation. Microsoft's behavior toward its developers, for example, does not seem to square with the claim that it is intent on driving out independent software producers:

> Microsoft doesn't court only the powers from other industries. It's also spending $85 million this year ministering to the needs of 300,000 computer software developers. It subsidizes trade-show space for hundreds of partners. And it's not above lavishing attention on small companies when it needs their support. . . . "The platforms that succeed are the ones that appeal to developers," admits Alan Baratz, president of Sun Microsystem Inc.'s JavaSoft division. He calls Microsoft's hold on the developer community its "crown jewel."[20]

More broadly, there seems to be a paucity of evidence to support the concern that the pace of innovation is insufficiently rapid. The pace of innovation in the computer industry is generally regarded with some awe. Certainly, the Windows market does not appear to have suffered from stifled development of applications.[21]

Finally, there seem to be tremendous rewards to those who do innovate in this industry. Even in the instance of Netscape, a supposed victim of Microsoft's power, the founders walked away with hundreds of millions of dollars. Does this discourage others from taking the same path? Unless and until careful research answers these sorts of questions, any antitrust action would be premature and potentially dangerous to the software industry and the economy as a whole.

A Real Danger to Innovation

The nature of software markets requires that software producers continually add functionality to their products. Unlike most other products, software never wears out. If Big Macs never change, McDonald's can keep selling them because consumers still want to purchase Big Macs that are just like the ones that they ate the day before. This is true for most goods, which eventually need replacement. But because software lasts forever, with no diminution in quality, there is no reason for consumers to purchase a word processor or operating system more than once unless new improved versions come to market. Undoubtedly, improvement will mean additional functionality.

To aid in understanding this, consider what it means to improve software. Software could be made to run faster and perhaps more intuitively, with no additional functionality. But this is not likely to win over many new customers. First, consumers will discover that speed improvements are likely to come when they replace their old computers with faster ones. Further, although intuitive interfaces are useful, practice overcomes inherent design imperfections. So the natural inclination of consumers would be to stick with any familiar version of a program (or operating system) unless the newer version could perform some useful tasks not available in the old version. This requires adding functionality not found in previous versions.

Added functionality can be seen in every category of software. Word-processors have far more functionality than they used to—spelling and grammar checkers, mail-merge programs, and thesauruses represent only a small portion of the additional functions that were not included with the original generation of word processors. Spreadsheets, database programs, and nearly every other category of program also have far more functionality than before.[22] That is one reason why new software seems to fill our ever-expanding hard drives, which have hundreds or thousands of times the storage capacity of earlier machines.

The consumer benefits in many ways from this added functionality—in spite of the gripes often heard by some reluctant upgraders. These large programs almost always cost far less than the sum of the prices that the individual component products used to command. The various components also tend to work together far better then separate components because they are made for each other. If it were not the case, consumers would not purchase new generations of software products.

As this process of adding functionality to programs continues, it is possible that the number of small companies specializing in add-ons will shrink. But is this any reason to prevent creators of word processors from including grammar checkers and thesauruses? Should the producers of dominant programs be forbidden to add functionality while producers of less successful programs are allowed to add new functions? That hardly seems a recipe for success. Do we really believe that innovation was retarded because add-on companies feared that they might have been put out of business? Do we even know if they have been put out of business? That those programmers are no longer working on new ideas? Again, questionable logic and a dearth of evidence make these claims suspect.

Yet it appears that some of Microsoft's critics, including those within the government, have proposed freezing the operating system, putting in jeopardy any additional added functionality. If this proposal were accepted for the operating system, it would also seem to apply to other categories of software. The results would be disastrous for software producers, who would have no new sales except to new computer users; for computer manufacturers, who would find little demand for more capable hardware; and most importantly for users, who would be forced to use seriously crippled software. The proposal to freeze Windows reflects a view that all the useful things have already been invented. Few proposed antitrust policies are as dangerous as this one.

Rights to the Desktop: The Irrelevance of the "Browser Wars"

At the Senate hearings, and in the media, considerable attention has been given to the claim that Microsoft's desire to prevent original equipment manufacturers (OEMs) from removing the Internet Explorer icon from the desktop was somehow inimical to competition. This section explains why Microsoft and OEMs might each want to control the placement of desktop icons and provides an economic framework for deciding who should be allowed to control the desktop icons. Ultimately, though, it turns out that icon placement should probably not matter even to the computer and software industry, much less to antitrust enforcers.

Control of the desktop might be valuable because, as a practical matter, all computer users see the desktop. In principle, desktop placements of "advertisements," whether a program or a message, could be sold to companies interested in such exposure. For example, assume that an icon for America Online appears on the desktop. Consumers interested in an online service might just click on the icon and begin the process of becoming an America Online customer. Knowing this, a company such as America Online might be willing to pay the controller of the desktop for a good placement of its icon.[23]

Assume for the moment, then, that these icon placements are indeed valuable. The next subsection explains why, nonetheless, regulators should not care whether Microsoft or OEMs control icon placement. Following that, the discussion critically reexamines the assumption that control of icons should matter even to the computer industry.

A Simple Theory of "Desktop Rights"

If placing icons on the desktop can generate revenues, it should not be surprising that both OEMs and the owner of the operating system (Microsoft) each will claim the right to place the icons. Economic analysis allows us to examine whether it makes any difference who has this right. It also may provide some guidance as to who should get this right.

The Coase theorem can help to explain the tradeoffs involved.[24] If the rights to place desktop icons were well defined, and if there were no transactions costs or wealth effects,[25] the Coase theorem tells us that regardless of who initially has these rights, they would end up where they have the greatest value.

Consider the following example. If the rights to sell desktop placement were worth $5 to Microsoft and $10 to OEMs, then OEMs would wind up controlling the desktop icons regardless of who initially had the rights. If Microsoft initially controlled the desktop, OEMs would be willing to pay up to $10 to Microsoft for these rights, and Microsoft would be better off selling the rights to OEMs. It would do this by raising the price of the operating system by more than $5 (but no more than the $10 that OEMs would pay) and granting OEMs the right to place the icons.

If, on the other hand, OEMs initially control desktop placements, Microsoft would be willing to lower the price of the operating system by up to $5 in exchange for the right to control icon placements. OEMs would prefer to keep the rights themselves, however, because they can generate more than $5 in revenues by maintaining this control. In either case, OEMs wind up with the rights, and both parties share the $10 in extra revenue brought about by icon-placement sales. Although the two parties might be expected to fight over the rights, it makes no difference to the rest of us who gets the rights. By analogy, as almost all microeconomics textbooks explain, if the government subsidizes gasoline purchases it makes no difference whether automobile drivers or service stations receive the subsidy, because in either case the subsidy would be shared in exactly the same way.

Sometimes the assumptions of the Coase theorem are not met. For example, if negotiations between OEMs and Microsoft were not feasible, efficiency considerations would require that the property rights be assigned to the party who can generate the highest value for desktop placements.[26] Because Microsoft and OEMs are already negotiating over other aspects of the desktop (e.g., price), however, there is little reason to believe that the market will not work efficiently. Because this is a matter of contract, property rights can be defined and transacted within the contract.

Thus, the current anxiety regarding desktop placements is misplaced. As long as the parties freely enter into new contracts, neither party will benefit from a legal stipulation of who initially controls the desktop. It should not matter at all to the government who has the rights.

The reader may naturally ask, "If it makes no difference, why is there fighting over who places the icons?" There are two answers. First, there is little evidence that Microsoft and OEMs disagree. It is Microsoft's competitors who are complaining. Second, it is not unusual in such circumstances for there to be contract disputes or strategic behavior. Two parties can negotiate a contract, then subsequently dispute their understanding of the terms of that contract. If, for example, OEMs are receiving a lower price from Microsoft because Microsoft thought it controlled desktop placement, but now OEMs have a chance to sell icon placement while remaining under a fixed contractual price for Windows, it would not be surprising that a dispute would arise.

Is Icon Placement Valuable?

In order for icon placement to be valuable, it must generate future revenues. America Online benefits in the previous example because consumers could not use its services without paying a monthly fee. Having its icon on the desktop increased the chances that consumers would sign up for the service.

For a typical software product to be on the desktop, however, it is usually the case that the software is already installed on the computer, and thus already purchased. The icon placement only increases its likelihood of use. The only additional benefits to the software producer from having the consumer *use* the software after purchasing it is that the consumer might purchase upgrades or ancillary products.

For the Netscape and Microsoft browsers there are several reasons why the icon placement might be important. (This analysis ignores any future revenues from upgrades, inasmuch as both companies have agreed not to charge for browsers or upgrades.) It is possible that Netscape and Microsoft might be able to trade off the success of their browsers to sell software specializing in serving up Web pages (known as servers) because of their large presence among the base of users and the (presumably) assured compatibility with these browsers.

There is another possible reason for the Web browser icon to have value. When a browser is first put into use, it goes to a default starting location on the Internet.[27] If large numbers of Web users (surfers) view a particular location, advertising revenues can be generated as some popular locations on the Internet, such as Yahoo, have discovered. Yahoo in fact paid Netscape many millions of dollars to provide Netscape users an easy way to reach the Yahoo page. Netscape and Microsoft, although somewhat late to this game, both are working on new start pages (to which the browsers will be preprogrammed to go) in the hopes of enticing users to stay at their Web sites. It is thought that browsers might become a potent revenue generating force by leading consumers to particular pages.

There are serious reservations to the claim that the browser icons are valuable for the control they provide of the start page, however. First, it is possible, and quite easy, for users to alter the start page. Would it make sense for radio stations to pay automobile dealers to have car radios set at certain stations when the cars leave the new car lot? They don't—mainly because it is so easy to change stations. Is it really that much more difficult for consumers to change the icons on the desktop? This is an empirical question whose answer may change as consumers become more accustomed to operating their browsers.

And there is an even more fundamental impediment to the claim that desktop placement is important for browsers: Just having the icon on the desktop is insufficient to gain access to the Internet. Clicking on that icon will not connect users to the Internet. For that, they will have to use one of many Internet service providers. The Internet service provider will almost certainly provide its own browser, independent of what icon is on the desktop.[28] Therefore, it is hard to see how the icon on the desktop at the time of sale provides much value at all.

Finally, the concept of detailed governmental control over desktop placement leads to other seemingly endless and seemingly absurd questions. What about the Start button in Windows? The order of programs tends to be alphabetical. Should the government be concerned about the ordering of these programs, and who gets the rights to order these programs? Has anyone investigated whether the various color schemes found in Windows work to benefit Microsoft's icons over the alternatives? Is the screen saver in Windows that shows the Microsoft Windows icon moving around anticompetitive in its subliminal effects? In conclusion, and in all seriousness, we should ask this: Should the government really be involved in these types of decisions?

The Trial So Far

The trial is playing out as this book is going through its copyediting stage. The rules for the evidence appear highly unusual: Only twelve witnesses for each side, and the only evidence heard in court is the cross examination.

So far, the level of evidence put forward by the government appears to be, from an economic vantage, disappointing, largely based on anecdotes and email. The economic case consists of theories proposed by the government purporting to demonstrate how Microsoft is trying to protect its monopoly in operating systems through illegal tactics. The government's case lacks almost any empirical examination of the economic conditions in software markets. There has been, as far as we can tell, no methodical examination of prices, quantities, or just about any other economic magnitudes.

Franklin Fisher, who the government put on as its final witness, attributes to network effects an enhancement of monopoly power and a barrier to entry. He seems to accept the theoretical view that network effects slow down changes in market shares. He seems, like many other economists, to believe in tipping and lock-in. The empirical support for these views? As far as we can tell, none. As is often the case, theory is itself is supposed to be persuasive, even if it is theory that has never been demonstrated to have any predictive or descriptive power, nor any empirical support.

As we have seen in chapters 7 and 8, the evidence from the software markets does not show slow changes in market shares. Instead, market changes occur at breakneck speed. There was no support for the concepts of tipping. And throughout the book we have failed to find any evidence of lock-in. To our knowledge, no one has presented any evidence contrary to our findings in the software industry.

Professor Fisher also accepts the idea that predation makes sense in this case. Microsoft, in his view, tried to destroy Netscape in order to protect Windows from potential competition with Java. The problem, of course, is that even if Java were a threat to Windows, and it is not clear that it ever was, predation is not going to get rid of that threat, as explained above. And there are other logical explanations for giving away the browser or including it in the operating system. Because Professor Fisher conducts no empirical economic analysis, he cannot distinguish between these hypotheses. Instead, he used email and memos to try to make his case.

As something of an aside, Professor Fisher also claims that a tie-in sale would increase profits for Microsoft even if the two tied products were used in fixed proportions. This is an error on Fisher's part, inasmuch as it is impossible for a tie-in with fixed proportions to increase profits for a monopolist if there are no other monopolists in related industries.[29]

Both Professor Fisher and the government's other economics witness, Frederick Warren-Boulton, did make one claim about pricing in the industry. The claim had to do with the fact that prices of hardware seem to have fallen more than prices of software, or more specifically, the prices of the operating system. The problem with this statement, even if true, is that it is totally irrelevant to the issue at hand. Hardware prices and software prices would not be expected to bear any particular relationship to one another. Do we expect the prices of corn flakes and milk to move together, or automobiles and gasoline, or socks and shoes? Theory and commonsense empirics both are in agreement that the answer to this last question is no. Although we can understand how difficult it is to resist appealing to incorrect arguments that might strengthen one's position with judges or juries, it is still disappointing that these two respected economists would make such claims. Unfortunately, this appears to be about the only empirical evidence regarding Microsoft's monopoly put forward by either of the two economists.

But Microsoft's case, unfortunately, has not gone well under cross examination, certainly not in the perception of reporters and many commentators. The government's attorney has chosen to focus less on the quality of the main body of evidence put forward by Microsoft's witnesses and more on dramatic inconsistencies (on fairly trivial points) that have the effect of weakening the credibility of Microsoft's witnesses.

The most extreme instance of this consisted of several videotape demonstrations that were badly botched by Microsoft witnesses over issues that were not really central to the antitrust questions at hand. The most notorious instance occurred during the cross examination of James Allchin, Microsoft's senior vice-president in charge of Windows. After presenting a tape purporting to demonstrate that removing Internet Explorer from Windows hurt the performance of Windows, Mr. Allchin was forced to concede that the tape shown in court was not the tape he described, after he had sworn that it was. These video foul-ups were staggering public relations fiascoes that should never have been allowed to happen in a trial of this magnitude. They reflect badly on Microsoft's defense team.

Similarly, the government criticized Microsoft's economics expert, Richard Schmalensee, on the consistency of his report with some of his earlier writings. Although there were some apparent inconsistencies, the press made a much larger issue of it than it did when Professor Fisher was confronted with seeming inconsistencies between his testimony and his earlier writings. The government also scored major publicity points by finding internal email within Microsoft that criticized the validity of some survey's used by Professor Schmalensee in his analysis.

The majority of Professor Schmalensee's report, however, was ignored in the cross examination. His report, unlike that of the government economists, contained considerable empirical evidence, including a limited examination relating product quality with market success. In addition, Professor Schmalensee demonstrated that the price of Windows was almost certainly less than the monopoly price, a conclusion consistent with our findings in application markets. According to news reports, this analysis was greeted with a good deal of skepticism, apparently for no reason other than the fact that his estimate of monopoly price was so much higher than current prices.

At this time the press seems certain that Microsoft has lost, but they never heard the direct evidence and may well have not read it. The court, on the other hand, is required to read the direct testimony. Whether the government's strategy of discrediting witnesses instead of evidence will work is yet to be known. It will be a shame if a poor defense causes the theory of lock-in to become entrenched in antitrust analysis.

Implications

The theories of path dependence and lock-in are relatively new to the economic literature. These theories have not won over the economics profession after years of debate, and they have not made their way into many economics textbooks. Nor do these theories draw on first principles in obvious and secure ways. That does not make theories of path dependence and lock-in bad economics, or wrong economics, or inappropriate topics for academic research. On the contrary, it makes the academic debate that much more important. It does make these theories, however, a poor foundation for public policies that could effect the progressive nature of the American economy.

If we were treating a dying industry, even speculative economic medicine might be worth a try. But the computer and software industries continue to astound most people with the rates both at which products improve and at which prices decline. It makes no sense to submit such a robust patient to the risks of economic quackery.

In the main text of the book we have shown that there is a poor connection between theories of path dependence and the real-world behaviors of entrepreneurs and consumers. We also discussed the disconnect between the alleged empirical support for these theories and real events. Contrary to the lock-in claim, and contrary to some popular stories of markets gone awry, good products do seem to displace bad ones. Because there is no real support for the supposition that markets fail in increasing-returns environments, there is no more basis for antitrust in increasing-returns markets than in any others.

There might even be less reason to apply antitrust to such markets. Our most basic theory of increasing returns implies that monopoly or near-monopoly equilibria are likely. Where people do value compatibility, or where increases in firm scale really do lower costs, dominant formats or single-producer markets will probably result at any particular moment. This certainly was a prominent finding in our examination of software markets. There is no point in the government's attacking serial monopolists competing to continue their dominance into the next period.

Furthermore, consumers benefit from serial monopoly. Anything else will frustrate the urge for compatibility, unnecessarily raise costs, or both. So monopoly outcomes need not imply that anything has gone wrong or been done wrong. Monopolies that are undone by the government may lead only to monopolies that are redone in the market. The faces may change, but market structure may not. If we insist that natural-monopoly industries be populated by several firms kept at inefficiently small shares, we are likely to find these markets taken over by foreign companies without such restrictions.

In such markets, firms will compete to be the monopolist. It is in this competition that products that create more value for consumers prevail against those that create less value. Notice what that means. The very acts of competition that bring about the market tests of these products—the strategies that save us from inferior keyboards—will look like monopolizing acts. That is because they are. They determine which monopoly prevails until better products prompt new campaigns to capture an increasing returns market.

Many of the other claims that surround the new antitrust debate are disconnected, not only from real-world observations, but also from any real theoretical support. One such claim is that Microsoft would like to crush any would-be direct competitor. It probably would. Theory and history, however, do not tell us how predation could ever work in a world in which assets are perfectly durable. Further, as we have seen, Microsoft has been visibly unsuccessful in crushing anything except when their products are better than the opposition. They had to resort to an attempt to buy the uncrushed Intuit; they have barely dented America Online with the much ballyhooed Microsoft Network; and they only began to erode Netscape's near-monopoly when their own browser came up to snuff. Microsoft's products, which dominate in the Windows environment, also are the better products, and have often dominated first in the Macintosh market.

There is, finally, the vaguely posed claim that Microsoft stifles innovation—another disconnect. The claim fails to conform to several prominent features of the PC landscape. First, Microsoft courts and supports its many software developers, who now number in the hundreds of thousands. Second, the personal computing industry, by any practical standard of comparison, seems to be astonishingly innovative.

Finally, and most important, antitrust doctrines brought to bear against Microsoft cannot be constructed so that they will apply to Microsoft alone. If doctrines emerge that the biggest operating system must be kept on a short leash, then why not also restrain a big producer of database software that sets the standards for that activity, or the biggest producer of printers, or scanners, or modems, or microprocessors, and so on? If these new technologies do exhibit increasing returns, or important reliance on standards, or network effects, or instant scalability, then we are likely to see high concentration in all of these areas. Unless we are to embark on a relentless attack on whatever it is that succeeds, we need to acknowledge that the constructive competitive actions that firms take in this environment—new products, new capabilities, new deals—will often hurt competitors by the very fact that they make consumers better off.

Notes to the Appendix

1. A portion of this essay first appeared as "Dismal Science Fictions: Network Effects, Microsoft, and Antitrust Speculation," *Policy Analysis* 324.

2. Susan Garland, "Commentary: Justice vs. Microsoft: Why It Has a Case," *Business Week* (November 17, 1997), p. 147.

3. Alan Murray, "The Outlook: Antitrust Isn't Obsolete in an Era of High-Tech," *Wall Street Journal* (November 10, 1997), p. A1.

4. We are not, however, aware of any formal studies that examine market shares and prices in high-tech markets.

5. See "Declaration of Kenneth J. Arrow," in *Memorandum of the United States of America in Support of Motion to Enter Final Judgment and in Opposition to the Positions of IDE Corporation and Amici* (January 17, 1995).

6. John R. Wilke and David Band, "Microsoft Allies in 'Active Desktop' Are Subpoenaed in Antitrust Probe," *Wall Street Journal* (February 5, 1998), p. B6.

7. See Gary L. Reback et al. (1995).

8. RealAudio files of Nader's conference, held in Washington, D.C., on November 13–14, 1997, and called "Appraising Microsoft and Its Global Strategy," are available at <http://www.appraising-microsoft.org/day1rm.html>.

9. This is not to say, however, that antitrust laws as written are ideal. If there really were serious problems with lock-ins to inferior technology, we might want to rewrite the antitrust laws. For reasons set forth here, however, there is no evidence supporting that supposition.

10. Tie-in sales may allow the monopolist to capture more of the surplus created by the monopolized good, may spread risk, may contribute to quality control, or may provide a cheap means for monitoring intellectual-property infringement. Such effects of tie-ins do not require monopolization of a second market. Further, where tie-ins are profitable for any of these reasons, they may contribute to economic efficiency. See Liebowitz (1983). Bundling is very common for all kinds of goods. People buy season tickets, cars with tires and transmissions, and houses with microwaves and furnaces. Bundling can be explained by efficiencies of either production or purchase and commonly occurs in highly competitive markets.

11. This analysis ignores natural gas, which in fact is usually cheaper than oil where it can be had.

12. Although this explanation has been around in antitrust economics for some time, it is formalized in Whinston (1990).

13. Furthermore, the existence of economies of scale in heating oil make it likely that someone else has already monopolized the industry, in which case extending the monopoly from furnaces to oil would cause no economic harm; it would mere-

ly change the identity of the monopolist. The furnace monopolist is likely to benefit if it can avoid dealing with an oil monopolist who can share in the furnace monopolist's profits, or lead to lower joint profits if the two monopolists each try to take larger shares of the profit.

14. Fisher, in his direct testimony (p. 20) claims that even with fixed proportions there is a potential gain because of the potential "metering" effect of tie-ins. We cannot go into the details here, but Fisher is incorrect, as demonstrated in Liebowitz (1983).

15. This does not hold true if a different firm monopolizes the tied market, as discussed in note 13. However, consumers suffer no harm if the other monopolist is merely replaced by Microsoft, and thus there is no reason that antitrust should care about that outcome.

16. The most famous of these cases is John D. Rockefeller's Standard Oil. See John McGee (1958).

17. See F. M. Scherer's text *Industrial Market Structure and Economic Performance* (2d ed., Rand McNally, 1980), where he states, "One conclusion relevant to public policy follows immediately. No single firm size is uniquely conducive to technological progress. There is room for firms of all sizes" (p. 418). Similarly, William Shughart's text *The Organization of Industry* (Irwin, 1990) states, "Industrial creativity does seem to depend on something other than pure size" (p. 356).

18. It is also the case that Microsoft now boasts one of the corporate world's biggest annual research and development budgets at $2.6 billion, almost a quarter of its 1996–97 sales revenue. Bill Gates nonetheless recently announced plans to double Microsoft's R&D budget. See "Gates expects Microsoft's research budget to double," *Minneapolis Star Tribune* (March 18, 1998), p. 5D.

19. Note that many small startups have in fact gained access to enormous amounts of capital in the equities market when they were able to convince investors of the potential value of their ideas. These would include Netscape, Yahoo, and many other Internet companies.

20. Steve Hamm, "The Secrets to Microsoft's Might," *Business Week* (January 19, 1998), available on the World Wide Web as part of the hardcopy story "Microsoft's Future."

21. Surely it is difficult to argue that the software market has been insufficiently innovative in recent years. Nonetheless, it remains very difficult to prove that the industry has been *optimally* innovative.

22. For example, word processors now contain draw packages, paint packages, graphing packages, dictionaries, thesauruses, grammar checkers, equation editors, outliners, and so forth. Spreadsheets now routinely include spell checkers, graphics

packages, statistics programs, financial programs, programming languages, linear and nonlinear programming routines, and so forth. Even fax programs now contain optical character recognition software (to convert faxes to text), draw packages to create cover pages, and so forth.

23. This was supposedly the main ingredient in a well-publicized deal whereby America Online agreed to include Internet Explorer on its installation disks (although users could use Netscape's browser if they so desired). See John R. Wilke And David Bank, "AOL, MCI Are Subpoenaed in Microsoft Antitrust Case," *Wall Street Journal Interactive Edition* (February 20, 1998).

24. This refers to a paper by Ronald Coase that is the most highly cited paper in the field of economics, and one of the contributions for which he received the Nobel prize. See Coase (1960).

25. *Transaction costs* include such things as the costs of finding parties willing to conduct business, the costs of negotiating deals, and the costs of arranging for payment and delivery. The term *wealth effects* refers to the fact that parties enriched or impoverished by an initial entitlement to a good might skew final outcomes in a market because the initial entitlement will alter their consumption patterns. Whoever has the initial entitlement to a glass of water in a desert will, for example, probably end up drinking it.

26. Who is most likely to maximize the value of desktop placement? The ability to generate value in desktop placement depends largely on the costs of searching, marketing, and negotiating desktop placement with both users and placement purchasers. In this case, it might appear that that Microsoft would be able to transact at lower costs with placement purchasers than could OEMs, arguing for giving Microsoft the property rights. First, OEMs are not included in the upgrade market, and thus Microsoft already would be negotiating for these desktop placements. The additional costs for Microsoft's controlling OEM placements would seem trivial. Second, each OEM would likely duplicate the marketing, search, and negotiation costs of other OEMs. On the other hand, OEMs often sell other software to customers of which Microsoft has no knowledge. Although the placement of these icons could be preordered in a particular way, this might impose its own inefficiencies. It is conceivable that this would tilt the result toward giving OEMs property rights. The bottom line is that at this time it remains unclear who can maximize desktop value.

27. Early in the history of the Internet, it was possible to have a browser and not know what to do to get started. Start pages cropped up to help consumers learn to maneuver their way around the Web.

28. For example, both America Online and AT&T's Worldnet Internet services use a version of Internet Explorer that is specially set up to go to America Online's and AT&T's home pages, respectively. Note that control of the start page is a Coasian problem analogous to the icon placement problem.

29. See Liebowitz (1983) for a proof of this point.

Appendix B
The Trial

As we went to press with the first edition of this book, the Microsoft trial was well under way. As we discussed in the first appendix, the initial phases of the trial did not go well for Microsoft. The trial continued in much the same vein. Microsoft's defense clearly was not making any serious impression on Judge Thomas Penfield Jackson. In November 1999, Judge Jackson issued his findings of fact (discussed below), a harshly worded decision in which he adopted much of the government's case. The government prosecutors could hardly have asked for more.

Shortly after issuing his findings of fact, Judge Jackson appointed Richard Posner—a distinguished academic lawyer, jurist, and leading figure in what is often referred to as the Chicago school of law and economics—to mediate settlement negotiations. Because of Posner's stature, this move was regarded as creating the best chance of a settlement and a signal that Judge Jackson would prefer such an outcome. But the talks failed—a failure widely attributed to disagreements between the Department of Justice (DoJ) and the states' attorneys general.

The scathing findings of fact foreshadowed the findings of law, issued in early April 2000, which found Microsoft guilty of all counts but one. There was much talk in the press that the government would ask for some sort of breakup. The proposal that seemed to receive the most attention early on and that Microsoft's adversaries were pushing would break Microsoft up in such a way that Windows would be sold by three competing companies. The competing proposals and other aspects of the case drew the attention of academics and other commentators.[1]

After that, the government and Microsoft submitted remedy their proposals. The government's proposed remedy included a breakup that would create two companies, one specializing in operating systems, the other containing all other Microsoft products. In the end, the judge requested minor fine-tuning of the government's proposal, then adopted it essentially word for word.

Probably the most surprising aspect of the remedies phase, given the severity of the court's remedy, was the absence of any real process. The trial itself did not include discussion of remedies, and it was widely expected that submissions and witnesses would discuss both the appropriateness and the consequences of the potential remedies. But although the future of Microsoft was at stake and the potential impact on the economy was large, the company was given less than two weeks to respond to the government's proposed remedies, and no witnesses were heard.

In a series of interviews after the decision, Judge Jackson made several statements that seemed most unusual, but that indicated his frame of mind. These statements imply that he based much of his decision on his view of the veracity of Microsoft's witnesses rather than on the logic of what they were saying. He indicated that he made so few changes to the government's remedy because he did not feel competent to propose remedies on his own, a remarkable admission.[2]

As we write this epilogue, the Supreme Court has just ruled that Microsoft's appeal will be heard by the Court of Appeals for the D.C. Circuit. The government had asked that the appeal go directly to the Supreme Court, on the basis of a little-used provision of the law that allows appeals to skip over the Court of Appeals where an expedited review is in the national interest. The Supreme Court's rejection of the government's request is thought to be a blow to the government's case because the D.C. Circuit appeals court had previously ruled that Microsoft's addition of the browser to the operating system was a legal integration.

In discussing the court's findings and final order at this stage, we run the risk that subsequent events will eclipse the issues we consider here. Yet taking stock at this point serves a purpose. Whatever the appeals process brings, Judge Jackson's findings and the litigation that brought them are legal history.

Given the enormity of the remedy, its tenuous relationship to the subject matter of the case, and the peculiarities of the process that brought it about, it will most likely be modified or discarded on appeal. Nevertheless, it deserves our scrutiny, for the appeals process, whatever the outcome, will probably go on for several years, during which time the remedy will remain the subject of debate and speculation. Further, even if this remedy doesn't survive the appeals process, it provides a useful example of the reach of government power under the antitrust laws and the belief that bureaucratic arrangements, even those that are hastily engineered, can improve on market outcomes. Finally, the remedy may restructure the software industry, establishing how the courts will deal with companies that establish and maintain important standards.

The Justice Department's success in the Microsoft trial has emboldened it to bring forward other cases that share certain similarities with the Microsoft case. In the Mastercard/Visa case, for example, the government argues that credit-card organizations have hampered innovation, a theme it previously used in the Microsoft case. As in the Microsoft case, the Mastercard/Visa case appears to have been brought at the behest of a competitor—in this case, American Express. Once again the government appears to be ready to protect competitors—especially well-connected competitors—instead of competition, using theories that stray far from established economic doctrines that ordinarily provide both the foundation and limitation for antitrust.

Network concerns continue to play a major role in antitrust activity. The European Commission cited network effects as a justification for modifying the AOL—Time Warner merger, and U.S. authorities have raised related concerns. The DoJ also succeeded in derailing the deal between Worldcom and Sprint.

This activity is part of a broader trend toward increased intervention in the economy. The DoJ filed almost five hundred cases between 1994 and 1999. Mergers have either been blocked, as was the case for Staples and Office Depot, or have been saddled with follow-on regulation, as occurred with the FCC conditions imposed on the SBC-Ameritech merger. Increasingly, antitrust is used as a lever to obtain concessions that are unrelated to core antitrust concerns, a move toward general regulation of the market and away from protection of competition.

Judge Jackson's Rulings

The Role of Lock-in

Lock-in claims of various sorts were made throughout the Microsoft case. As we noted in the preceding appendix on antitrust economics, before the case was even filed, Microsoft's rivals used lock-in theories to argue that the government needed to play an active role in overseeing market choices of technologies. Lock-in claims were an important part of the government's case at trial and, in the end, were central to Judge Jackson's findings and to the explanation for several of the most important features of his remedy. Needless to say, given the arguments that we have made in this book, we find the court's use of lock-in to be fundamentally flawed. At best, lock-in theories are new and largely unexplored conjectures with no empirical support. It would be surprising, therefore, to rest such an important legal matter on economic arguments that have little theoretical or empirical foundation.

In his findings of fact, Judge Jackson refers to the lock-in problem as either the "intractable chicken-and-egg problem," the "collective-action problem," the "positive-feedback loop," or, more frequently, the "application barrier to entry."[3] His version of the lock-in story as applied to software operates along these lines: even if everyone preferred OS/2, we all (including application programmers) might think that everyone else is going to stick with Windows, and so we each choose Windows to get its large set of applications. In short, we all use Windows because we all use Windows.

For Judge Jackson, this barrier is the source of Microsoft's monopoly power.[4] In his own words (paragraph numbers are as they appear in the findings of fact),

> 39. Consumer demand for Windows enjoys positive network effects. . . . The fact that there is a multitude of people using Windows makes the product more attractive to consumers. . . . The main reason that demand for Windows experiences positive network effects, however, is that the size of Windows' installed base impels ISVs [independent software vendors] to write applications first and foremost to Windows, thereby ensuring a large body of applications from which consumers can choose. The large body of applications thus reinforces demand for Windows, augmenting Microsoft's dominant position and thereby perpetuating ISV incentives to write applications principally for Windows. This self-reinforcing cycle is often referred to as a "positive feedback loop."
>
> 40. What for Microsoft is a positive feedback loop is for would-be competitors a vicious cycle. . . . The small or non-

existent market share of an aspiring competitor makes it prohibitively expensive for the aspirant to develop its PC operating system into an acceptable substitute for Windows. . . . Even if the contender attracted several thousand compatible applications, it would still look like a gamble from the consumer's perspective next to Windows, which supports over 70,000 applications.

41. In deciding whether to develop an application for a new operating system, an ISV's first consideration is the number of users it expects the operating system to attract. Out of this focus arises a collective-action problem: Each ISV realizes that the new operating system could attract a significant number of users if enough ISVs developed applications for it; but few ISVs want to sink resources into developing for the system until it becomes established. Since everyone is waiting for everyone else to bear the risk of early adoption, the new operating system has difficulty attracting enough applications to generate a positive feedback loop. The vendor of a new operating system cannot effectively solve this problem by paying the necessary number of ISVs to write for its operating system, because the cost of doing so would dwarf the expected return.

The reader will find this logic very familiar. Relabel "application barrier to entry" as "prerecorded-movie barrier to entry," and you have the VHS/Beta story discussed in chapter 6.[5]

But the judge's argument is faulty not only because it is analogous to other faulty lock-in arguments. The flaws of his argument stand on their own. The collective-action problem can be addressed more creatively than the judge presumes. In this regard, the last sentence of paragraph 41 is technically wrong. The owner of the hypothesized rival operating system (OS) could afford to pay ISVs to write applications so long as the OS owner could contract to receive a percentage of the application revenues. Such an agreement would be reasonable because an OS owner who helps fund applications should be able to ask for some compensation when such funding policies increase the revenues of the application company by increasing the size of the market.[6]

If the new OS is enough better than Windows that it ought to displace Windows, the net value produced by the new OS will be greater than the value produced by Windows, which means that revenues from the combined operating system and applications would more than cover the costs of writing or porting new programs. (The judge never addresses this issue of relative quality, but the prospect of the failure of products that cost more than they are worth does not suggest any real social problem.) Thus, by taking ownership stakes in applications, the owner of a worthwhile operating system would find expected returns larger than the costs. Of course, this approach might be expensive, but it is very likely that only a small number of programs—the popular programs that generate the vast majority of revenues—would need to be ported to a superior platform to make it successful. This resolution is not hypothetical: most providers of operating systems have offered some applications, and the quest for the "killer-app" that can establish an operating system is well known.

The judge's chicken-and-egg theory makes it difficult to explain how Microsoft ever overcame the applications barrier in the first place. After all, programmers wouldn't have written programs for Windows "until it became established," and there would have been no users without programs. Yet Microsoft did overcome this seemingly impenetrable barrier.[7] Although the judge is correct in stating that Microsoft did not have to confront and overcome an incumbent with 70,000 applications,[8] implying that the first mover has an advantage, it also did not have anywhere near as large a potential audience of computer users (with mice!) as currently exists, a disadvantage for the first mover when Microsoft introduced Windows.

One might suppose that the same factors that allowed Microsoft's operating system to flourish could work on behalf of a superior alternative, but the judge insists that no new entrant could overcome these factors. He even suggests that the failure of OS/2 and the Macintosh to dislodge Windows is evidence in favor of the barriers-to-entry theory. Looked at through the lens the judge adopted, the economic world is populated by helpless producers and hapless consumers. Inertia reigns, market errors are common, and monopolists remain forever entrenched. But the actual reasons for the failure of these operating systems are more prosaic.

In fact, OS/2 did start out with plenty of developers, but was more expensive than Windows, required beefier computers, routinely crashed during installation, didn't work with many printers and video cards, and seemed invented to create a monopoly.[9] Similarly, Macintosh's disappointing performance has much to do with its high price, Apple's unwillingness to port its operating system to other hardware, and Apple's general disdain for providing backward compatibility.[10]

Conventional economic reasons readily explain these products' lack of success, requiring no speculation about collective action, chickens and eggs, or other theories about barriers to entry.

The Logic of the Court's Findings

Judge Jackson's findings of fact and law repeat the government's theory almost verbatim. The judge found Microsoft to have a monopoly in *operating systems*—i.e., Windows. This finding is an important step in the legal logic of the case. Because Netscape had and continues to have a relatively large share of the browser market, Microsoft could not be argued to hold a monopoly in the browser market, particularly considering that it overcame Netscape's dominance and clearly constituted new competition during the period of time that the trial addressed. Thus, for Microsoft to be found guilty of monopolization under section 2 of the Sherman Act, its battle with Netscape would have to be related to the operating system. To establish a connection between the operating system and the browser, the government asserted that Netscape and Java were a threat to Windows.

How is it that the browser could be considered a competitor to Windows? Because it is possible for programmers to write programs that work within the Netscape browser (using the Java language), it is possible to imagine a scenario where so many programs are written for the Netscape browser that computer purchasers care only about whether programs run in the Netscape browser. Any operating system could run the browser, so the underlying operating system would become irrelevant, and Windows would lose its grip on the market. Thus, the judge concluded, in order to protect its OS monopoly, Microsoft contrived to reduce Netscape's market share to a level he estimated to be 40 percent in 2001. He asserted that a market share of 40—50 percent would be insufficient for Netscape to be a viable threat to Windows. He further argued that for Netscape to live up to its potential, it needed to be the "standard" in the browser market.

There are two problems with Jackson's claims. First, Netscape's failure to pose a viable threat to Windows was not for lack of market share. If developers had been inclined to write programs that ran in the Netscape browser, as Judge Jackson claimed they were, then surely 40 percent of the

Windows market plus Netscape's larger share of the Unix, Macintosh, and the other markets would provide a potential market large enough to keep programmers happily raking in revenues. In addition, given the ready availability of Netscape, developers could have anticipated that the introduction of a worthwhile Netscape-based product would have prompted millions of additional Windows users to install Netscape on their computers.

Second, it requires a leap of faith to agree with Jackson's premise that middleware (programs that allow other programs to run on top of them) will evolve to be a viable alternative to a standard OS. There have always been middleware programs. For example, many programs were written to run on top of Lotus 1-2-3. But no middleware has ever become a platform for mainstream programs or a serious alternative to an operating system.[11] The strongest support offered for the government's middleware theory was some evidence that at least one senior Microsoft executive thought that the middleware threat was serious; otherwise, the theory has no real-world support.[12]

The government's theory, as adopted by the court, is that Microsoft engaged in a broad range of activities to destroy Netscape in order to protect its Windows monopoly from competition. Microsoft's allegedly predatory actions included all of its efforts to advance Internet Explorer, including building a better browser and enlisting support from independent software producers (ISPs) and original equipment manufacturers (OEMs). But this theory ignores important features of the browser market. Perhaps most interestingly, it ignores the fact that other operating systems, such as OS/2 and the Macintosh OS, like Windows, include a browser.

To conclude that Microsoft's investments in the browser were predatory, the court ignored its own finding that Microsoft's efforts to build a browser improved the breed. And to conclude that giving away Explorer could only be predatory, the court ignored other potential sources of revenue from success in browsers, including server revenue, portal revenue, and Windows revenue.

The Remedy[13]

The remedy proposed by the government and adopted by Judge Jackson contains two components. Receiving the lion's share of attention has been its structural component, which breaks Microsoft into two separate companies—an applications company and an operating-system company. The structural remedy includes certain conduct restrictions, such as preventing the two companies from recombining and severely limiting business between them. The restrictions that accompany the structural remedy have a duration of ten years.[14]

The second component of the remedy is a separate set of conduct restrictions that have a duration of three years. As we discuss below, these provisions impose potentially enormous costs on Microsoft with very little in the way of expected benefit to the consumer.

The structural remedy appears fairly simple at first blush. As is often the case, however, the devil is in the details. The beginning text of the more than five-thousand-word remedy contains the substantive part of the structural remedy:[15]

> 1.c The Plan shall provide for the completion, within 12 months of the expiration of the stay pending appeal set forth in section 6.a., of the following steps:
>
> 1.c.i. The separation of the Operating Systems Business from the Applications Business, and the transfer of the assets of one of them (the "Separated Business") to a separate entity along with (a) all personnel, systems, and other tangible and intangible assets (including Intellectual Property) used to develop, produce, distribute, market, promote, sell, license and support the products and services of the Separated Business, and (b) such other assets as are necessary to operate the Separated Business as an independent and economically viable entity.

These provisions divide Microsoft into two companies, one built generally along the lines of an applications company (the Applications Business, or AppCo) and the other along the lines of an operating systems company (the Operating-Systems Business, or OpCo). We use the term *generally* because the proposed division of assets and products, in combination with the restrictions on the two companies doing business with one another, does not separate the OS components from the applications company in obvious, customary, or efficient ways. Section 7 of the remedy, which defines terms, articulates the court's division of the existing business:

> 7.c. "Applications Business" means all businesses carried on by Microsoft Corporation on the effective date of this Final

Judgment except the Operating Systems Business. Applications Business includes but is not limited to the development, licensing, promotion, and support of client and server applications and Middleware (*e.g.,* Office, BackOffice, Internet Information Server, SQL Server, etc.), Internet Explorer, Mobile Explorer and other web browsers, Streaming Audio and Video client and server software, transaction server software, SNA server software, indexing server software, XML servers and parsers, Microsoft Management Server, Java virtual machines, Frontpage Express (and other web authoring tools), Outlook Express (and other e-mail clients), Media player, voice recognition software, Net Meeting (and other collaboration software), developer tools, hardware, MSN, MSNBC, Slate, Expedia, and all investments owned by Microsoft in partners or joint venturers, or in ISVs, IHVs [independent hardware vendors], OEMs or other distributors, developers, and promoters of Microsoft products, or in other information technology or communications businesses.

In short, the AppCo gets all the software applications except the operating system, no matter how closely an application might be tied to the operating system. Provision 2.b.ii prevents the AppCo and OpCo from conducting business with one another for a period of ten years after implementation of the breakup plan. The division of properties in section 1.c, together with these trade restrictions, will impose substantial inefficiencies. Next, we examine certain features of the remedy. We demonstrate that the remedy is inconsistent with the court's findings of fact and in the long run will weaken, not strengthen, the world of computing that surrounds the Windows operating system.

The Unlikely Benefits of the Breakup

The government alleges that breaking up Microsoft will benefit the economy. Such a conclusion does not follow from well-established principles, but rather relies on conjectures about economics and on speculation about the behavior of both of the successor companies.

First, note that the OpCo will not directly compete with the AppCo, so, unlike most imposed breakups, this structural remedy does not create direct competitors. Thus, the court's remedy will not directly alter market power in either of these markets.

The government asserts that competition will nonetheless increase, articulating two possible ways that this increase might occur. But to support this argument, the government had to contradict the findings of fact and ignore other realities of this market.

Strengthening of Alternative Operating Systems

The government asserts that although this breakup does not increase the number of competitors in the OS market, competition will nevertheless be enhanced. The government and its experts suggest that having a separate AppCo will strengthen the competitive position of alternative operating systems (particularly Linux) to the extent that these alternative operating systems might overcome the application barrier to entry.[16] They argue that because the AppCo will no longer have a financial interest in Windows, it will no longer have an incentive to protect Windows from other operating systems and may therefore find it desirable to promote other operating systems to reduce Windows' power.

This argument makes two key assumptions. First, it assumes that the AppCo will find it profitable to port its programs to Linux. Second, it assumes that the porting of the AppCo's products to Linux will have an important impact on Linux's relative competitive position. The first of these assumptions is contradicted by current market evidence, the second by the court's own findings.

There is little reason to believe that the AppCo will find it profitable to port its programs to Linux. The government bases much of its claim on the fact that Corel ported the WordPerfect Office suite to Linux.[17] But Corel's action cannot be taken as a harbinger of profitable opportunities. As we write this epilogue, Corel has alerted investors of the possibility of bankruptcy, and it has just received an emergency injection of $30 million to keep it afloat for the next few months.[18] Corel's financial predicament was well known when the government was writing its brief, and it was also well known that Corel's recent business decisions were highly unusual, influenced perhaps by its declining fortunes.[19]

Meanwhile, virtually no other major desktop applications have been ported to Linux, including those from such market leaders as Intuit, Symantec, Lotus, Adobe, or Quark.[20] The AppCo is no more likely than any of the other desktop ISVs to find it profitable to port applications to the Linux operating system.

And even if the AppCo did port its office suite to Linux, that wouldn't overcome the application barrier to entry, at least not according to the theory of that applications barrier put forward by the plaintiffs and accepted by the court. Microsoft Office consists of five or six very popular applications.[21] But the court's applications-barrier-to-entry theory clearly states that the addition of such a small number of applications would not make Linux a viable substitute for Windows. For example, in paragraph 40 of the findings of fact, the judge states:

> To provide a viable substitute for Windows, another PC operating system would need a large and varied enough base of compatible applications to reassure consumers that their interests in variety, choice, and currency would be met to more-or-less the same extent as if they chose Windows. Even if the contender attracted several thousand compatible applications, it would still look like a gamble from the consumer's perspective next to Windows, which supports over 70,000 applications.

Again, in paragraph 44:

> Although Apple's Mac OS supports more than 12,000 applications, even an inventory of that magnitude is not sufficient to enable Apple to present a significant percentage of users with a viable substitute for Windows.

Notice also that although the Mac OS has Microsoft Office among its applications, the court did not consider the Macintosh a serious competitive challenge to the Microsoft OS. Ironically, it was Microsoft, in criticizing the applications-barrier-to-entry theory, that claimed that a key for a successful operating system depended not so much on the total number of applications as on having a few very good products in the most popular categories of applications. But the government and the judge rejected this claim. For Judge Jackson and the government to turn their backs on the findings of fact and suggest now that a handful of applications can overturn the applications barrier to entry suggests a rather casual attitude toward those found facts.

New Competitors in Operating Systems?

The government and its experts have also suggested that the proposed structural remedy will lead to new competition in operating systems. They speculate that the AppCo will expose sufficient application programming interfaces (APIs, or code that allows other programs to call on certain functions in another program) in the AppCo office product that it might turn into a middleware competitor to Windows.[22] This idea that middleware might rise up to become an operating system is an interesting theoretical notion, but one that again lacks factual support.

Several application companies in the desktop PC market have attained large market shares. Some of these cases are presented in chapters 8 and 9. As we noted above, thousands of mini applications were written for Lotus 1-2-3, and special hardware was even created specifically to allow it to use more memory than the operating system would normally permit. Yet there is no evidence that Lotus 1-2-3 ever had the type of general desktop applications written for it that would have made it a competitor to the operating system current at that time, the far simpler DOS. Similarly, when WordPerfect was the dominant word processor, it was ported to work on all major desktop operating systems, including DOS, the Macintosh, the Amiga, and the Atari ST. Yet it too never threatened to usurp DOS's position as an operating system.

There is no real-world history to support the claim that the AppCo will become a competitor to the OpCo. On the contrary, in other circumstances in which there has been a dominant application in an important market, there has been no movement toward an OS function for that application. At best, the government's claim must be viewed as highly speculative.

Finally, the government's supporting experts have claimed that the AppCo might take actions to weaken the competitive position of the OpCo.[23] This claim is an application of a more general theory that a dominant producer at one stage of a production process will have an incentive to weaken any market power of producers in other stages.

Operating systems and applications can be understood as different "stages" in the production of computer services. This argument is related to the double-marginalization problem discussed below.[24]

Although this theory is grounded in fundamental economic reasoning, it is not at all clear that the breakup would alter the competitive landscape in any important way. The number of well-financed potential competitors in this industry is quite large—including IBM, Intel, AOL, Texas Instruments, Dell, and even Sony. The addition of one more firm into this mix is unlikely to alter the competitive environment significantly.

Likely Harms of a Breakup

The forced breakup of any company is likely to impose serious costs. Firms become organized in a particular way in order to maximize their effectiveness. Those that are organized particularly well—that serve customers well and at low costs—survive; those that do not, perish. The most effective prosper. Microsoft has been an extraordinary success story. Its effectiveness in contributing to the creation of the personal computing world had made it the most valuable company in the world in terms of market capitalization. To assume that Microsoft could be rearranged like so many Lego blocks on the basis of a few months inquiry ignores what we understand about the evolution of enterprise.

Price Increases

A theoretical problem well known to economists occurs when two firms with market power produce complementary products: the double-marginalization problem. Each firm attempts to charge a markup that would maximize its own profits, taking the other firm's markup as given. The consequence is a higher set of prices than would be chosen by a single firm selling the two goods jointly. Thus, under the assumption that both the AppCo and the OpCo will have market power, prices would be expected to increase following the breakup. Both a declaration by the government's expert Carl Shapiro and an amicus brief by Litan, Noll, Nordhous, and Scherer acknowledge this problem.[25]

Although this mutual influence is one of the few things about the case that prompts widespread agreement among economists, it is not the real problem. The real problem concerning price is that Microsoft has long pursued a low-price, high-volume strategy. This strategy has paid off by allowing Microsoft to establish and maintain standards and to extend the use of its products to millions of consumers and businesses. The potential for large price increases comes from the possibility that one or both of the successor companies would abandon this strategy.

The analysis in chapters 7 to 9 demonstrates the historical effect of Microsoft's low-price strategy on software prices. The price decline attributable to Microsoft's influence is quite large. After the breakup, however, new leadership will exist in one or both companies, and each will choose a pricing strategy. If software prices in the markets in which Microsoft participates had fallen only at the rate that prices have fallen in other software markets, they would be at about double where they are now. If the successor AppCo were to raise prices to that level, the impact will be very significant.

Also, the price of Windows, by any reasonable estimate, is now far below the profit-maximizing *monopoly* price. According to a recent estimate by two economists not particularly friendly to Microsoft, the monopoly price of Windows is $813 (an estimate that is probably low because it assumes a very low price for computers).[26] Thus, if the OpCo were to abandon the low-price strategy, the increase in Windows' price could be quite large.

Disruption Costs

A breakup will also impose direct costs of reorganization, even if Microsoft is allowed to determine how to conduct the breakup (within the time and product constraints the government has imposed). These costs include physically relocating workers; transferring assets; setting up business plans for the new companies; dealing with morale problems among workers somewhat uncertain of their future; setting up separate accounting systems, health plans, and pensions; allocating overhead between the companies; paying capital market costs; and so forth.

These costs, although likely to be substantial, will not in themselves be catastrophic. After all, spin-offs occur with some regularity in the economy. It is important to note, however, that because this breakup will occur according to the government's timetable and plan, the reorganization costs can be expected to be larger than the costs of a similarly situated voluntary spin-off, which would be conducted in a manner planned to minimize these costs. Further, voluntary spin-offs typically occur along product lines that have operated as independent establishments well prior to the separation.

Even greater disruption is likely to occur to the businesses that provide Windows-based software products and to the consumers and the producers who use them. Changes in Microsoft marketing, engineering, and support staff; the prospect of a dramatic change in pricing policies; the fact of buying software packages from two different suppliers; and concerns about compatibility and continuity of products will increase both costs and uncertainty in the software industry.

Loss of Synergies

There are good reasons to believe that Microsoft's structure offers important economic efficiencies. First, there is Microsoft's own success. Second, there is the observation that most companies that have succeeded at providing operating systems have also provided applications. Third, there is a body of economic theory that argues that the boundaries of firms are not arbitrary, but rather develop to capture efficiencies that cannot be captured in separate enterprises.

Both the applications and the OS groups benefit from being part of the same company. For the most part, these advantages are the ordinary run-of-the-mill synergies that one expects between company units working on complementary products—what are sometimes called economies of scope. For example, OS programmers will be better able to fashion an operating system that meets the needs of programmers if the OS programmers have spent some time working as application programmers or have interacted frequently with application programmers. We would expect important benefits to arise from this type of cross-pollination. Of course, there would still be value in asking outside ISVs to provide input as well in order to broaden the source of information.

Although some of these synergies can be approximated by transactions between separate firms, such efforts are likely to be more expensive and less efficacious. For example, the OS company could rely more extensively on requests from application companies on how to improve the operating system, or it could hire application programmers from other companies to gain more continuous feedback. But hiring workers from outside to supply this feedback is far more costly than transferring workers internally. Also, such a practice imposes costs on the firm that is losing personnel to the OS company, without any offsetting benefits. Sporadic and formal information-gathering activities are likely to be more expensive and less informative than the informal but continuous interactions found in a single firm that can internalize these synergies.

Furthermore, the inherent problems of dividing Microsoft's integrated software products, the personnel who develop them, and ongoing research projects also cause direct losses of synergy. As we discuss below, the breakup specifies a poor allocation of those assets and products, with most products going to the AppCo, no matter how much more sensible it might have been to place them with the OpCo.[27]

The Impact of the Conduct Provisions

In addition to the conduct provisions that accompany the court's structural remedy, which apply for ten years, there are separate conduct provisions that last for three years. Nine major categories are given for the three-year conduct restrictions, with many of these categories having two or three subcategories of rules.

Some of these restrictions will impose large costs on Microsoft, its developer base, and consumers. Often, these remedies needlessly apply a wrecking ball where a scalpel would work far better. In this section, we highlight some of the provisions likely to fare poorly in a cost-benefit examination. It should be noted that the actual meaning of some of the provisions remains a matter of discussion. No doubt these matters will be the subject of continuing litigation if the court's final order is implemented.

Fragmenting Windows: The Binding Middleware Provision

One seemingly innocuous three-year provision will allow OEMs to choose which components of Windows they wish to install on their machines. It will further require Microsoft to discount the price of Windows to OEMs for components that the OEMs leave out of their computers:

> 3.g. Restriction on Binding Middleware Products to Operating System Products. Microsoft shall not, in any Operating System Product distributed six or more months after the effective date of this Final Judgment, Bind any Middleware Product to a Windows Operating System unless:
>
> i. Microsoft also offers an otherwise identical version of that Operating System Product in which all means of End-User Access to that Middleware Product can readily be removed (a) by OEMs as part of standard OEM preinstallation kits and (b) by end users using add-remove utilities readily accessible in the initial boot process and from the Windows desktop; and
>
> ii. when an OEM removes End-User Access to a Middleware Product from any Personal Computer on which Windows is preinstalled, the royalty paid by that OEM for that copy of Windows is reduced in an amount not less than the product of the otherwise applicable royalty and the ratio of the number of amount in bytes of binary code of (a) the Middleware Product as distributed separately from a Windows Operating System Product to (b) the applicable version of Windows.

This remedy requires a la carte pricing for operating systems.

On its surface, who could be against such flexibility? Are not a restaurant's customers better off if the seller cannot include items in the meal that the consumer doesn't want? This approach sounds reasonable, at least at a superficial level. Yet it is often more efficient, for both consumers and producers, for meals to be sold as prix fixe bundles rather than a la carte.

Of course, paying only for what you use makes sense when the price of individual components is related in some fashion to cost or value. In Judge Jackson's remedy, however, the a la carte prices of the individual items are determined by the amount of computer code rather than by the usefulness, importance, novelty, creation cost, or market price of a component.[28] This pricing rule is equivalent, in the restaurant analogy, to pricing a menu item by the number of letters in the name of the item.

Lettuce and spaghetti would have higher prices than steak and lobster—a pricing system that is clearly nonsensical, whether for our hypothetical restaurant or for OEMs, which will be given the inane incentive of choosing components of Windows based in part on the number of bytes of code they contain.

That inefficiency pales, however, next to the consequences of degrading the Windows standard. Operating systems are not like restaurants. If everyone eats something different at a restaurant, we celebrate the diversity in tastes. If everyone's operating system has a different set of features, a very serious problem arises—the operating system is no longer a standard.

Any standard loses its value to consumers if it fragments. Metric measurement would lose its value if we each selected our own personal size for a meter. Part of the value of Windows is that it presents a standard to both users and developers of software.

Nevertheless, the government's remedy seems to invite OEMs to fragment the Windows standard. Further, the government's remedy does not have any provisions requiring OEMs to disclose to consumers when they are selling threadbare versions of Windows. Such disclosure might not do much good anyway because it would be largely indecipherable to typical computer users.

Let's look, for example, at audio compression (one of the components that can currently be turned off in Windows 98). The way Windows now works, software developers can count on all users having access to these sound-decompression routines because these routines are normally turned on during Windows installation. Even if they have been turned off, it is relatively easy for software developers to provide instructions to users on how to turn them back on because the routines reside on the Windows CD.

But under the government remedy, software developers will no longer be able to count on users having access to audio-compression routines. OEMs will be given a financial incentive to sell machines with "stripped-down" versions of Windows. Some OEMs might decide to reduce their costs by not including needed audio-compression routines. On Christmas morning, when little Johnny turns on the computer to play his new video game, there will be no sound if his parents purchased a computer missing those routines.[29] The software developer now has one very unhappy customer.[30] Multiply this problem by many potential middleware products, and it is easy to see how consumers will suffer from a fragmented market. This problem is potentially enormous.[31]

Nevertheless, the government asserts that this concern is unwarranted and that only a handful of products would be affected.[32] It isn't clear to us exactly what products would fit into the category of middleware products or where the audio-compression example fits in,[33] both of which have to do with the definition of *middleware product:*

7.r. "Middleware Product" means

i. Internet browsers, email client software, multimedia viewing software, instant messaging software, and voice recognition software, or

ii. software distributed by Microsoft that

1. is, or has in the applicable preceding year been, distributed separately from an Operating System Product in the retail channel or through Internet access providers, Internet content providers, ISVs or OEMs, and

2. provides functionality similar to that provided by Middleware offered by a competitor to Microsoft.

Perhaps the government's discussion will provide guidance to courts that are called on to interpret this issue. Even if the government is correct, however, and only a relative handful of products is affected, a potential problem still exists. If some versions of Windows have voice recognition and others do not, and if some versions have video streaming and others do not, the potential for a serious fragmentation problem is real even with only five or ten middleware products that might or might not be included with Windows.

The government's response to concerns about fragmentation can only be described as extraordinary. It claims that when OEMs remove Microsoft middleware programs, the underlying code will still remain resident, to be called by other programs. The government states: "Section 3.g., requires that OEMs and end users be able to remove access only to the middleware product—in this case the browser—not to APIs or code."[34] In essence, it is asking Microsoft to hide the middleware program from view and refund its "price," but to keep its functionality intact. Under this interpretation, the government would be correct in its claim that there would be no fragmentation. Nevertheless, under this interpretation, Microsoft would be providing essentially the full Windows program to OEMs and end users, but granting discounts for the features that have been hidden. Of course, OEMs would then have every incentive to "remove" (i.e., hide) all such middleware products because their consumers get the products either way.[35]

Interestingly, the government's proposed interpretation thwarts the very purpose of this provision. The government would like other manufacturers of middleware to have greater opportunity to have OEMs install their software.[36] Yet if the Microsoft middleware is included for free, what incentive do OEMs have to include competing software from other producers? Exactly the same incentive as if the Microsoft middleware were a part of Windows and no discount were offered. This provision, under the government interpretation, cannot achieve the ends that the government desires. Only under the alternative interpretation—the interpretation that points to fragmentation—do alternative producers of middleware have an increased likelihood of OEMs purchasing their products.

The government might more readily achieve a la carte OS pricing by requiring that OEMs have the right to remove features for appropriate discounts, but also requiring OEMs' full disclosure that components have been removed.[37] This way, if fragmentation occurs, it will at least be along lines that consumers have chosen. Or, if consumers value standardization, they will be able to ensure that they are obtaining a standard version.

Reduced Innovation in the Operating System

The remedy also has the potential to hamper innovation in the operating system. Part of this potential problem comes from the "Binding Middleware" restriction discussed in the previous section. Obviously, if OEMs can use new middleware innovations without paying for them, Microsoft will have less incentive to create these innovations. Similarly, the restricted trade between the OS company and the application company has the potential to reduce innovation in the operating system. Voice-recognition technology can illustrate this problem.

Voice recognition is going to become much more useful to computer users in the next few years. It will be particularly useful for users with visual impairment or with disabilities hindering the use of their hands.

Currently several firms produce voice-recognition software, including IBM, Lernout & Hauspie, and Dragon Systems, with prices ranging from about $100 for basic versions to several hundred dollars for more advanced versions. The software has been improving, but still leaves much to be desired. Most of these programs allow voice recognition to be used with a handful of other programs, usually Microsoft Office and one or two others.

Including voice recognition in the operating system has important advantages over having it as a stand-alone program.[38] If it is part of the operating system, every firm writing applications for Windows, instead of just a handful, can take advantage of voice recognition, using the feature built into Windows, just as they currently draw on mouse operations or printer drivers. Consumers will also benefit because the cost of voice recognition, based on the historical precedent of Windows pricing, will probably be only a few dollars instead of the few hundred dollars that it now takes to purchase a stand-alone program.[29]

One would expect that absent the remedy's trade restrictions, Microsoft would adopt the voice-recognition software that provides the best combination of price and functionality because that combination would create the greatest net value for consumers and would therefore have the most favorable influence on Windows' profitability. This might entail using a product designed in-house or licensing the product from a third party.

How then does the government's remedy impede this process? First, provision 2.B.ii essentially prevents the two former Microsoft companies from doing business with one another for a period of ten years, what we call the "no-trade clause":

> 2.B After Implementation of the Plan and throughout the term of this Final Judgment, the Operating Systems Business and the Applications Business shall be prohibited from:
> ii. entering into any Agreement with one another under which one of the Businesses develops, sells, licenses for sale or distribution, or distributes products or services (other than the technologies referred to in the following sentence) developed, sold, licensed, or distributed by the other Business;
> Section 2.b.ii shall not prohibit the Operating Systems Business and the Applications Business from licensing technolo-

gies (other than Middleware Products) to each other for use in each others' products or services provided that such technology (i) is not and has not been separately sold, licensed, or offered as a product, and (ii) is licensed on terms that are otherwise consistent with this Final Judgment.

Because voice recognition is specifically defined as a middleware product, the last sentence does not overrule 2.b.ii.

One other element of the judgment that might seem to control the business relationship between the AppCo and OpCo is section 1.c.ii:

> 1.c.ii. Intellectual Property that is used both in a product developed, distributed, or sold by the Applications Business and in a product developed, distributed, or sold by the Operating Systems Business as of April 27, 2000, shall be assigned to the Applications Business, and the Operating Systems Business shall be granted a perpetual, royalty-free license to license and distribute such Intellectual Property in its products, and, except with respect to such Intellectual Property related to the Internet browser, to develop, license and distribute modified or derivative versions of such Intellectual Property, provided that the Operating Systems Business does not grant rights to such versions to the Applications Business. In the case of such Intellectual Property that is related to the Internet browser, the license shall not grant the Operating Systems Business any right to develop, license, or distribute modified or derivative versions of the Internet browser.

This paragraph does not seem to be entirely clear and is likely to provide more fodder for litigation. How does *intellectual property* differ from *products*? Which products or intellectual properties were developed by the OpCo, and which by the AppCo? If intellectual properties were developed using programmers from each division, how are they to be classified?[40]

Microsoft has made a very substantial investment in voice recognition. Under the government remedy, voice-recognition software goes to the AppCo. Suppose that the efficient outcome would be for the AppCo voice-recognition software to be included in the OpCo operating system.

This outcome would presumably be disallowed. Instead, the OpCo would have to deal with one of the other voice-recognition vendors and be forced to include an inferior product in Windows. Because, according to the remedy, Microsoft is out of the competition to provide voice-recognition software for Windows, and if voice recognition does indeed become part of the OS standard, then Microsoft's voice-recognition project will need to be sold off or scrapped. This is just one example of how innovation in the operating system can be affected.

Reduced Competition in Non-Desktop Markets

Although the remedy is draped in the language of increased competition, certain aspects of it seem designed specifically to reduce competition, particularly in the high-end server markets.

Windows NT (now Windows 2000) is Microsoft's entry in the high-end server and workstation market. These products were not part of the case. Further, there can be no serious claim that NT has a monopoly in the server/workstation market,[41] where Microsoft is the challenger to entrenched incumbents such as IBM and Sun. The presence of NT clearly enhances competition in this market, but the government's remedy seems intent on reducing such competition.

Once again, this shortcoming of the remedy has to do with the specific division of programs and the no-trade clause. Important components of Microsoft's server software (e.g., transaction server software and the others listed in note 27) are given to the AppCo. Windows 2000 without its server software is a high-end operating system so emasculated as to be noncompetitive. The benefits of reduced competition in the server market will redound to firms such as Sun, IBM, and Oracle that have a large stake in high-end (and high-priced) servers and workstations.

Even if the murky intellectual property clause 1.c.2 is understood to allow some cross-licensing, a new set of problems arise. There would then be two competing versions of the software, with each version based on the same original code, which would create confusion among consumers and hinder the adoption of these programs.

It is interesting how this particular feature of the remedy comports with the politics of this antitrust case. Sun and Oracle have been strong political supporters of the case. They now stand to benefit from reduced competition.

Rules on Sabotage

The aim of provision 3.c is to put in place a system to punish Microsoft should it alter the operating system intentionally to sabotage the performance of a competitor's software product. It is difficult to disagree with this aim. After all, intentionally degrading the performance of a competitor's product is both economically inefficient and the antithesis of fair and unfettered competition.

The text of this provision is as follows:

> 3.c. Knowing Interference with Performance. Microsoft shall not take any action that it knows will interfere with or degrade the performance of any non-Microsoft Middleware when inter-operating with any Windows Operating System Product without notifying the supplier of such non-Microsoft Middleware in writing that Microsoft intends to take such action, Microsoft's reasons for taking the action, and any ways known to Microsoft for the supplier to avoid or reduce interference with, or the degrading of, the performance of the supplier's Middleware.

Although the prevention of sabotage is a reasonable goal, there are problems with this provision as an operational rule. First, it doesn't distinguish between an action that is taken to sabotage a competitor and an action that is merely an unavoidable by-product of changes in technology. Only the former needs to be prevented. Neither does this provision define the meaning of *performance,* which leaves the door open for the provision to be used to impose costs on Microsoft for actions that clearly have nothing to do with sabotage. Finally, it would seem that the only sure way for Microsoft not to run afoul of this provision would be for the operating system to remain 100 percent backward compatible forever, a very inefficient result.

For example, is a 0.1 percent slowdown the type of degradation that this type of provision intends to address? What if the program runs 5 percent slower but is more stable? A more likely result is that the program runs faster on some machines but slower on others, depending on the hardware configuration. What then? This is the computer-science version of economists' problems with index numbers such as price indexes. They struggle with it just as we do.

This provision could impose unreasonably burdensome costs on Microsoft for no apparent purpose. And because the remedy applies the no-sabotage provision to the more general category *middleware* as opposed to *middleware product,* the number of products that might qualify could be quite large. It doesn't seem very difficult to focus on what this provision is trying to accomplish and to find a lower-cost solution. One possibility would be to impose a large fine if an arbitrator determined that Microsoft altered a Windows component solely to sabotage another firm's application.

OEM Flexibility in Product Configuration

Provision 3.a.iii prevents Microsoft from entering into contracts with or otherwise restricting an OEM from modifying the Windows desktop, start-up folder, favorites, and other defaults. The purpose of this provision is to ensure that non-Microsoft products can be put on the desktop and thus improve their competitive position. However, an important distinction should be made between the purpose of this provision and its actual implementation.

The purpose, as we read it, would be to prevent Microsoft from prohibiting free contracting between OEMs and other parties—or, in other words, to open up the ability to contract. Allowing free contracting is always a pro-competitive activity (as long as it is not a contract to collude). The actual implementation of this proposal, however, is just the opposite. It forbids Microsoft from contracting even when such contracting would be clearly beneficial. Therefore, it is anticompetitive.

Assume, as is always the economist's prerogative, that an Internet service provider, say Earthlink, wants to have its icon put on the desktop and is willing to pay a sufficiently high price to outbid others. Earthlink could negotiate with Microsoft to put its icon on the desktop, or it could negotiate with dozens of OEMs to put the icon on the desktop. Transaction costs are likely to be lower in negotiating with only a single agent, Microsoft, as opposed to negotiating with dozens of OEMs.

In the first appendix, we argue that there are good reasons to expect that contracting will ensure an efficient result, regardless of who owns the property rights. If the same result prevails regardless of property-rights assignment, then why should it matter if Microsoft is not allowed to sell the desktop space? The answer, once again, is efficiency. If trans-action costs are minimized when Earthlink has only a single negotiation, then it is socially efficient to allow Microsoft to sell the desktop space. Under provision a.iii, however, Microsoft cannot contract with OEMs to prevent OEMs from altering the desktop. Microsoft, therefore, cannot guarantee that the desktop space it sells will actually contain the icon it promises. Only OEMs can guarantee that they will deliver what they sell. The market, in this case, will not be able to achieve the efficient result of having Microsoft sell the desktop space.

If the motivation of this provision is to ensure that Microsoft cannot keep certain competitors from having icons on the desktop, the provision should have been written to state just that.

Integration, Innovation, and Maintenance

Microsoft's decision to sell its browser, Internet Explorer, as a part of the operating system has been absolutely central to this case. Not surprisingly, the court's treatment of the browser is the aspect of this case most likely to affect antitrust doctrine.

In the trial, much was made of whether the browser really was integrated into Windows. Unfortunately, much of the focus on this issue became the computer-science issue of whether the browser could be removed without disabling the operating system, which is irrelevant. A watch will still work if you remove the second hand.

The real issue is whether integration yields benefits—better products or lower costs—that could not have been accomplished by the purchase of separate goods. The D.C. Circuit Court of Appeals, in its earlier ruling on the issue of browser integration, said as much: "The short answer is thus that integration may be considered genuine if it is beneficial when compared to a purchaser combination."[42] That court also took note of the court's limitations in assessing product quality, concluding that "The question is not whether the integration is a net plus but merely whether there is a plausible claim that it brings some advantage."[43]

Judge Jackson's findings of law take issue with this statement, offering the argument that two separate products exist if consumers perceive two markets for two goods. Whatever the outcome of the Microsoft antitrust case, this rule is bad economics that would undermine antitrust practice and damage both competition and innovation. Consumer perception of two separate markets would offer very poor guidance on the permissibility of product integration. Let's look at an analogous example.

Twenty-five years ago, a thriving industry provided aftermarket rust-proofing for automobiles. New-car buyers in the northern United States and Canada took their cars to aftermarket rustproofers or had dealers arrange rustproofing before delivery. But starting in the mid-1970s and accelerating dramatically in the early to mid-1980s, automobile manufacturers began to incorporate extensive rustproofing. They improved designs and made heavy use of galvanizing and other coatings. Integrating rustproofing into manufacturing and design worked much better than adding it on. Today, consumers expect integrated rustproofing and long-term warrantees on rust resistance. The small aftermarket for rustproofing that remains is mostly confined to restored older cars and repaired newer ones. No doubt the aftermarket rustproofers that were crowded out by manufacturers' improvements bewailed the loss of their market, but consumers are much better off.

Here and in a host of other examples (having to do with everything from shirts and buttons to cars and tires), the fact that consumers perceive separate markets provides no useful indication about the advantage of integration.

Judge Jackson attempts to ground his finding of two separate products in consumer sovereignty, drawing on the *Jefferson Parish* and *Eastman Kodak* cases:

> The significance of those cases, for this Court's purposes, is to teach that resolution of product and market definitional problems must depend upon proof of commercial reality, as opposed to what might appear to be reasonable. In both cases the Supreme Court instructed that product and market definitions were to be ascertained by reference to evidence of consumers' perception of the nature of the products and the markets for them, rather than to abstract or metaphysical assumption as to

the configuration of the "product" and the "market." . . . In the instant case, the commercial reality is that consumers today perceive operating systems and browsers as separate "products," for which there is separate demand.[44]

There are two problems with this statement. First, consumers can perceive separate markets, even when the benefits of integration overwhelm the costs. Separate markets exist for cars and rustproofing or for shirts and buttons, cars and tires, yet few people object to these integrations. Interestingly, an additional consideration for the *Jefferson Parish* court was whether significant numbers of consumers, perceiving separate markets, were being forced to buy something that they didn't wish to buy from the defendant. Second, with changes in technology, both cost-benefit comparisons and consumer perceptions can change. So the "commercial reality" that "consumers today perceive" does not resolve much. In 1975, consumers undoubtedly perceived separate markets and products for cars and rustproofing. A contract that compelled consumers to buy added-on rustproofing only from authorized car dealers might well have flunked a cost-benefit test, while harming independents such as Ziebart. But ten years later, few would have disputed the benefits of factory manufactured-in rust resistance. Where technology change offers new-product integration, a rule that compels a look at consumer perceptions as though frozen in time will be harmful.

This particular form of innovation—adding functionality to existing products—is especially important for the software industry. We noted in the first appendix that because software is durable, sales of software will depend heavily on product improvements. Product improvements will consist largely of adding functionality to existing products.

Maintaining Standards

A standard is a terrible thing to waste. If the owner-producer-provider of a standard is not permitted to update the standard or the products that embody the standard, the standard will perish. Efficiency in the market for standards therefore requires that producers be permitted to incorporate innovations in their products. In our analysis of standards and technology choice in chapter 3 and elsewhere, we show that standards offering the largest surpluses could be expected to prevail in the marketplace. In part, this outcome would occur because the owners of more productive standards would be willing to invest more to establish their products. But suppose that once a standard is established, improvements are prohibited or somehow handicapped. Such a prohibition might have two harmful effects. First, it might mean that the best available product—an improved version of the established standard—would be prohibited. Second, it might prompt unwarranted instability in standards, forcing consumers to invest unnecessarily in products based on new standards.

The connection to the Microsoft case will be evident to the reader. The findings of law can be understood to mean that because Windows is the standard for personal computing, Microsoft will be prohibited from extending Windows by adding new functionality to the standard if any competitor offers that functionality as an add-on. The court's remedy reinforces that position by making it much more expensive for Microsoft to add new features to Windows. If the district court's interpretation of the rules on product integration are adopted into antitrust law, Windows will be a weaker standard that may well give way prematurely to a rival not hobbled by this legal restriction—at least not initially—and other standards will be weaker, less flexible, and less enduring.

Conclusions

The government has chosen and the judge has approved a defective remedy. Its key defect is its logical inconsistency with the claims made in the case. It is difficult to avoid concluding that the purpose of the so-called remedy is not correction, but punishment.

No one disputes that breakups are costly. The government's own experts agree that software prices are likely to rise, an obvious disadvantage to consumers. The capricious allocation of products, the fragmentation of the operating system, the rules forbidding trade between the split-up companies, all impose clear and significant costs. The intentional handicapping of OS products that played no role in this case will work only to decrease competition in the server and handheld markets. Synergies will be lost.

When the theory of an antitrust case is based on a defective view of markets, it is not surprising that the findings are flawed or that the proposed remedy will do more harm than good. The Microsoft case is based largely on a theory of lock-in through network effects, an insecure foundation at best. Network theories, we have argued, ought not be enshrined in our antitrust laws. They can be so enshrined only if conjecture is elevated above evidence.

NOTES TO THE APPENDIX

1. The three-Windows proposal was given its most detailed exposition in a paper by Thomas Lenard of the Progress and Freedom Foundation, a think tank nominally in favor of free markets and reduced government intervention: Thomas M. Lenard, *Creating Competition in the Market for Operating Systems: A Structural Remedy for Microsoft* (Progress and Freedom Foundation, 2000). Oracle funded a study proposing the same type of breakup: Robert J. Levinson, R. Craig Romaine, and Steven C. Salop, "The Flawed Fragmentation Critique of Structural Remedies in the Microsoft Case," draft dated January 20, 2000. A critique of the proposal, based on its high costs, can be found in Stan J. Liebowitz, *Breaking Windows: Estimating the Cost of Breaking Up Microsoft Windows* (Association for Competitive Technology and the ASCII Group, April 30, 1999), and also in *A Fool's Paradise: The Windows World after a Forced Breakup of Microsoft* (Association for Competitive Technology, February 25, 2000). Tom Hazelitt and George Bittlingmayer, in a cleverly named paper, "DOS Capital," examine the impact of the case on stock prices of firms in related industries, concluding that stock market participants view the government's prosecution as bad for the high-tech economy. All of these papers can be found at <http://www.ssrn.com>. Additionally, John Lott weighed in with a timely book—*Are Predatory Commitments Credible?* (University of Chicago Press, 1999)—disposing of many game-theoretic arguments being used to support predation claims. Richard McKenzie's book *Trust on Trial* (Perseus, 2000) explores, among other things, the political background of the case.

2. See James V. Grimaldi, "Reluctant Ruling for Judge; Jackson Says He Would Still Prefer Out-of-Court Settlement" *Washington Post,* June 8, 2000, p. A1. The judge is quoted as saying, "It's important you understand what my function is here. . . . I am not an economist. I do not have the resources of economic research or any significant ability to be able to craft a remedy of my own devising."

3. *United States v. Microsoft, Inc.,* Civil Action no. 98-1232 DDC.

4. Judge Jackson's definition of the market leaves out all competitors to Windows. The Macintosh, for example, is not really a substitute for Windows

according to the judge, which implies that Windows must also not be a substitute for the Macintosh and that therefore the Macintosh is a monopoly in its market, as he defines it.

5. A "barrier" that did not prevent the video recorder market from working properly. VHS, the market standard, appears in its turn to be in the process of being overcome, this time by DVDs, which are not even capable of recording programs.

6. Actually, a number of alternative arrangements might work: vertical integration, applications developers being given a share of the OS firm and vice versa, reciprocal commitments to develop products, etc.

7. But this success was neither immediate, obvious, or easy. As discussed in chapter 7, Windows 1.0 and Windows 2.0 were notable flops. It wasn't until Windows 3.0, almost five years after the first incarnation, that Windows steamrolled to a large market share. The reason? It was the first version of Windows that worked well.

8. This number may wildly overstate the number of real applications in use. For a critical evaluation of the 70,000 applications claim, see Richard McKenzie, *Microsoft's "Applications Barrier to Entry": The Missing 70,000 Programs* (Cato Institute, August 31, 2000).

9. The story of OS/2 involves a juicy irony regarding monopoly and barriers to entry. In its original incarnation, there were to be two versions of OS/2, regular and lite. The regular version would run only on machines with the IBM Microchannel architecture, a proprietary standard limited to IBM brand PCs. The lite version, missing networking and communication features, was intended to run on other computers. If successful, this option would have moved all business users to IBM PCs and allowed other computer manufacturers to merely share in the home/small-business market. The judge could have learned a thing or two about attempted monopolization if he had investigated this story. He might also have viewed the victory of Windows in a different light had he investigated more deeply.

10. The Macintosh was incompatible with both the Apple II and the Lisa, the two machines that preceded it.

11. There have been many middleware programs such as Lotus 1-2-3 or Hypercard for the Macintosh, language programs such as Basic or C, and many others. Each of these middleware applications had a very large number of programs written to use their features, but none became a serious alternative to an operating system.

12. In fact, James Barksdale, Netscape's president, testified that Netscape ever had any serious likelihood of competing with Windows as an operating system:

> Q.: Do you believe in 1995 that it was possible for Navigator to serve as a substitute for at least the platform characteristics of Windows?
> A: No.

Q.: And Netscape, as a company, did you not hold that belief?
A.: We have always believed, and we still believe, that it can substitute for some of the characteristics; we have never maintained, in any serious way, that it could substitute for all of it. (trial transcripts, October 20, 1998, p.m. session, p. 73)

13. This section is based in part on an analysis Liebowitz did for the Association for Competitive Technology, which was entered into the record as an affidavit included with the brief that the Association for Competitive Technology introduced into the remedy phase of the hearings.

14. See sections 2.b.i and 2.b.ii of the remedy.

15. For the complete text, go to: <http://www.microsoft.com/presspass/trial/jun00/06-07finaljudg.asp>.

16. Plaintiffs' Memorandum in Support of Proposed Final Judgment, p. 9. U.S. DoJ cases can be viewed at <http://www.usdoj.gov/atr/cases/f4700/4771.htm>.

17. On page 29 of the Plaintiffs' Memorandum in Support of Proposed Final Judgment (corrected May 2, 2000), we find: "In spite of Microsoft's claims at trial about the vitality of Linux, it has refused to port Office to Linux; by contrast, competitor Corel, unconstrained by a need to protect an operating system monopoly, has found it profitable to port its Office suite to Linux." Carl Shapiro also argues that Corel's behavior supports the government's view that a Microsoft application company would port its office suite to Linux (see page 9 of his declaration in favor of the government's remedy).

18. See, for example, Julian Beltrame, "Corel Cash Crunch May Spur Spinoff of Some Product Lines," *Wall Street Journal* online, July 20, 2000.

19. Corel has been willing to place bets with longer odds than most other software producers, as evidenced by the fact that it was one of the very few major ISVs to port its office suite to Java, although that too proved to be a highly unsuccessful undertaking. See Lee Gomes and Don Clark, "Java Stirs Fervor among Users But Hasn't Lived Up to Promise," *Wall Street Journal*, Interactive Edition, August 27, 1997.

20. This information comes from querying the Web site, <http://www.thelinuxstore.com>.

21. Word, Excel, PowerPoint, Outlook, and, depending on the specific suite, FrontPage, or Access.

22. See, for example, paragraphs 102 and 103 in "Declaration of Rebecca Henderson." U.S. DoJ can be viewed at <http://www.usdoj.gov/atr/cases/ms.remediespapers.htm>.

23. See "Declaration of Carl Shapiro," p. 7.

24. This theory can probably be traced to Bresnahan. See, for example, "New Modes of Competition: Implications for the Future Structure of the

Computer Industry," in *Competition, Innovation, and the Microsoft Monopoly: Antitrust in the Digital Marketplace,* edited by Jeffrey Eisenach and Thomas Lenard (Progress and Freedom Foundation, 1999), p. 155.

25. Page 49 of the amici brief contains a discussion of the double-marginalization problem, as does page 14 of the "Declaration of Carl Shapiro."

26. Chris E. Hall and Robert E. Hall, "Toward a Quantification of the Effects of Microsoft's Conduct," *American Economic Review* 90 (May 2000): 188–191. They assumed a computer price of $1,000, whereas Dataquest recently estimated the price to be closer to $1,700.

27. The list of applications given to the AppCo that seem better suited to the OpCo include Internet Explorer, BackOffice, Internet Information Server, SQL Server, streaming audio and video server software, transaction server software, SNA server software, indexing server software, XML servers and parsers, Microsoft Management Server, voice-recognition software, NetMeeting, and developer tools.

28. Actually, it is not exactly the size of the code within Windows. Section g.ii states that the price of Windows must be reduced by the ratio of the size of the middleware code *measured by the size of a separately distributed version of the middleware* relative to the size of Windows. One additional problem is that a separately distributed version would likely include code that has nothing to do with the functioning of the middleware product, but instead with transferring the product from the disk or Internet to the computer—that is, code for checking the system, binding the code to the system, and so forth.

29. Many computer-game users have experienced this type of problem because the hardware (e.g., sound cards) in PCs is not fully standardized, and the game developers write their games to work with only the leading sound cards because it would be too expensive to do otherwise. Although the packaging usually states the hardware requirements, many users are not sufficiently sophisticated to know whether the program will work on their machines. The packages currently state whether the product works with DOS, Windows 3.1, Windows 95, and so forth, but doesn't have to specify which components of the operating system are installed because the operating system is standardized and the user has easy access to all components. Under provision 3.g, the package would have to list all the "middleware" programs that need to be installed into the operating system in order for the program being purchased to work. Such a list will add a great deal of extra complexity into the purchase decision because consumers, who often barely know which operating system their computer uses, will need to have a far more intimate knowledge of their machine to interpret these restrictions.

30. Defenders of this remedy might claim that the game developer could include on the distribution CD, along with the game, those components of

Windows that are needed to run the game but that might have been removed by an OEM. In that case, however, the cost of the game would go up, needlessly raising prices for those customers who already have that Windows component installed.

31. A particularly specious government claim is that fragmentation, if it occurred, would be nothing new because Microsoft already allows consumers to remove many components of Windows with the add/remove software feature built into Windows. This assumption is mistaken, however, because the code is always there to replace any features of Windows not included in a particular installation. If fragmentation were to occur from this middleware provision, it would be different from what occurs with current Windows flexibility in installation. There is a certain consistency in the government's argument, however. It makes sense that the government wouldn't perceive a fragmentation problem because it seems to view the removal of middleware in Windows as a nonpermanent result, akin to the current add/remove feature of Windows .

32. On page 62 of the Plaintiffs' Reply Memorandum in Support of Proposed Final Judgment (May 17, 2000), we find: "Microsoft ignores the definition of 'Middleware Product' (§ 7.p), which is the term to which Section 3.g., applies and which is much narrower than 'Middleware' (§ 7.o). That definition ensures that the anti-binding provision will apply to only a small group of products."

33. Would the audio compression be the type of middleware product that section 3.g would proscribe? It doesn't fit section 7.r.i. Audio codecs do provide functionality similar to that offered by Microsoft competitors, fitting section 7.r.ii.2. Audio compression has been distributed separately by third parties, but we do not know if Microsoft would have been considered to have distributed it separately from the operating system as required by 7.r.ii.1 (these codecs are automatically downloaded, for example, by Windows Media Player if needed). These are the types of problems that make interpretation of the remedy so murky.

34. Found on page 63 of the Plaintiffs' Reply Memorandum in Support of Proposed Final Judgment.

35. We assume that "stand-alone" middleware products, which will be hidden or missing, are of little direct value to consumers. Using voice recognition as an example, a stand-alone program is likely to be of limited value because people are going to want to use voice recognition within their favorite word processor. More generally, a stand-alone program is likely to be of little extra value to software that is truly middleware because the purpose of middleware is, by definition, to be used by other programs.

36. On page 61 of the Plaintiffs' Reply Memorandum in Support of Proposed Final Judgment, we find: "Forced bundling injures consumers directly and injures competition by increasing the costs rival software vendors must incur to get their products distributed effectively."

37. This is a bit tricky. If the discount were equal to the market price of such software, we would find that the price of Windows would quickly go to zero or less because Windows is inexpensive relative to many third-party products (e.g., voice recognition). Instead, the various middleware products would together have to be deemed worth a certain portion of the total Windows price, and the individual components would share that amount in some relation to their market value.

38. The analogy here that might make the point more transparent is the situation with DOS and printer drivers. DOS did not include any printer drivers, meaning that each software developer had to create his or her own printer drivers. Because there were hundreds of printers, this approach was very expensive and time consuming, as well as being grossly inefficient. The effort involved in writing printer drivers was independent of the number of units sold, so this cost fell disproportionately on small ISVs, making it more difficult for them to compete with large ISVs. Microsoft's inclusion of printer drivers in Windows allowed ISVs, without cost, to have their programs print to any printer with a driver—a move that was clearly efficient and benefited small ISVs the most.

39. The cost to consumers of features such as disk compression, disk fragmentation, undelete programs, fax software, Internet-sharing software and so forth have been added into Windows at a rate of pennies on the dollar compared to the previous stand-alone prices.

40. The definition of *intellectual property* given in section 7 is "copyrights, patents, trademarks and trade secrets used by Microsoft or licensed by Microsoft to third parties."

41. The same argument can be made for the Windows CE operating system and the future X-box game machine. In both of these markets, the most successful firms produce both the hardware and the operating system, which the remedy would not allow Microsoft to emulate.

42. *United States v. Microsoft, Inc.*, 147 F. 3d 935 (D.C. Cir. 1998).

43. Ibid.

44. *United States v. Microsoft, Inc.*, Civil Action no. 98-1232 DDC, Findings of Law, p. 29.

Bibliography

Arthur, W. B. 1990. Positive feedbacks in the economy. *Scientific American* 262: 92–99.

————. 1989. Competing technologies, increasing returns, and lock-in by historical events. *Economic Journal* 99: 116–131.

————. 1994. *Increasing Returns and Path Dependence in the Economy.* Ann Arbor: University of Michigan Press.

Beeching, W. 1974. *A Century of the Typewriter.* New York: St. Martin's.

Binger, B. R., and E. Hoffman. 1989. Institutional persistence and change: The question of efficiency. *Journal of Institutional and Theoretical Economics* 145: 67–84.

Brigham, Joan-Carol. 1997. The drawing/diagramming and illustration software markets 1995–2000. IDC.

Calabresi, G. 1968. Transactions costs, resource allocation and liability rules: A comment. *Journal of Law and Economics* 11:67–74.

Card, David. 1996. PC office suite, word processor, and spreadsheet markets review and forecast, 1995–2000. IDC.

Carlton, D. W., and J. M. Klamer. 1983. The need for coordination among firms, with special reference to network industries. *University of Chicago Law Review* 50: 446.

Cheung, S. N. S. 1973. The fable of the bees: An economic investigation. *Journal of Law and Economics* 16: 11–33.

Chou, D., and O. Shy. 1990. Network effects without network externalities. *International Journal of Industrial Organization* 8: 259–270.

Church, J., and N. Gandal. 1992. Network effects, software provision, and standardization. *Journal of Industrial Economics* 40: 85–104.

————. 1993. Complementary network externalities and technological adoption. *International Journal of Industrial Organization* 11: 239–260.

Coase, R. H. 1960. The problem of social cost. *Journal of Law and Economics* 3: 1–44.

———. 1964. The regulated industries: Discussion. *American Economic Review* 54: 194–197.

———. 1974. The lighthouse in economics. *Journal of Law and Economics* 17: 357–376.

Dahlman, C. 1979. The problem of externality. *Journal of Law and Economics* 22: 141–163.

David, P. A. 1985. Clio and the economics of QWERTY. *American Economic Review* 75: 332–337.

———. 1986. Understanding the economics of QWERTY: The necessity of history. In W. N. Parker, ed., *Economic History and the Modern Economist*. New York: Basil Blackwell.

———. 1992. Heroes, herds and hysteresis in technological history: 'The battle of the systems' reconsidered. *Industrial and Corporate Change* 1: 129–180.

Demsetz, H. 1969. Information and efficiency: Another viewpoint. *Journal of Law and Economics* 10: 1–22.

———. 1982. *Economic, Legal and Political Dimensions of Competition*. Amsterdam: North Holland.

Dvorak, A., N. L. Merrick, W. L. Dealey, and G. C. Ford. 1936. *Typewriting Behavior*. New York: American Book Co.

Economides, N. 1989. Desirability of compatibility in the absence of network externalities. *American Economic Review* 79: 1165–1181.

Ellis, H. S., and W. Fellner. 1943. External economies and diseconomies. *American Economic Review* 33: 493–511.

Farrell, J. 1988. Sylvia, ice cream and more. *Journal of Economic Perspectives* 2: 175–182.

Farrell J., and G. Saloner. 1985. Standardization, compatibility, and innovation. *Rand Journal* 16: 70–83.

———. 1986. Installed base and compatibility: Innovation, product preannouncements, and predation. *American Economic Review* 76: 940–955.

———. 1992. Converters, compatibility and control of interfaces. *Journal of Industrial Economics* 40: 9–36.

Foulke, A. T. 1961. *Mr. Typewriter: A Biography of Christopher Latham Sholes*. Boston: Christopher.

Franz, W. 1990. Hysteresis: An overview. *Empirical Economics* 15: 109–125.

Gleick, J. 1987. *Chaos: Making a New Science*. New York: Penguin.

Goldschmid, H., M. Mann, and J. F. Weston. 1974. *Industrial Concentration— The New Learning*. Boston: Little, Brown.

Gomes, L. 1998. Economists decide to challenge facts of the QWERTY story. *Wall Street Journal* (February 25), p. B1.

Gould, S. J. 1991. The panda thumb of technology. In *Bully for Brontosaurus*. New York: W. W. Norton.

Herkimer County Historical Society. 1923. *The Story of the Typewriter: 1873–1923*. New York: Andrew H. Kellogg.

Hirshleifer, Jack, and David Hirshleifer. 1998. *Price Theory and Applications* (6th ed.) Upper Saddle River, N.J.: Prentice Hall.

Kahn, A. E. 1988. *The Economics of Regulation: Principles and Institutions*. Cambridge, Mass.: MIT Press.

Katz, M. L., and C. Shapiro. 1985. Network externalities, competition, and compatibility. *American Economic Review* 75: 424–440.

———. 1986. Technology adoption in the presence of network externalities. *Journal of Political Economy* 94: 822–841.

———. 1992. Product introduction and network externalities. *Journal of Industrial Economics* 40: 55–84.

Katzner, D. 1993. Some notes on the role of history and the definition of hysteresis and related concepts in economic analysis. *Journal of Post Keynesian Economics* 15: 323–345.

Kinkhead, R. 1975. Typing speed, keying rates, and optimal keyboard layouts. *Proceedings of the Human Factors Society* 19:159–161.

Kirsch, David A. 1998. From competing technologies to systems rivalry: the electric motor vehicle in America, 1895–1915. Ph.D. dissertation, Stanford University.

Kitch, E. W. 1977. The nature and function of the patent system. *Journal of Law and Economics* 20: 265, 275–280.

Klopfenstein, B. C. 1989. The diffusion of the VCR in the United States. In M. R. Levy, ed., *The VCR Age*. Newbury Park, Calif.: Sage Publications.

Knight, F. H. 1924. Some fallacies in the interpretation of social cost. *Quarterly Journal of Economics* 38: 582–606.

Kobayashi, B., and L. Ribstein. 1996. Evolutions of spontaneous uniformity: Evidence from the evolution of the limited liability company. *Economic Inquiry* 34: 464–483.

Krugman, P. 1994. *Peddling Prosperity*. New York: W. W. Norton.

Krugman, P. 1998. The legend of Arthur: A tale of gullibility at *The New Yorker*. *Slate* (www.slate.com). Posted Wednesday, January 14.

Landes, W. M., and R. A. Posner. 1987. Trademark law: An economic perspective. *Journal of Law and Economics* 30: 265–309.

Lardner, J. 1987. *Fast Forward*. New York: W. W. Norton.

Liebowitz, S. J. 1983.Tie-in sales and price discrimination. *Economic Inquiry* 21: 387–399.

———. 1985. Copying and indirect appropriability: Photocopying of journals. *Journal of Political Economy* 93: 945–957.

Liebowitz, S. J., and S. E. Margolis. 1990. The fable of the keys. *Journal of Law and Economics* 33: 1–26.

———. 1994. Network externality: An uncommon tragedy. *Journal of Economic Perspectives* 8: 133–150.

———. 1995*a*. Don't handcuff technology. *Upside* (September): 35–42.

———. 1995*b*. Path dependence, lock-in and history. *Journal of Law, Economics, and Organization* 11: 205–226.

———. 1995*c*. Are network externalities a new source of market failure? *Research In Law And Economics* 17: 1–22.

———. 1996. Should technology choice be a concern for antitrust? *Harvard Journal of Law and Technology* 9: 283–318.

———. 1998*a*. Network externality. In *The New Palgrave Dictionary of Economics and the Law*. London: Macmillan.

———. 1998*b*. Path dependence. In *The New Palgrave Dictionary of Economics and the Law*. London: Macmillan.

———. 1998*c*. Path dependence. In *European Encyclopedia of Law and Economics*. London: Edward Elgar.

Loffredo, M. 1992. The Word Processing Software Market Review and Forecast, 1993–1998. IDC.

———. 1993. Word Processing Market: DOS, Windows, OS/2, and Macintosh. IDC.

———. 1994. The Word Processing Software Market Review and Forecast, 1994–1999. IDC.

Lopatka, J. E., and W. Page. 1995. Microsoft, monopolization, and network externalities: Some uses and abuses of economic theory in antitrust decision making. *The Antitrust Bulletin* 40: 317–369.

Mandeville, B. M. 1762. *The Fable of the Bees*. New York: Capricorn.

Mares, G. C. 1909. *The History of the Typewriter*. London: Guilbert Pitman.

Margolis, S. E. 1987. Two definitions of efficiency in law and economics. *Journal of Legal Studies* 16: 471–482.

Matutes, C., and P. Regibeau. 1992. Compatibility and bundling of complementary goods in a duopoly. *Journal of Industrial Economics* 40: 37–54.

McGee, J., Predatory price cutting: The Standard Oil (N.J.) case. *Journal of Law and Economics* 1 (1958): 137–169.

Miller, L. A., and J. C. Thomas. 1977. Behavioral issues in the use of interactive systems. *International Journal of Man-Machine Studies* 9: 509–536.

Mokyr, J. 1991. Evolutionary biology, technological change and economic history. *Bulletin of Economic Research* 43: 127–147.

Navy Department. 1944. *A Practical Experiment in Simplified Keyboard Retraining—A Report on the Retraining of Fourteen Standard Keyboard Typists on the Simplified Keyboard and a Comparison of Typist Improvement from Training on the Standard Keyboard and Retraining on the Simplified Keyboard.* Department of Services, Training Section. Washington, D.C.: Navy Department, Division of Shore Establishments and Civilian Personnel.

The New Palgrave: A Dictionary of Economics. 1987. John Eatwell, Murray Milgate, and Peter Newman, eds. New York: Stockton Press.

New York Times. 1888. Typewriters contest for a prize. August 2, p. 2.

———. 1889*a*. Remington still leads the list. January 9.

———. 1889*b*. Wonderful typing. February 28, p. 8.

———. 1955*a*. Revolution in the office. November 11.

———. 1955*b*. U.S. plans to test new typewriter. November 11.

———. 1956*a*. Pyfgcrl vs. Qwertyuiop. January 22.

———. 1956*b*. Key changes debated. June 18.

———. 1956*c*. U.S. balks at teaching old typists new keys. July 2.

Norman, D. A., and D. E. Rumelhart. 1983. Studies of typing from the LNR research group. In W. E. Cooper, ed., *Cognitive Aspects of Skilled Typewriting.* New York: Springer.

North, D. C. 1990. *Institutions, Institutional Change, and Economic Performance.* New York: Cambridge University Press.

Pigou, A. C. 1912. *Wealth and Welfare.* London: Macmillan.

———. 1920. *The Economics of Welfare.* London: Macmillan.

———. 1924. Comment. *Economic Journal* 34: 31.

Rae, J. B. 1965. *The American Automobile.* Chicago: University of Chicago Press.

Ribstein, L., and B. Kobayashi. 1996. An economic analysis of uniform state laws. *Journal of Legal Studies* 34: 131–199.

Roe, M. J. 1996. Chaos and evolution in law and economics. *Harvard Law Review* 109: 641–668.

Shughart, W. F. 1990. *The Organization of Industry.* Homewood, Ill.: Irwin.

Sloan, A. P. 1972. *My Years with General Motors.* New York: Anchor Books.

Standard and Poor's Stock Guide. 1996. New York: McGraw-Hill.

Stigler, G. J. 1941. *Production and Distribution Theories.* New York: Macmillan.

Strong, E. P. 1956. *A Comparative Experiment in Simplified Keyboard Retraining and Standard Keyboard Supplementary Training.* Washington, D.C.: U.S. General Services Administration.

Tirole, J. 1988. *The Theory of Industrial Organization.* Cambridge, Mass.: MIT Press.

van Vleck, V. N. 1997. Delivering coal by road and by rail in Great Britain: The efficiency of the "Silly Little Bobtailed Coal Wagons." *Journal of Economic History* 57: 139–160.

Wall Street Journal. 1990. Santa Fe Institute engages in research with profit potential. May 8.

Wardley, M. 1997. PC spreadsheet market review and forecast, 1996–2001. IDC.

Whinston, M. 1990. Tying, foreclosure and exclusion. *American Economic Review* 80: 837–859.

Williamson, O. E. 1993*a*. Contested exchange versus the governance of contractual relations. *Journal of Economic Perspectives* 7: 103–108.

———. 1993*b*. Transaction cost economics and organization theory. *Industrial and Corporate Change* 2: 107–156.

Yamada, H. 1980. A historical study of typewriters and typing methods from the position of planning Japanese parallels. *Journal of Information Processing* 2: 175–202.

———. 1983. Certain problems associated with the design of input keyboards for Japanese writing. In W. E. Cooper, ed., *Cognitive Aspects of Skilled Typewriting.* New York: Springer.

Young, A. A. 1913. Pigou's *Wealth and Welfare. Quarterly Journal of Economics* 27: 672–686.

Zinsmeister, K. 1993. Japan's MITI Mouse. *Policy Review* 64: 28–35.

Index

AB. *See* Average benefit
Add-ons, 302
Adobe, 206, 208, 231n11, 284
Adoptions, payoffs and, 57, 57 (table)
Advertising, 242
Aftermarket rustproofers, crowding out of, 300, 301
Aldus, 206, 208, 231n11
All-in-one programs. *See* Office suites
Allchin, James, 265
Allocation, 1, 56, 68, 240
Amazon, 110
American Express, 275
American Standards Association, 29
America Online, 268, 272n28; icon placement for, 260, 262; Internet Explorer and, 271n23; pricing by, 233n33
Ameritech, SBC merger and, 275
Amiga, 285
Ami Professional, 142, 158n9, 184, 189, 199n24; cost of, 191; growth of, 180; market share for, 141; MS Word and, 186, 188, 191; review of, 188
AmiPro for Windows, 182, 188
Ampex Corporation, 120-21
Antitrust, 14-16, 17, 270n15; cases, 275, 300, 303; doctrines, xiv, xv, 299; freeze proposal and, 259; return-to-scale industries and, 15; software industry and, 249, 258
Antitrust laws, 245, 269n9; government power under, 275; predatory pricing and, 252
Antitrust theory: lock-in theory and, 247, 249; Microsoft investigation and, 247-48, 267-68; network technology and, 249-55; rethinking, 246
Antonoff, Michael: on Lotus 1-2-3, 165
AOL, xvi, 224, 255; charges by, 226, 233n35; Time Warner merger and, 275
Apache, 88
APIs, 292
AppCo. *See* Applications Business
Appeals process, 274
Apple, 284; Digital Research and, 144; DOS compatibility and, 133n7; GUI and, 129; Macintosh and, 304n10; Microsoft and, 195; operating system of, 3, 144, 278; suit by, 159n12
Apple II, 163, 179

Application companies, operating system and, 289
Application programmers, 288
Applications, 304n8; operating systems and, 285, 286
Applications-barrier-to-entry theory, xv, 276, 277, 284, 285
Applications Business (AppCo): defined, 281-82; Linux and, 284; market power of, 286; middleware and, 285; OpCo and, 281, 282, 285, 289, 294-95, 306n27; prices and, 287; software applications for, 282; voice-recognition software and, 295-96; Windows and, 283, 285
Appropriation, 21, 40n1
Arthur, Brian, 58, 117; briefs by, 248; on diminishing returns, 80; on inefficiency, 57; on technology/increasing returns, 56; on VHS/Beta, 133n3
Ashton-Tate, 164, 186
Association for Competitive Technology, 305n13
Associations, 68
Atari, 163; GUI and, 129
Atari ST, 141, 149, 285; operating system of, 144
Audio compression, 291, 292, 307n33
Autarky value, 93
AutoVision, 121, 123
Average benefit (AB): MB and, 78; MC and, 79; network participants and, 77-78

BackOffice, 282, 306n27
Backward compatibility, 222; benefits/costs of, 142, 143; path dependence and, 140
Bain, Joe: on market share/monopoly behavior, 196
Baratz, Alan: on Microsoft/developer community, 257
Barksdale, James: testimony by, 232n28, 304-5n12
Barriers-to-entry theory, 277, 278, 279
Beeching, Wilfred, 36, 37
Beta, 19, 277; failure of, xi; review of, 124; superiority of, 56; survival of, 125; VHS vs., 6, 10-11, 16, 55-56, 60, 70, 92, 120-27, 133n3; world share for, 124
Betamax, 121, 122, 123
Bittingmayer, George, 84n10

315

About the Authors

Stan J. Liebowitz is professor of managerial economics and academic associate dean in the School of Management at the University of Texas at Dallas, and research fellow at The Independent Institute, in Oakland, California. He received his Ph.D. in economics from UCLA, and he has previously been on the faculty at the University of Rochester, University of Western Ontario, and, as the John Olin Visitor, University of Chicago. Dr. Liebowitz has written on the topics of copyright and technology, broadcasting regulation, pricing practices, and mortgage discrimination.

Stephen E. Margolis is professor of economics and head of the economics department in the College of Management at North Carolina State University, and a research fellow at The Independent Institute in Oakland, California. He has also been on the faculty at the University of Western Ontario and has been a visiting faculty member at the Fuqua School of Business and the University of Michigan Business School. Professor Margolis received his Ph.D. from UCLA, and his research includes work on housing markets, pricing of medical services, monopolistic competition, and economic efficiency in the law.

Professors Liebowitz and Margolis have jointly written numerous scholarly articles on the subjects of network effects and lock-in that have appeared in the *Journal of Economic Perspectives; Journal of Law, Economics and Organization; Harvard Journal of Law and Technology; Journal of Law and Economics; Research in Law and Economics; New Palgrave Dictionary of Economics and the Law;* and *Encyclopedia of Law and Economics.* In addition, their more popular articles have been published in the *Christian Science Monitor, Investor's Business Daily, Orange County Register, Reason, San Francisco Chronicle, Upside,* and the *Wall Street Journal.*